Palgrave Studies in Agricultural Economics and Food Policy

Series Editor
Christopher Barrett
Cornell University
Ithaca, New York, USA

Agricultural and food policy lies at the heart of many pressing societal issues today and economic analysis occupies a privileged place in contemporary policy debates. The global food price crises of 2008 and 2010 underscored the mounting challenge of meeting rapidly increasing food demand in the face of increasingly scarce land and water resources. The twin scourges of poverty and hunger quickly resurfaced as high-level policy concerns, partly because of food price riots and mounting insurgencies fomented by contestation over rural resources. Meanwhile, agriculture's heavy footprint on natural resources motivates heated environmental debates about climate change, water and land use, biodiversity conservation and chemical pollution. Agricultural technological change, especially associated with the introduction of genetically modified organisms, also introduces unprecedented questions surrounding intellectual property rights and consumer preferences regarding credence (i.e., unobservable by consumers) characteristics. Similar new agricultural commodity consumer behavior issues have emerged around issues such as local foods, organic agriculture and fair trade, even motivating broader social movements. Public health issues related to obesity, food safety, and zoonotic diseases such as avian or swine flu also have roots deep in agricultural and food policy. And agriculture has become inextricably linked to energy policy through biofuels production. Meanwhile, the agricultural and food economy is changing rapidly throughout the world, marked by continued consolidation at both farm production and retail distribution levels, elongating value chains, expanding international trade, and growing reliance on immigrant labor and information and communications technologies. In summary, a vast range of topics of widespread popular and scholarly interest revolve around agricultural and food policy and economics. The extensive list of prospective authors, titles and topics offers a partial, illustrative listing. Thus a series of topical volumes, featuring cutting-edge economic analysis by leading scholars has considerable prospect for both attracting attention and garnering sales. This series will feature leading global experts writing accessible summaries of the best current economics and related research on topics of widespread interest to both scholarly and lay audiences.

More information about this series at
http://www.springer.com/series/14651

John W. Mellor

Agricultural Development and Economic Transformation

Promoting Growth with Poverty Reduction

John W. Mellor
Cornell University
Ithaca, New York
USA

John Mellor Associates, Inc.
Washington, District of Columbia
USA

Palgrave Studies in Agricultural Economics and Food Policy
ISBN 978-3-319-65258-0   ISBN 978-3-319-65259-7   (eBook)
https://doi.org/10.1007/978-3-319-65259-7

Library of Congress Control Number: 2017950561

Cover image © Nigel Cattlin / Alamy Stock Photo
Cover design by Fatima Jamadar

Printed on acid-free paper

This Palgrave Macmillan imprint is published by Springer Nature
The registered company is Springer International Publishing AG
The registered company address is: Gewerbestrasse 11, 6330 Cham, Switzerland

FOREWORD

After the heyday of the Green Revolution, a generation of scholars and policymakers took agriculture for granted. Then the global food price crises of 2007–2012 reawakened appreciation of the central role agriculture plays in the process of economic development locally and globally.

John Mellor was among the earliest and most influential champions of that fundamental truth. His landmark 1961 *American Economic Review* paper with Bruce Johnston, "The role of agriculture in economic development" was, along with the Nobel Laureate W. Arthur Lewis' classic 1954 paper, absolutely foundational to subsequent understanding of how agricultural development ignites economic growth and poverty reduction at larger scales. That 1961 paper drew on Mellor's own intensive field research in south Asia in the 1950s, which set the stage for a career of careful empirical investigation and deep engagement with the messy realities of agricultural and food policy around the world. A sequence of heavily cited studies—most notably his 1966 book *The Economics of Agricultural Development* and his 1976 work *The New Economics of Growth*—built up the evidence base that helped prompt Green Revolution investments by underscoring the crucial role of institutional and technological change in agriculture, and of public investment in agricultural research and extension, in spurring economic transformation. While public intellectuals feared that population growth would bring mass famine, Mellor and others charted a course that instead helped usher in a period of historically unprecedented reduction in poverty and hunger. A burgeoning academic literature today is now rediscovering the old truths first articulated by Mellor and his collaborators.

Mellor was unusual not only in the extraordinary intellectual impact of his scholarship on subsequent research, but equally in the practical impact he had on real world policymaking. As a Cornell University professor, he influenced a generation of talented students, several of whom went on to highly influential careers of their own, most notably his doctoral advisee Lee Teng-Hui, who served as President of the Republic of China (Taiwan) from 1988 to 2000. Serving as Chief Economist of the United States Agency for International

Development in the early 1970s, including during the world food crisis of 1973–74, Mellor exerted considerable influence over the United States government's response to unfolding events of immense humanitarian consequence, as well as those of other governments. Indeed, Mellor's sage influence helped prompt the creation in 1975 of the International Food Policy Research Institute (IFPRI). Mellor then served as IFPRI's Director General from 1977 to 1990. That period secured for IFPRI an enviable reputation as the global leader in policy-oriented research on food and agricultural policy to reduce hunger, malnutrition, and poverty and to stimulate economic growth, environmental sustainability, and human development. In the quarter century since he ran IFPRI, Mellor has served as a prized adviser to a range of senior government officials around the world, remaining remarkably active as a global thought leader to this day.

Hence my great excitement that John Mellor has written this volume. Very rarely do we students get the opportunity to learn from the expert insights of an early giant of the field reflecting on more than half a century's research and practical experience in the field, much of it sparked by his own path-breaking work. The questions Mellor and his collaborators pursued decades ago remain highly topical today. We continue to struggle to understand how best to ignite inclusive economic growth that can rapidly and sustainably reduce the extreme poverty that still disfigures much of the world, especially in rural areas of Africa and Asia. The linkages between the farm and non-farm sectors, although indisputably substantial, remain underappreciated and only weakly understood. The appropriate role of government in these domains remains hotly disputed. On these and other key issues, Mellor has a vantage point like no other. By virtue of the extraordinary longevity and stature of his contributions, Mellor's insights merit careful study, perhaps especially where they buck current prevailing beliefs.

The central theses Mellor advances in this volume are powerful in their implications. Mellor argues that small commercial farmers, rather than large-scale farms or poorer, semi-subsistence producers, are the key engines of economic growth and poverty reduction. A significant portion of that impact comes through local general equilibrium effects through labor markets and those farmers' demand for non-tradable goods and services, both of which generate high multiplier effects that concentrate gains among the poor. Pervasive rural factor and product market imperfections and the significant public good elements of investments in, especially, agricultural research and extension, necessitate a central role for government. That requires more substantial public sector spending and activity than has been the case in most developing countries over the past generation. These claims challenge some conventional wisdom today and invite rigorous testing of many subsidiary hypotheses.

More than 50 years after his seminal work spawned a generation of scholars to pursue research agendas he advanced, John Mellor offers in this volume more than a powerful valedictory address from one of the field's giants. He again challenges the agricultural and development economics community to engage in research that makes a difference. It is a tremendous privilege to introduce a volume that any serious student of agricultural development and economic transformation needs to read. The unsurpassed historical sweep of Mellor's observations, drawing on an extraordinary career of great scholarly and practical impact, make Mellor's insights as timely in the early twenty-first century as they were in the mid-twentieth century.

Cornell University   Christopher B. Barrett

PREFACE

My intention is to explain how rapid agricultural growth accelerates the economic transformation to a modern economy and most important why it is the prime instrument for removing rural and much of overall poverty. From that I explain why modernization of agriculture is essential to filling that role and state what the initial conditions and requirements for that modernization are. The focus is on low- and middle-income countries—the ones striving to become high income and modern. Modernization of agriculture is of great importance to progress in those countries.

The reader should come away with a clear, integrated picture of why and how to develop agriculture. That picture is quite different to much of the academic analysis and practice of foreign assistance agencies and many low- and middle-income governments. It is consistent with the practice of several governments that have been highly successful in achieving rapid agricultural growth and poverty reduction. That consistency is in part because I closely observed and learned from them.

I take clear positons throughout the book, based on my own research and reading, and my lengthy and wide ranging experience drawn from living in rural areas, doing and administering research, senior government experience, and a recent 25-year period of interacting within low- and middle-income country governments.

The topic of this book is broad and so the relevant literature is vast. A comprehensive review is not possible. I cite research that draws different conclusions to mine as well as some in agreement and emphasize review papers. The citations lead to a further broadening of the literature for those who wish to pursue topics in depth. Quantification of key relationships between accelerated agricultural growth, the economic transformation and poverty reduction is either original to this book or an extension of my previous work with several colleagues. All that empirical work is reproducible from spreadsheets that are made available.

For the purposes of this book much of the survey data based research has two shortcomings: First, it fails to differentiate the non-poor commercial small commercial farmers who produce the bulk of agricultural output from the comparably large number of farmers who are at subsistence or below subsistence levels and produce but a small fraction of agricultural output. Second, it fails to distinguish the geographic areas in which modernization is under way with accelerated agricultural output growth from those that remain predominantly in slow moving traditional agriculture. As a result, it understates the potential for growth and diverts attention from the means of that growth.

The Economics of Agricultural Development, the predecessor to this book, was published 50 years ago. Ten years after publication it won the American Agricultural Economics Association award for research of lasting value. It is of course dated. It refers to Japan as a developing country and it was before the birth control pill. However, the errors are largely of omission rather than commission. (See the annex on intellectual history at the end of this book.) What has changed in the intervening 50 years is copious research on every facet of the subject and an extraordinary diversity of experience.

I had the good fortune to have an extraordinary set of people open the way to the diverse experiences that led to this book. Those experiences fall into four classes: The discipline of years of field research, teaching and learning from students, and leading the staff of a large research institute; the derived wisdom from close interaction with farmers, intensively in India, Ethiopia, Pakistan, and the United States, and more fleeting in many other African, Asian, and Latin-American countries; the healthy cynicism from a stint as Chief Economist of the US foreign assistance program and years of interaction at the field level with foreign aid missions; and a sense of reality from the most recent 25 years meshing research results and country experience in interacting with caring officials at all levels of low- and middle-income country governments.

Bruce Johnston my co-author in a much quoted *American Economic Review* article and two review articles in *The Journal of Economic Literature* was an early leader for many of the ideas in this book. He brought experience with the post war land reforms in Japan and introduced me to the seminal Japanese thinkers about agricultural development, Professors Ohkawa and Ishikawa.

F. F. Hill, Cornell University and later the Ford Foundation, guided my efforts to understand development problems of the then backward southern United States and had the faith to entrust me with starting a major academic program on agricultural development long before it became fashionable. I owe a lot to my Cornell colleagues. I also learned from Hill how he and his associates built the government instituted Farm Credit Administration and saw it become farmer managed and farmer owned—such a grand lesson about agricultural finance. The early US agricultural institutional history is valuable to understanding current needs and I was tied to that through my senior associates at Cornell.

Hla Myint, Oxford, taught me how important it was to leaven academic research with knowledge of how governments operate and their limitations. J. R. Hicks and Roy Harrod (Oxford) taught me the value of rigorous theory and Tommy Baloch (also Oxford) taught me that being an American is not always so good, an unpleasant experience that later became very helpful.

My greatest debt is to Arthur Mosher who said that having done a thesis on agricultural development in the then backward southern United States was not enough and arranged for my family to spend a year and a half in rural India, where I worked closely, interviewing each of them every week, with a sample of 30 Indian farmers. I owe those farmers and their families a lot and I am disappointed that I have had so little impact on improving their lot. I was once accused in public of generalizing from India—no, I generalized from 30 farm families in India—of course a bit leavened by meeting farmers in many other countries.

Ralph Cummings (Rockefeller Foundation) brought me back to India to work at the Indian Agricultural Research Institute, and I learned immensely from him how to run a technical assistance program so it actually builds national capacity instead of stunting it. Dan Parker, Administrator, USAID, took me as a young academic, into government, reporting directly to him and with a large staff to research pressing issues of foreign aid. Those were the days when US foreign aid officials were writing respectable and influential academic journal articles.

Then Sir John Crawford, took a flyer on me to build The International Food Policy Research Institute right at its start, which brought intimate contact with a large group of outstanding researchers and government officials. That period included for several years chairing the CGIAR center directors, enlarging my view of the hard sciences that are at the core of dynamic agricultural growth. Reading all the IFPRI research reports and commenting on them and interacting with government aid agencies and recipients gave me a sense of knowledge and knowledge gaps. During those years I benefitted immensely from Uma Lele's (World Bank) long and intensive work on all aspects of agricultural development in Africa.

Finally, another huge debt to Prime Minister Meles, Ethiopia who showed me that a government can indeed achieve rapid growth in agriculture—it is not just some academic figment of the imagination—and through his staff an apprecia-tion of why some of what I recommended was not possible. In that context, I interacted at all levels with practical participants in effective cooperatives and learned first-hand the problems of these important institutions. Throughout I interacted with traders, learning of their problems and contributions.

It is obvious that following from each of these I was privileged to learn from a legion of their associates. It has been a long journey, that I hope is not yet over.

Chris Barrett (Cornell) took time from his extraordinarily demanding pres-sures to read the drafts carefully and to give comments that made a major difference to this book. Liz Bageant his associate, gave the blunt (but tactfully put) commentary that forced major changes from the early draft. Similarly, for the publisher's anonymous reviewers.

In writing this book, I received excellent research assistance, covering a wide range of careful and thoughtful statistical and library search, from Akbar Naqvi. In the modern computer age perhaps the most important debt is to Zarmina Said and her sister Homa who patiently saw me through hundreds (two per day on average!) of book ending computer crises and endured my hysterics while they were doing it. And then my books are well written because I do what my editor says to do and Linda Dhondy was especially helpful on this book.

Thank you all, thank you, I hope I have done justice to the opportunities you have given me.

Washington, DC, USA   John W. Mellor
May 2, 2017

Contents

LIST OF FIGURES

LIST OF TABLES

CHAPTER 1

Introduction

This chapter first summarizes the two "big ideas" that are the subject of this book. These ideas differ from current central tendencies in thinking about the agriculture of low- and middle-income countries and poverty reduction. That is followed by definition of the concepts that are central to the analysis in this book—geographic area and national income level, four types of households (small commercial farm, large-scale/feudal farm, rural non-farm, and urban), economic transformation, agricultural modernization, and rapid agricultural growth.

THE BIG IDEAS

The rapid growth of small commercial farmer dominated agriculture accelerates the economic transformation and is essential to the rapid decline in dominantly rural poverty.

Small commercial farmers dominate agricultural production in most low- and middle-income countries. They are not poor and spend a substantial portion of their incremental income from farming on labor-intensive non-tradable goods and services from the large, rural, non-farm sector. That is central to poverty reduction. Those farmers are central to the exposition throughout this book.

Much of the academic literature (e.g., Collier and Dercon 2014; Dercon and Christiaensen 2011), foreign aid policy, and even government officials of low- and middle-income countries presume and act as though farmers are poor with a consequent inability to finance change or take risks. They are implicitly depicted as an average of what we define as small commercial farmers and the rural non-farm population. This book is a major departure from that conventional wisdom with profound implications for all aspects of agricultural growth and its role in economic transformation and poverty reduction.

The rural poor are concentrated in the rural non-farm sector and their employment and income increase comes from increased local demand for non-farming activities. That demand comes from the small commercial farmer

© The Author(s) 2017
J.W. Mellor, *Agricultural Development and Economic Transformation*,
Palgrave Studies in Agricultural Economics and Food Policy,
https://doi.org/10.1007/978-3-319-65259-7_1

and is the dominant means of reducing poverty in both low- and middle-income countries. Many households in the rural non-farm sector also do some farming, earning a portion of their income from that source.

Because small commercial farmers dominate agricultural growth and foster rapid growth in the rural non-farm sector this plays an important role in economic transformation. That not only speeds up economic transformation but disburses urbanization from the major central city to a geographically dispersed set of smaller towns and cities. That in turn influences the path of growth as upper-middle-income and high-income status is achieved.

Open trading regimes are favorable to agricultural growth. However, because of the rapid growth of the non-tradable rural non-farm sector the trade component will be lower in this strategy than in those that have been most favored over the past few decades.

The impact of expenditure by small commercial farmers on the rural non-farm sector is measured under fast and slow agricultural growth regimes and is found to be dominant in poverty reduction in both low- and middle-income countries, and also dominant in gross domestic product (GDP) growth in low-income countries, while being important but not dominant in middle-income countries. The impact of expenditure by high growth rate small commercial farmers is compared to that from large-scale farmers and the urban sector and is found to be the dominant source of increased employment and rural poverty decline.

For the past few decades, much of the thinking and practice of rural poverty reduction, especially among influential foreign aid donors, has focused directly on the poorer geographic regions and subsistence and below subsistence farmers. That has provided a welcome palliative to the recipients but fails to achieve a long-term reduction in poverty.

Since poverty is most dramatically illuminated by hunger, and severe malnutrition, the conditions for food security are analysed throughout. The findings are consistent with the view of Noble Laureate Amartya Sen that famine, hunger, and poverty are due to lack of income on the part of the poor, not lack of food in the economy. However, the relationship is more complex. It is only through a rapid increase in agricultural production by small commercial farmers that the income can be generated that reduces dominantly rural poverty. There has been an unfortunate tendency of Sen's followers to conclude, incorrectly, that growth in agricultural production is not important to food security and poverty reduction. That wrong conclusion strengthened the shift of foreign aid away from agricultural growth. Barrett (2010) in a science paper places this discussion in the current hierarchy of food security discussions.

Government has a prominent role if small commercial farmer dominated agriculture is to grow rapidly.

If government is not explicit about the importance of agriculture and does not make large expenditure and rapidly build key government institutions to foster agricultural growth the sector will not grow rapidly and rural poverty levels will decline slightly or not at all. Failure by government is the story in much of Sub-Saharan Africa, in a few low-income Asian countries, and increasingly so in middle-income countries of Asia. That is why poverty reduction has slowed. Recent decades have seen foreign aid and much academic effort focused on "privatization" and neglect of the central role of government in modernization of agriculture and hence on poverty reduction.

Of course agriculture is preeminently private sector—farmers are private sector as is the bulk of input and output marketing firms. However, they become more motivated in the context of clear government emphasis on their role in reaching national objectives and they require essential, constantly improving, complementary government services including rural roads, electrification, education and major government institutions always including research and extension, and many modest services such as statistics provision and market analysis.

There are four big problems: obtaining an explicit emphasis on agriculture; appropriating adequate funds; developing the government's institutional capacity; and knowing when and how to withdraw from some activities as the private sector grows and modernizes.

A large, widespread, extension service and the field efforts of research can bring substantial rural political support to governments. Indeed, it is surprising that more low-income country governments have not sought popular support in rural areas by large-scale, nationwide, government research/extension systems contributing to a large increase in income of the politically influential, small commercial farmer. Perhaps that is because so many low-income country governments do not rely significantly on popular democratic processes.

It is apparent that the explicit role of government with respect to agriculture is very different and far greater than its explicit role in the industrial or service sectors. Of course that means that over reach with all its negative effects is also possible. The exposition in Part 3 will monitor that role carefully.

There has been a tendency in recent decades for foreign aid to focus on encouraging the private sector, without recognizing that the greatest need of the agricultural private sector is rapid growth in agricultural production that requires specific government actions and institutions. A six percent growth rate as a minimum doubles the size of the private sector in 12 years. The reality has been neglect of key government functions, particularly compared to the golden age of foreign assistance to agriculture in the 1960s–1980s. That is particularly important given the tendency of contemporary low- and middle-income country political systems to be far more urban oriented than was true of most contemporary high-income countries when they were in low- and middle-income status.

SHARE OF GOVERNMENT EXPENDITURE ON AGRICULTURE

How large should the government effort to forward accelerated agricultural growth be? The African Union's major effort to provide a strategy for agricultural development, the Comprehensive Africa Agriculture Development Programme (CAADP) (2010), has a carefully analysed and researched numerical recommendation: governments should spend a minimum of ten percent of their total expenditure on agriculture. The International Food Policy Research

Institute (IFPRI) (2016) reports that for Africa that share declined from 3.5 percent in 2003–2008 to 3.0 percent for 2008–2014!

The CAADP recommendation is important to the exposition in succeeding chapters. Those chapters will emphasize critical areas that must receive priority in planning and implementation. But there are many essential functions of government with respect to a modern agriculture that are too mundane and detailed for attention in a grand strategy and in this exposition. A review of all the departments in a well-functioning Ministry of Agriculture would show area after area essential to a well-functioning modern agriculture. Those include detailed regulatory functions essential to a healthy agriculture, special planning functions, statistical systems, and data collection. If budget is provided for the priorities but insufficient for these many essential functions of government then the priorities will not be met.

DEFINITIONS

The following definitions are central to the analysis in this book and are stated and quantified in the following sections.

Defining Countries by National Income Level and Geographic Location

This book analyses low- and middle-income countries. As defined by the United Nations, low-income countries average $648 per capita income, middle-income $4729, and high-income $37,793. Low-income countries are almost entirely in Sub-Saharan Africa and South Asia (Table 1.1). Sub- Saharan Africa is divided nearly equally between low-income and middle-income countries, while South Asia is one-quarter low-income and three-quarters middle-income. East Asia and the Pacific is two-thirds middle-income and one-third high-income. Analysis in this book is heavily on Asia, which has been emphasized in foreign aid since the end of World War II, and Sub-Saharan Africa which started later than Asian countries but is now heavily favored by foreign aid donors.

Table 1.2 provides a sense of the wide variation among low- and middle-income countries. The table arranges selected countries within geographic areas

Table 1.1   Proportion of population in low-, middle-, and high-income countries, by region

Region	Low income (%)	Middle income (%)	High income (%)
East Asia & Pacific	5.4	64.9	29.7
South Asia	25.0	75.0	0
Europe & Central Asia	0	33.3	66.7
Latin America & Caribbean	2.4	53.7	43.9
Middle East & North Africa	0	61.9	38.1
North America	0	0	100
Sub-Saharan Africa	54.1	41.7	4.2

Source: Regions are from World Bank; percentages calculated from country and lending groups World Bank Data

Table 1.2 Economic indicators for selected countries

Country	GDP per capita (US$)	% of rural population	GDP per capita growth rate (%)	Agricultural growth rate (3-year average) %	Manufacturing as % of GDP	Wheat yield (3-yr. avg.)[a]	Rice yield (3-yr. avg.)[b]	Maize yield (3-yr. avg.)[c]
Bangladesh[d]	1086.8	66	4.8	3.3	17	29,897	44,050	66,223
Pakistan	1316.6	62	2.6	3.0	14	27,750	24,193	41,231
India	1581.5	68	6.0	2.2	17	31,203	36,452	25,926
Indonesia	3491.9	47	3.7	4.2	21	N/A	51,409	48,989
China	7590.0	46	6.7	4.3	30	50,390	67,315	59,658
Ethiopia	573.6	81	7.5	5.8	4	23,660	28,136	32,448
Rwanda	695.7	72	4.5	5.0	5	21,153	55,602	21,544
Tanzania	955.1	69	3.6	3.2	6	9786	24,835	13,812
Ghana	1441.6	47	1.6	4.2	5	N/A	26,243	17,748
Nigeria	3203.3	53	3.5	4.6	10	10,566	19,059	16,060
Bolivia	3124.1	32	3.8	4.2	13	11,693	25,604	26,509
Guatemala	3673.1	49	2.1	4.4	20	21,768	29,384	20,790
Egypt	3365.7	57	0.0	3.0	16	65,875	95,487	77,426
Japan	36,194.4	7	0.1	1.8	19	39,905	67,215	26,857
France	42,725.7	21	-0.3	-0.7	11	74,034	49,950	60,862
USA	54,629.5	19	1.6	1.4	12	30,771	84,866	94,820

[a]Food and Agriculture Organization of the United Nations *Statistics Division* (FAOstat) dataset: 2012–2014 average for wheat yields for all countries, units are Hg/Ha

[b]FAOstat: 2012–2014 avg. for rice/paddy yields for all countries

[c]FAOstat: 2014–2014 avg. for maize yields for all countries

[d]Bangladesh qualifies as a low-income country according to the World Bank, despite having a GDP per capita above the maximum number for low-income countries, assumingly because of the fact that its growth in GDP per capita in 2014 was an anomaly in comparison to other years where it was comfortably below the number

by per capita income. It is striking that over a wide range of incomes the proportion of the population that is rural remains at a very high 46 percent up to 81 percent. This suggests that even middle-income countries as a group still have a large population of rural poor, in turn suggesting failure in agricultural growth of the small commercial farmer.

Across these sets of countries as incomes rise the share of the rural population and the share of agriculture in GDP trends down and the share in services trends up. The share in industry increases substantially from low to middle income and then drops. On growth rates, that for GDP is the same for the two low- and middle-income sets and then drops substantially for high-income countries.

Agriculture is at the lower end of the range for rapid growth in the low-income countries. It drops substantially below that for the middle-income countries and even lower for the high-income countries. The moderately high level for low-income countries is the product of a small number with substantially higher growth rates than the average and the bulk significantly lower. There is at most modest evidence of catch-up growth in agriculture.

Poverty

In this book, the World Bank's extreme poverty line is used to define the poor. Conceptually that requires income to provide a basic diet of sufficient calories for a moderately active life plus the other essentials met by families at that level of calorie consumption. In 1996 that was defined as a dollar a day and is increased with inflation. The World Bank at the same time also defined moderate poverty as less than two dollars a day.

Extreme poverty is of course a very low-level definition. It is used here because it is clearly defined and is the ultimate in abject poverty, associated with high death rates with a likely unfavorable impact on the physical and mental development of children. Although concentrated in South Asia and Sub-Saharan Africa, extreme poverty is widespread with well over one billion people so classified. The number in moderate poverty is in the order of twice the number in extreme poverty. The proportionate incidence of poverty has been increasing in Sub-Saharan Africa, while it has been declining elsewhere, albeit at a diminishing rate.

Non-monetary measures of poverty such as life expectancy, childhood mortality, literacy, the gap between female and male literacy, and other measures are also used as indicators of progress and various composites of several measures calculated. Most of these measures have been improving somewhat more rapidly than the monetary measure. However, in a broad sense the various measures of poverty are moderately correlated.

Small Commercial Farmers

Agricultural production in most low- and middle-income countries is dominated by small commercial farmers (e.g., Mellor and Malik 2017; Jayne et al. 2006). They produce the bulk of agricultural output and are the source of the income growth the expenditure of which lifts the rural poor out of poverty. They are central to the exposition throughout this book.

For low- and middle-income countries the small commercial farmer is defined at the lower end as having enough land to produce sufficient food to lift the family's consumption above the World Bank defined poverty line. At the upper end, they have insufficient land (income) to support an urban import and capital-intensive lifestyle. They live in the rural areas along with other rural people and have a rural-based consumption pattern. They are generally thought of as the backbone of rural society. These farmers are not poor by the standards of their community, are commercial, selling a minimum one-third of their production, to derive the non-food items in the above poverty line level of living. The class as a whole markets well over half of its output and that rises over time. They are able to bear risk, to invest capital from their own income, and are interested in raising their farm income. Almost all their income comes from farming (Table 1.5).

Tenant farms are treated in principle like owner-operated farms. If they have enough land to generate an above poverty line income they are counted as small commercial farmers. Those that qualify as small commercial farmers are not common and will not be discussed separately. If they have enough income to support an urban lifestyle they are counted as large commercial farmers. They too are a rarity as a percentage of farming. If they generate farming income at the poverty level or lower, after subtracting the rent payment, then they are rural non-farmers. In a feudal system, as in much of Sindh Province, Pakistan, essentially all fall into the rural non-farm class.

This definition is not stated in terms of farm area. That is because the area encompassing the small commercial farm category varies according to a wide range of factors including land productivity. For any specific situation the definition can be converted to an area definition, as is done in the tables in this chapter and the next. Data for the rural household classes are presented for Ethiopia, Punjab, Pakistan, and Sindh, Pakistan to illustrate three quite different circumstances.

Ethiopia is broadly representative of low-income countries with respect to these household classes (see Jayne et al. 2006). Small commercial farmers dominate agricultural production (Table 1.3). They represent a little over half of the rural households but farm 77 percent of the land. The bulk of the farms are between 0.75 and 5.0 hectares. Large-scale farms occupy ten percent of the land. The rural non-farm population represents somewhat less than half of the rural households but only farms 13 percent of the land.

Punjab, Pakistan represents a situation in which the small commercial farmer also dominates production, comparable to Ethiopia, but with a substantially larger large-scale farm component. Note that the rural non-farm sector is far larger than in Ethiopia, at 80 percent of the rural households, but farms the same percentage of the land: 12 percent. There is current literature (e.g., Collier and Dercon 2014) arguing for agricultural growth in low-income countries to be centered on large-scale commercial farms; hence the representation, here and in Chap. 2, of a province that has a prominent place for such farms.

Table 1.3   Relative importance of major rural household types, Ethiopia, Punjab, Sindh

Region	Small commercial farmer households (%)	Small commercial farmer land (%)	Rural non-farm households (%)	Rural non-farm land (%)	Large-scale/ feudal households (%)	Large-scale/ feudal land (%)
Ethiopia	54	77	46	13	Less than 1	10
Punjab	20	70	80	12	Less than 1	18
Sindh	11	42	89	2	Less than 1	56

Source: Mellor and Malik (2017)

Sindh, Pakistan represents a vastly different situation with 56 percent of the land in feudal holdings and only 42 percent in small commercial holdings. Chapter 7 will quantify the implications of that for growth and poverty reduction. The rural non-farm sector is even larger than in Punjab at 89 percent of the rural population but farms only two percent of the land. Later chapters will show the deleterious effect of these circumstances on poverty reduction. Although feudal agricultures are now uncommon, they once played an important role and hence the focus on such an example.

Small commercial farmers spend half of their incremental income on the local rural non-farm sector. That sector provides labor-intensive goods and services that are non-tradable—that is they do not have a market outside of the local community. Examples are house improvements, local furniture, traveling by bus with local drivers and conductors, local school tutoring, and a wide range of services.

Table 1.4, with data from Pakistan, shows that the market for all non-farm production is almost entirely local. The tehsil (administrative division) is the lowest administrative level. This is an important feature of the rural non-farm sector in low- and middle-income countries. The table for Pakistan frames the issue very clearly and is particularly convincing since Pakistan is a country in which urban areas are widespread with maximum opportunity to provide a market for the rural non-farm sector.

There is a large literature corroborating that it is rural households and farmers specifically who provide the market for the large rural non-farm sector. Gavian et al. (2002) provide a detailed study specifically for Egypt, which like Pakistan has a widespread urban system. Mead and Liedholm (1998) generalize broadly from a large number of studies specifically noting that farmers are the prime market. Mellor and Malik (2017) discuss the issue at length.

Rural Non-Farm Households

Rural non-farm households are defined as those with insufficient land to reach the poverty level from farming—that is less land than the bottom of the range for small commercial farmers. Relatively few well-to-do rural households own plots smaller than the bottom of the small commercial farm range. The bulk of the

Table 1.4   Sources of demand for rural non-farm enterprises, Pakistan (%)

Location of demand	Production	Services	Trade
Same tehsil	74	98	100
Different tehsil in the same district	15	1	0
Different district in the same province	7	0	0
Other province	2	0	0
Other country	1	0	0

Source: Malik (2008)

rural non-farm households are poor and the bulk of the poor are rural non-farm. Long-term poverty reduction in low- and middle-income countries must focus on how growth can raise incomes in these households.

The rural non-farm households (top two rows) rely on a diverse set of income sources, largely as wage earners (Table 1.5). On average, those with land derive half of their income from crop and livestock production. Essentially all in the rural non-farm class are net purchasers of food. Landless rural non-farm households derive essentially all of their income from non-farming activities. The small commercial farmers derive essentially all of their income from farming. As stated above and in Table 1.4 the demand for what they provide comes almost entirely from the same tehsil, the lowest level administrative unit. The local small commercial farmers are the prime source of demand for their goods and services and hence determine their prosperity.

In Ethiopia this group represents 46 percent of rural households and farms 13 percent of the land. In Pakistan, they constitute those with under three acres of land (Table 1.2). They comprise 79 percent of rural households, 83 percent of impoverished households, and 61 percent of these households fall under the poverty line. Two-thirds of these households are landless. This class farms only eight percent of acreage available in Pakistan.

Large Commercial/Feudal Farmers

Large commercial and feudal landholders have sufficient agricultural income to take on urban-oriented consumption patterns (widespread focus groups participated in by the author and colleagues in Pakistan and East Africa provided this description). They commonly live in urban areas. For Pakistan they are defined as those with more than 75 acres of farmed land. Such farms comprise 18 percent of the area in Punjab, thus they are an important but not dominant category (Table 1.2). They are more important in a few East African countries, but never dominant, except in the Union of South Africa. Both large commercial farmers and feudal landowners spend their income in urban areas substantially on capital- and import-intensive goods and services that create little employment, and of course none in rural areas (focus groups and individual informants in Ethiopia and Pakistan, including the chairman of the large farmers' association in Pakistan).

Table 1.5   Percentage share of each source of income in total income, by size of farm, Pakistan, 2010–2011

Size of farm (acres)	Crop income	Livestock income	Wages and salaries	Business income	Rental and pension income	Other transfer income	Remittances	Total income
Landless	0	3	56	19	4	2	15	100
More than zero but less than 3 acres	27	20	24	13	3	2	12	100
3 to less than 5 acres	51	22	13	5	1	1	7	100
5 to under 12.5	65	17	8	4	1	1	4	100
12.5 to under 25	73	16	5	2	1	1	2	100
25 to under 50	70	17	4	3	1	0.2	5	100
50 to under 75	85	10	1	2	2	0.1	0.2	100
75 and above	80	8	5	5	1	0	1	100
Total	28	11	34	13	3	2	10	100

Source: Pakistan Bureau of Statistics HIES 2010–2011

Large commercial farms tend to have technically competent management, relatively small labor forces, substantial mechanization, and a high level of factor productivity. Where governments do not provide the institutional infrastructure essential to the success of small commercial farmers, the large commercial farmers are more productive than the small commercial farms. That gives the wrong impression that the future of high productivity lies with them, even though they rarely control a high proportion of the land. Rather, this book emphasizes that governments need to provide those institutions and services to the small commercial farmer.

The owners of feudal holdings are similar to large commercial farms in having urban high-income oriented consumption patterns and therefore have little impact on rural poverty reduction. They are typically urban dwelling absentee owners. They are a major feature of Sindh province in Pakistan where they occupy 56 percent of the cropped area. Because of the difficulty of managing labor, such absentee owners normally allocate small plots of land to a family and collect revenues on a sharecropping basis. Essentially all sharecropped land is in large feudal holdings since small scale renters normally receive cash rent. That is because the renter wants and can bargain for the management income. A substantial literature states the conditions under which sharecropping can be efficient and productive. Feudal systems in low- and middle-income countries tend not to meet those conditions. Sharecropping is of course entirely different in high-income countries.

It is notable that in feudal systems the proportion in poverty in each size of farm class is more than 50 percent higher on the sharecropped farms than on the non-sharecropped farms (Mellor and Malik 2017).

The fourth household category is the undifferentiated urban sector.

The Economic Transformation

Economic development is a process of radically increasing per capita national income, drastically reducing poverty, and as a central element of the latter to greatly improve food security and nutritional quality. The economy is transformed from a dominantly rural and low-productivity agricultural economy to one that is dominantly urban and non-agricultural. That includes a large scale shift of population and labor force from rural to urban areas. With that comes the rise of large cities and the concomitant development of the intellectual centers and cultural offerings central to any concept of a modern society. Agriculture eventually settles into a positon, particularly with the inclusion of the large rapidly growing sectors servicing it, as one of the many substantial sectors in the economy. The sum of these processes is referred to as the economic trans-formation. The appearance and the substance of the economy is radically transformed.

Agriculture, the initially dominant sector, has a central role to play in that transformation. However, to play that role requires a radical modernization of agriculture. Government is dominant in determining the progress of those forces. Not taking advantage of the transformative role of agriculture slows and delays economic transformation to the detriment of the growth rate, poverty reduction, food security and the broad welfare of urban and rural people.

Agricultural Modernization

The Oxford Dictionary defines modernization as to "Adapt (something) to modern needs or habits, typically by installing modern equipment or adopting modern ideas or methods: *a five-year plan to modernize Algerian agriculture.*"

The term is used here because the core of rapid agricultural growth is the development of modern scientific institutions using constantly evolving and advancing modern scientific methods and institutional structures. There is a whole set of new supporting institutions. The effect is a long term trend, radically increasing agricultural productivity. Eventually labor bottlenecks, particularly seasonal ones, are encountered and modern machinery begins to be used as well. Labor productivity increases at all stages of modernization. Particularly notable is the increased labor productivity from yield increasing agricultural technology. It is not a once and for all change but a dynamic continuum. The definition refers to agriculture and all its supporting institutions.

Rapid Agricultural Growth

How rapidly does agriculture have to grow to have a significant effect on economic transformation and poverty reduction? That rate must be sustainable over a substantial number of decades. A spurt of growth from a single research breakthrough or a run of favorable weather is not adequate. The reference growth rate used in this book is six percent.

It is agricultural growth per capita that determines the impact on overall growth rates and poverty reduction. In post Mejia Japan (1868) with very low population growth rates, a much lower rate of agricultural growth could be transformative compared to what is required in contemporary Africa with its very high population growth rates.

Typical low- and even middle-income country population growth rates are now over two and a half and sometimes as high as three percent. The agricultural growth rate must be significantly higher than that. As seen in the next chapter, one percent higher has little impact. So the agricultural growth rate in low-income countries must exceed four to five percent at least until the population growth rate declines. The average growth rate of value added in agriculture in Africa for 2008–2014 was a grossly inadequate 2.6 percent (IFPRI 2016).

Because of the land constraint, the agricultural growth rate is more constrained than that for urban industry. Thus we note that for agriculture, even for short periods, eight percent is never exceeded. So we might bracket the target range as between four to five percent and six to seven percent.

In the African Union's CAADP (2010) a large team of highly competent analysts gave considerable attention to an appropriate, and feasible, target growth rate for an agriculture expected to play a major role in economic transformation, income growth, and poverty reduction. Their considered judgement was to set a six percent growth rate target. The report with that target was unanimously signed off by all Chiefs of State of African countries. That is the reference target used in this book. It will be argued that because of more developed institutional structures and production biased towards commodities with even higher growth rates, that it is feasible in Asian countries as well.

What would a "natural" growth rate be in a traditional agriculture with little or no government institutional support? Most likely it would be similar to the population growth rate or a little higher. As rural population grows there is pressure from declining per capita incomes to utilize the increased labor to increase production. That labor would bring some marginal land into production and intensify labor input by, for example, better weeding and more composting (see Boserup 1965 for an extended discussion). One would expect some natural innovation by farmers to offset slightly reduced labor productivity. Thus it is reasonable to describe a base growth rate in a traditional agriculture with little effective intervention by government to be in the order of three percent. Thus, we see modernization as doubling the growth rate from three to six percent.

High-income countries, all of which have well developed institutional structures for maintaining research and technology-based growth, average a one to two percent agricultural growth rate. That may be the natural growth rate for agriculture once high-income status is reached. Low- and middle-income countries can reasonably achieve more than three times that rate because they, in agriculture, as for other sectors, are in a catch-up mode. At the six percent rate it will take several decades to catch up with the slowly progressing high-income countries.

Overview of Succeeding Sections and Chapters

The remainder of this book is divided into three parts. Part 1 analyses and quantifies the role of agriculture in the various aspects of economic transformation and poverty reduction; Part 2 describes, for the dominant inputs, labor, and land, the base context of traditional agriculture; Part 3 builds on that base to discuss each of the major institutional structures required to achieve the high growth rate in the agricultural sector necessary for it to play a substantial role in economic transformation.

REFERENCES

African Union. (2010). *Comprehensive African Agricultural Development Plan (CAADP)*. Addis Ababa: The New Partnership for Africa's Development.
Barrett, C. B. (2010). Measuring food insecurity. *Science, 327*(5967), 825–828.

Boserup, E. (1965). *The conditions of agricultural growth: The economics of agrarian change under population pressure.* Abingdon: Routledge.

Collier, P., & Dercon, S. (2014). African agriculture in 50 years: Smallholders in a rapidly changing world. *World Development, 63,* 92–101.

Dercon, S., & Christiaensen, L. (2011). Consumption risk, technology adoption and poverty traps: Evidence from Ethiopia. *Journal of Development Economics, 96*(2), 159–173.

Gavian, S., El-Meehy, T., Bulbul, L., & Ender, G. (2002). The importance of agricultural growth to SME development and rural employment in Egypt. In G. Ender & J. S. Holtzman (Eds.), *Does agricultural policy reform work? The impact on Egypt's agriculture, 1996–2002* (pp. 395–435). Bethesda: Abt Associates Inc.

International Food Policy Research Institute. (2016). *2016 Global Food Policy Report survey.* Washington, DC: International Food Policy Research Institute.

Jayne, T. S., Mather, D., & Mghenyi, E. (2006). *Smallholder farming under increasingly difficult circumstances: Policy and public investment priorities for Africa* (MSU international development working paper no. 86). East Lansing: Michigan State University.

Malik, S. J. (2008). Rethinking development strategy: The importance of the rural non-farm economy in growth and poverty reduction in Pakistan. *Lahore Journal of Economics, 13*(Special Edition), 189–204.

Mead, D. C., & Liedholm, C. (1998). The dynamics of micro and small enterprises in developing countries. *World Development, 26*(1), 61–74.

Mellor, J. W., & Malik, S. J. (2017). The impact of growth in small commercial farm productivity on rural poverty reduction. *World Development, 91,* 1–10.

PART I

Agriculture and the Economic Transformation

CHAPTER 2

The Economic Transformation

The economic transformation is the overriding feature of economic growth in low- and middle-income countries. The transformation is from a predominantly rural and agricultural nation to one that is predominantly urban with urban industry and services dominating the economy. It is accompanied by a demographic transition. The population growth rate first accelerates then slows and eventually declines. Health and life expectancy improve greatly.

In low-income countries rapid growth in the large agricultural sector has a dominant impact on the overall growth rate, the decline in poverty, and the speed of economic transformation. In middle-income countries rapid growth in a now relatively smaller agriculture continues to have a substantial impact on the overall growth rate but is still dominant in the decline in poverty.

The focus on growth, employment, and poverty is on per capita levels and hence changes in population growth rates are important. The demographic transition describes the changes in death rates, birth rates, and population growth that interact with the economic transformation.

This chapter has two components: First, discussion of the demographic transition that determines population growth rates and hence is central to per capita changes in income and employment. Second, a description of the variables that determine the extent of agriculture's impact on economic transformation, employment growth, and poverty reduction. That leads to Chap. 3 that provides numerical estimates, under various conditions, of the impact of alternative rates of agricultural growth on GDP, employment growth rates, and food security of low-income rural families.

THE DEMOGRAPHIC TRANSITION

The demographic transition is the extraordinary evolution of population growth from slow growth, with high death rates and birth rates and periodic fluctuations in death rates, to rapid population growth as death rates decline far faster than

© The Author(s) 2017
J.W. Mellor, *Agricultural Development and Economic Transformation*,
Palgrave Studies in Agricultural Economics and Food Policy,
https://doi.org/10.1007/978-3-319-65259-7_2

birth rates, to slow and even declining population growth with low birth and death rates. Population growth changes from little being subject to human control to increasingly being subject to that control.

Where there is underemployed labor, as is typical of poor rural areas in low- and many middle-income countries, a percentage point off the population growth rate is the near equivalent of a percentage point on the employment growth rate. Reducing the population growth rate by a percentage point, while being time consuming, requires little of the capital resources of growth, but does compete with agriculture for government institutional systems.[1] The demographic transition is much studied and over long time periods (e.g., Bocquet-Appel (2011) in relation to early agricultural growth; Lee (2003) over three centuries; in relation to technological change Galor and Weil (2000); in relation to the agricultural transition, Garenne and Joseph (2002).

Figure 2.1 presents the standard stylized picture of the demographic transition. It describes the course of birth rates and death rates and shows their effect on the population growth rate. Phase I is a period of birth rates being stable at a near biological maximum for those conditions and a death rate that fluctuates around that birth rate with food availability and health conditions. The population grows little or not at all. That was the condition of the world for most of human history with population spurts when settled agriculture occurred and with other major production advances.

Phase III is again a period of relatively small population growth as death rates are at a very low level and birth rates have declined to a similarly low level. Most of the population plans family size and implements the plan. At what level of

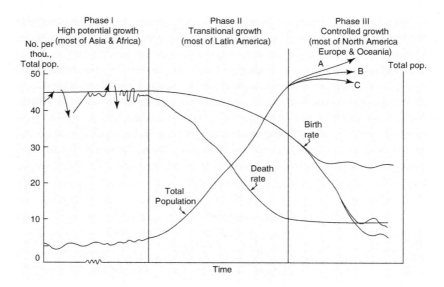

Fig. 2.1 Stylized population phases (Source: Author's construction)

growth it will be controlled depends on individual decisions that are a matter of private and public taste and to a certain extent subject to public policy. That population policy debate is ongoing in Japan and a number of European countries. If the cost of children to the family changes that might or might not influence family planning decisions depending on individual family values. But the result tends to be slow or even declining population growth.

Phase II is the one in which all low- and middle-income countries find themselves. That phase can best be understood as falling into two parts. The first part has death rates falling rapidly and birth rates declining at a slower pace—the gap between the two widening. That is a period of accelerating population growth, posing an increasingly difficult problem for economic growth and poverty reduction. The second part is a period of birth rates declining more rapidly than death rates and therefore a period of a declining rate of population growth. That is increasingly helpful to the growth rate. Modern birth control technology has compressed Phase II laterally. It now takes much less time to get through Phase II.

POLICIES FOR REDUCING BIRTH RATES

China has shown not only that it is possible to institute policies that radically reduce birth rates and human population growth rates but has also demonstrated the substantial implications of such policies. Describing that situation spotlights key issues about population policy. Following that is discussion of less intrusive, but nevertheless potentially effective, policies for reducing birth and population growth rates.

In 1979 China introduced the one child policy (see Hesketh et al. 2005). That was in the context of a low-income, substantially rural population, very large total population, very high population densities, and a clear understanding that income growth was constrained by rapid population growth. It was preceded by a period of moderately rapid decline in birth rates. The one child policy was in a context in which the bulk of development economists argued the urgent need to reduce birth rates.

With few exceptions it became illegal for a family to produce more than one child. The policy was rigidly enforced including forced abortions. The population growth rate declined rapidly to close to zero in ten years. There is no evidence of any depressing effect on economic growth. Thus the impact on per capita income and economic transformation was large. From a growth point of view, it was a highly successful policy. That of course ignores the individual loss of a larger desired number of children and the social impact of the draconian measures. However, there were two major macro-economic effects that are broadly considered undesirable.

First, instituted in a context of the societal importance of having a male child for support in old age and family continuity, it was natural that if only one child was allowed that should be a boy. A family was generally allowed to have a second child if the first was a girl – but no more. The sex ratio of births moved quickly to 20 percent more boys than girls. Aside from the social price of achieving that ratio it leads to an imbalance between males and females for marriage. One can argue that it will be substantially self-correcting in the long run (which may be a long time in coming!) as girls will eventually get increasingly large financial offers for marriage. But, for a long time a large number of boys will not be able to marry. A partial solution was to import girls for marriage from nearby lower-income countries (e.g., Vietnam). But that is proving at best a partial answer. Finally, the policy has changed. The result is a powerful argument against drastic policies for reducing birth rates. However, it is notable that in India a disproportion of boys has occurred in the context of now being able to make sex identification tests in the early stages of pregnancy.

Second, as the dramatic decline in birth rates works through the age distribution the proportion of the population of working age declines substantially. There will be a shortage of young workers to support retiring people and that just when the length of time in retirement is increasing due to greater longevity at the older ages. At the very least this change adds urgency to pushing up incomes, economic transformation, poverty reduction and of course accelerated agricultural growth, in the demographic window of lower dependency ratios. China has been taking advantage of that potential but many countries are not taking advantage of that important demographic window.

For a short period, India also instituted a program similar to China's one-child program. However, it soon collapsed amid negative public uproar.

Rapid expansion of urbanization, formal education, roads, and electrification are important changes that reduce birth rates, even without specific attention. Education is the most obvious, especially girls' education. Numerous studies are consistent in the importance of girls' education to a large set of variables from agricultural production to family planning (see Lutz and Samir 2011).

As modernization occurs the sources of important knowledge for family decisions shift from entirely within the village to, in a large part, out of the village. When knowledge is largely within the village the farmer's wife has as good or possibly better access than the husband and therefore her participation in family decision making is important. Her influence may be culturally determined to be indirect but it is substantial.

As the location of knowledge about farming technology, health, and education shifts out of the village to increasingly distant places the wife loses access and therefore influence relative to the husband. That need not happen. A concerted effort on many fronts is needed—including formal schools, access to extension agents, and provision of home economics extension agents. None of that happens naturally. It requires explicit attention to the objective of women's participation. The point here is that a decline in women's influence in the household also lessens their influence in joint family planning decisions.

Education leads to more knowledge available about health and nutrition and absorbing the knowledge increases women's role in the family. In Western Europe and North America there was a long tradition of strong home economics training programs that emphasized health and nutrition in a practical manner, working largely through the wives. Very few low- and middle-income countries have such programs.

Roads are critical to getting trained personnel into agricultural areas that are essential for modernization, and that applies to education and family planning as well. The same points apply to rural electrification. Poor transportation inhibits girls' participation in formal education more than boys so there is a gender and hence birth rate dimension to the infrastructure question. Similarly, physical infrastructure and micro-credit are particularly important to women's participation in the increased employment associated with rapid agricultural growth. That type of employment is traditionally important to women in rural areas. The more women who participate in the small businesses so important to the economic transformation, the greater their ability to influence birth rate issues and of course the greater their interest in that issue.

Directly following independence, India initiated and continues to this day a large-scale publicity program advocating a two-child family: one family two children. That program had many components and included large posters prominently posted everywhere depicting a happy family of husband, wife and two smiling children, one boy and one girl. There was a parallel large-scale organizational effort to publicize family planning. There were also substantial foreign aid technical assistance programs which were largely acceptable in that context. All that effort has been reduced in late-developing countries as in Africa.

These programs helped to bring a general view in rural areas of a three- or four-child family. That was not the two children of India's publicity. That would come soon to urban areas and later to rural areas. The effectiveness in early decades was low, probably due to the ineffectiveness of birth control methods at those times. With major improvements in birth control technology the publicity campaigns paid off in a significant decline in birth rates. However, it remained difficult for the administrative structures to fully meet the needs of rural women for access to birth control in a discreet manner essential to their participation.

It is reasonable to assume that intensive publicity efforts, accompanied by programs to ensure the ready availability of the full range of birth control technologies, are an important reason why birth rates have fallen much more rapidly in still low-income India compared to most other low-income countries and that such programs work reasonably well in achieving population growth rates that can be managed in the context of rapid agricultural growth.

The Demographic Dividend

In low- and middle-income countries a rapid decline in birth rates decreases the dependency ratio. There are fewer children to support. It increases the proportion of the population working. That is the demographic dividend (see Williamson 2013). It is a temporary window of opportunity. It is important to realize this potential by increasing employment opportunities and to do so before the proportion of aging elderly increases the dependency ratio. Employment-intensive, rapid agricultural growth helps obtain the demographic dividend. Many countries appear to be failing on this front.

Population Density

Population density is the population per unit of area. Population density is of course the product of population growth. However, once it has occurred, high density is a plus for economic growth. In rural areas high population density is normally a reflection of productive agricultural resources. Productive resources lead to higher incomes and in traditional low- and middle-income countries to faster population growth. Once the population has become dense it spreads overhead costs, such as roads and education, over more families and favors innovation from human interaction. Sparsely populated areas are difficult and expensive to develop.

Boserup (1965) shows how increasing population density leads to a change in technique towards land use intensity, an increase in productivity, and greater soil conservation. Tiffen et al. (1994) provide a nuanced, detailed analysis of the complex processes by which increasing population density led to a wide range of changes that increase production and concurrently introduce soil conservation measures (see also Hayami and Ruttan 1985).

VARIABLES THAT DETERMINE AGRICULTURE'S IMPACT ON THE ECONOMIC TRANSFORMATION

The processes by which rapid agricultural growth affects the economic transformation are complex (for book length treatment, see Mellor 1995, 1976). They start with the small commercial farmer and go through the rural non-farm population. Three variables dominate the size of the impact: the magnitude of increased income to the small commercial farmer from modernization and its expenditure on the rural non-farm sector; the size of the rural non-farm sector relative to the small commercial farm sector and the absolute size of both; and the employment elasticity of each rural sector (the percentage increase in employment derived from a given percentage increase in production). Prior to discussion of these variables is a brief review of cross-sectional studies of the impact of agricultural growth on poverty reduction.

The Dominance of Agricultural Growth in Poverty Reduction: Cross-Section Analysis

Several analyses, including from the World Bank (Ravallion and Datt 2002), Harvard University (Timmer 1997), the United Kingdom's Overseas Development Institute (Thirtle et al. 2003) document from quite different data sets and across different sets of countries that agricultural growth reduces poverty rapidly while industrial growth does not. The antecedent to these studies was a seminal paper by Ahluwalia (1978) that analysed fluctuations in Indian agricultural production, largely driven by weather, on poverty. That weather influence is corroborated by Christiaensen et al. (2011) and is important to our analysis of price relationships.

The World Bank's World Development Report for Agriculture (2008) provides a survey of a large number of analyses of the impact of agricultural growth on poverty reduction and concludes that agricultural growth has four times the impact on poverty reduction as growth in the sum of other sectors. Christiaensen et al. (2011) further confirmed the World Bank findings and noted that agricultural growth was associated with substantial rate of growth of labor productivity. Indeed, agricultural labor productivity grew much faster than urban industrial labor productivity. That is consistent with an assumption in the quantitative analysis in the next chapter. They also found the impact of agriculture on poverty reduction was greater for the under one dollar a day poor (1996 price levels) than for the two dollars a day poor. That is consistent with the assumption in the calculations in the next chapter that the rural non-farm sector is dominated by the extreme poor: the under one dollar a day.

These studies also show a lag in the full effect on poverty of agricultural growth. That is consistent with the process being complex, as described in this chapter. Timmer (1997) also shows that the favorable impact of agricultural growth on poverty reduction is greatly diminished if the agriculture is dominated by large-scale farms. That is also consistent with the exposition in this chapter.

The preceding studies do not explain how this relationship works. That sets the stage for a detailed explanation in this book which can now be done with full confidence in the relationship of agriculture with poverty.

Agriculture's impact on poverty reduction would be clear if agricultural production was generated primarily by those below the poverty line. Put simply, the rural poor would grow more food and consume it. Exposition later in this chapter shows that is not the case. The studies just cited, except for Christiaensen et al. (2011), implicitly assumed that direct relationship. We show that increased agricultural production comes almost entirely from the non-poor, small commercial farmer. That apparent anomaly is analysed, explained, and related to the economic transformation in the next sections of this chapter.

In the early years of the "green revolution" when sudden availability of highly productive new technology gave a huge boost to agricultural production in Asian countries that process was popularly derided because it was noted that production was from the commercial farms and not the poor, and hence was not driving down poverty. Griffin (1974) is representative of a substantial literature to that effect. The cross-section studies noted earlier describe a lag from the increase in agricultural production to the decline in poverty. That is the explanation for the initially apparent lack of "green revolution" impact on poverty. Poverty did soon decline markedly in the "green revolution" countries.

Expenditure by the Small Commercial Farmer
The driving engine of agriculture's impact on the economic transformation is the biological, science-based, technological change that radically increases the productivity and income of small commercial farmers. They produce the bulk of agricultural output in low- and middle-income countries. They spend half of their incremental income on the rural non-farm sector.

There is a large literature supporting this position. The initial study, for Malaysia, that provides the half of expenditure spent on the rural non-farm sector result was by Bell et al. (1982). That was followed by a large number of studies from the International Food Policy Research Institute (IFPRI) including a key paper (1983) and a book co-authored by Hazell and Ramasamy (1991), and a review paper by Delgado and his colleagues (1998). Studies by Mead and Liedholm (1998) of the rural non-farm sector confirm that farmers are the source of demand for the sector. That is further reinforced for Egypt by Gavian et al. (2002).

There are three striking impressions in observing areas of rapid agricultural growth. I draw on widespread travel across modernizing agriculture in eight countries of Asia and Africa and focus group discussions with officials in those areas—most notably the Provincial Governor of a prosperous rural province in Egypt, who impatiently noted "everyone knows that prosperous farmers bring vibrant market towns!".

The market towns in areas of rapid agricultural growth are vibrant places in stark contrast to the stagnant atmosphere in market towns surrounded by stagnant agriculture. New shops open regularly, there are crowded streets, a lot of bus traffic. Second, the villages are notable for the dramatic change in housing: thatched roofs, dirt floors, and mud brick walls are replaced by solid plastered brick and other solid durable materials. The amount of locally made furniture increases dramatically. Third is the frequency of bus travel. Everyone wants to travel, and rising incomes permit it. The buses are staffed and repaired locally (and frequently!). The better the infrastructure, the stronger all this derived growth.

Most of these goods and services are pure labor—there is little or no capital. Because of the large underemployment of labor in the rural non-farm sector, these labor-intensive goods and services are low in price compared to purchased goods from outside. Farmers have an ample incentive to continue spending heavily in the local area. As growth occurs these activities migrate to the nearby market towns where there are external economies for their activities. The suppliers of these goods and services note the changing needs of prospering farmers and so the composition changes over time, but remains labor intensive.

In addition to being labor intensive in production, these goods and services are also non-tradable, meaning there is no market for them outside the local area. Table 1.4 corroborates this. It is not urban income driving these enterprises. It is and must be local agriculture.

As agricultural modernization proceeds, labor bottlenecks appear that are met with farm mechanization, often initially with quite small machines. A few of the many workshops that do repairs, outside of agriculture as well as within, will gravitate to manufacturing a wide variety of items and selling outside the region. That forwards the process of development of larger market towns and a gradual disconnect from agriculture. Rapid agricultural growth fosters a disbursed pattern of urbanization, much of which eventually has little connection with agriculture but does benefit from relatively lower wage rates and household capital availability. That comes more fully in the middle-income stage of development.

Taiwan established a pattern of a high proportion of exports coming from medium-sized firms scattered in towns throughout the country (Lee 2003). Those firms started servicing agriculture. This is entirely different to the pattern of very large-scale industry centered in the major cities in South Korea, made possible by very large capital inflows from the United States. In most European and North American countries there is a pattern of disbursed urbanization that grew out of the agriculture-oriented market towns. Chicago was once a "cow town."

With half of incremental income spent in the rural non-farm sector, the other half is equally divided between increased food consumption and modern, urban supplied, manufactured goods. Those goods are retailed in the nearby market towns. The quarter of incremental income spent on urban supplied goods, is often modern such as cell phones, radios and even TVs as well as personal service goods. That quarter of income helps to drive increased urban production. However, it is less important than the half of income spent on the rural non-farm sector. That is partly because the former goes for capital-intensive goods often with an import content, and thus generates much less employment than in the labor-intensive rural non-farm sector.

Relative Size of the Rural Non-farm Sector

What is the percentage increase in income of the rural non-farm households generated by a given increase in income of the small commercial farm? Obviously the larger the increase in income, the greater the impact on poverty. Later chapters will quantify the effect of differences in the rate of growth of farm income. Likewise, the larger the small commercial farm sector, the bigger the impact. But the impact also depends on the relative size of small commercial farm and rural non-farm sectors.

If the rural non-farm sector is larger than the small commercial farm sector, then the percentage rise in income of the rural non-farm sector is proportionately less and vice versa if it is smaller. More precisely, to arrive at the percentage increase, the incremental expenditure by the small farmer sector has to be multiplied by the ratio of the sizes of the two sectors.

As will be shown for Pakistan, a long period of population growth with little growth in agriculture results in division of farms, more and more falling into the rural non-farm category, increasing poverty, and a diminishing impact of a given agricultural growth rate on rural non-farm incomes. Similarly, if slow, then urban growth backs up the rural non-farm population.

The rural non-farm sector spends some of its income on itself. That further increases the size of the sector as will be reflected later in the quantification section.

Employment Elasticity by Sector

The three rural household classes differ dramatically in the percentage increase in employment in response to a given percentage increase in income. These elasticities are very important and surprisingly there is very little measurement of them. The following relies on just a few studies and is based heavily on the underlying logic.

The small commercial farm in the context of yield-increasing technology change experiences substantial increase in labor productivity. It requires very little additional labor to harvest a larger crop and to use fertilizer. Data from the Indian Green Revolution showed that each ten percent increase in output from that technology resulted in only a three percent increase in labor used (Rao 1975). That is an employment elasticity of 0.3 (Rao 1975). That elasticity would be even lower for large commercial farmers because they are somewhat mechanized.

In sharp contrast, the rural non-farm sector, producing labor-intensive goods and services and operating at very low wage rates experiences very little increase in labor productivity as utilization rises. Increased demand will be met by increased supply of labor with little or no increase in productivity or wages. That will continue until the initially large supply of underemployed labor is absorbed.

Ellen McCullough (2016) in a detailed analysis cutting across several Sub-Saharan African countries of the World Bank's large data sets on labor utilization finds "vast reserves of underemployed labor." Those data are strongly supportive of the assumption that lack of demand is the constraint to expansion of the rural non-farm sector and that relief of the demand constraint is in a context of highly elastic supply of labor and an employment elasticity close to 1.0.

Thus the employment elasticity is conservatively estimated at 0.9. A ten percent increase in production of that sector's goods and services results in a nine percent increase in employment. Note that this exposition is fully consistent with Lewis's (1954) seminal position of "unlimited supplies of labor." However, the nature and location of that employment is radically different to Lewis's exposition. Our exposition is more nearly a two-stage shift to urban industry.

Rural labor markets do tighten surprisingly early in rapid growth. That is because of the big employment impact in the rural non-farm sector. As that happens, labor productivity for much of the sector can slowly increase—retail labor becomes more efficient, carpenters use somewhat better tools. The employment elasticity does not change much.

Data for the increase in urban employment in response to output increase give a mixed picture, but generally it is low. Some studies show no increase in employment even with quite a significant increase in urban manufacturing production. Urban manufacturing is in labor-intensive industries and tends to be connected to competitive international markets with the consequent need to increase labor productivity—that is, to reduce labor content. Some urban services have quite a high elasticity. The judgement reached is that 0.5 is the highest level to be found and is an average between quite a high elasticity for the services sector and a very low one for the manufacturing sector. We will use this as being conservative from the point of view of measuring agriculture's impact.

Note

1. Crist et al. (2017) make the case for "eventually reversing population growth," on the grounds of the already out of hand reduction in biodiversity with large spread effects. That would strongly reinforce the poverty reduction relationships discussed in this chapter. They also document the sharp decline in emphasis on reduced population growth rates attributing that in part to the view that the green revolution reduced the urgency of feeding an increased population.

References

Ahluwalia, M. S. (1978). Rural poverty and agricultural performance in India. *Journal of Development Studies, 14*, 298–323.

Bell, C., Hazell, P., & Slade, R. (1982). *Project evaluation in regional perspective: A study of an irrigation project in Northwest Malaysia.* Baltimore: Johns Hopkins University Press.

Bocquet-Appel, J. P. (2011). The agricultural demographic transition during and after the agriculture inventions. *Current Anthropology, 52*(S4), S497–S510.

Boserup, E. (1965). *The conditions of agricultural growth: The economics of agrarian change under population pressure.* Abingdon: Routledge.

Christiaensen, L., Demery, L., & Kuhl, J. (2011). The (evolving) role of agriculture in poverty reduction: An empirical perspective. *Journal of Development Economics, 96*(2), 239–254.

Crist, E., Mora, C., & Engelman, R. (2017). The interaction of human population, food production, and biodiversity practice. *Science, 356*(6335), 260–264.

Delgado, C. L., Hopkines, J., Kelly, V. A., Hazell, P., Mckenna, A. A., Gruhn, P., et al. (1998). *Agricultural growth linkages in sub-Saharan Africa.* Washington, DC: International Finance Corporation.

Galor, O., & Weil, D. (2000). Population, technology, and growth: From Malthusian stagnation to the demographic transition and beyond. *The American Economic Review, 90*(4), 806–828.

Garenne, M., & Joseph, V. (2002). The timing of the fertility transition in sub-Saharan Africa. *World Development, 30*(10), 1835–1843.

Gavian, S., El-Meehy, T., Bulbul, L., & Ender, G. (2002). The importance of agricultural growth to SME development and rural employment in Egypt. In G. Ender & J. S. Holtzman (Eds.), *Does agricultural policy reform work? The impact on Egypt's agriculture, 1996–2002* (pp. 395–435). Bethesda: Abt Associates Inc.

Griffin, K. B. (1974). *The political economy of agrarian change: An essay on the green revolution.* Cambridge, MA: Harvard University Press.

Hesketh, T., Lu, L., & Xing, Z. W. (2005). The effect of China's one-child family policy after 25 years. *New England Journal of Medicine, 353*(11), 1171–1176.

Hazell, P. B., & Röell, A. (1983). *Rural growth linkages: Household expenditure patterns in Malaysia and Nigeria* (Vol. 41). Washington, DC: International Food Policy Research Institute.

Hazell, P.B., & Ramasamy, C. (1991). *The green revolution reconsidered: The impact of high yielding varieties in South India.* Baltimore: John Hopkins University Press.

Hayami, Y., & Ruttan, V. W. (1985). *Agricultural development: An international perspective* (2nd ed.). Baltimore: Johns Hopkins University Press.

Lee, R. (2003). The demographic transition: Three centuries of fundamental change. *The Journal of Economic Perspectives, 17*(4), 167–190.

Lewis, W. A. (1954). Economic development with unlimited supplies of labour. *The Manchester School, 22*(2), 139–191.

Lutz, W., & Samir, K. C. (2011). Global human capital: Integrating education and population. *Science, 333*(6042), 587–592.

McCullough, E. B. (2016). Labor productivity and employment gaps in sub-Saharan Africa. *Food Policy, 67*, 133–152.

Mead, D. C., & Liedholm, C. (1998). The dynamics of micro and small enterprises in developing countries. *World Development, 26*(1), 61–74.

Mellor, J. W. (1976). *The new economics of growth: A strategy for India and the developing world*. Ithaca: Cornell University Press.

Mellor, J. W. (Ed.). (1995). *Agriculture on the road to industrialization*. Baltimore: Published for the International Food Policy Research Institute (IFPRI) by Johns Hopkins University Press.

Rao, C. H. (1975). *Technological change and the distribution of gains in Indian agriculture* (Vol. 17). Delhi: Macmillan Company of India.

Ravallion, M., & Datt, G. (2002). Why has economic growth been more pro-poor in some states of India than others? *Journal of Development Economics, 68*(2), 381–400.

Thirtle, C., Lin, L., & Piesse, J. (2003). The impact of research-led agricultural productivity growth on poverty reduction in Africa, Asia and Latin America. *World Development, 31*(12), 1959–1975.

Tiffen, M., Mortimore, M., & Gichuki, F. (1994). *More people less erosion: Environmental recovery in Kenya*. London: Overseas Development Institute.

Timmer, C. P. (1997). *How well do the poor connect to the growth process?* (CAER Discussion Paper No. 17). Cambridge, MA: Harvard Institute for International Development.

Williamson, J. G. (2013). Demographic dividends revisited. *Asian Development Review, 30*(2), 1–25.

World Bank Group. (2008). *World development report 2008: Agriculture for development*. Washington, DC: World Bank Group.

CHAPTER 3

Measuring the Impact of Agricultural Growth on Economic Transformation

This chapter measures the impact, by household sector, of rapid growth in agricultural production on income and employment growth and food security. It does so by accommodating the variables described in the preceding chapter in a spreadsheet and calculating and comparing the effect of a six percent and a three percent growth rate in agricultural production. The difference in impact is large.

The next section presents the methodology, followed by application to two different agricultural production growth rates and then the effect of converting feudal land holdings to small commercial farms. The applications are to a low-income country and two quite different provinces within a middle-income country. A sensitivity test of change in the employment elasticities is also carried out and shows the results sensitive to that assumption.

METHODOLOGY

We use a simplified growth accounting framework and multipliers based on the assumptions underlying two sector economic-based fixed price models. We assume a regionally tradable output (agriculture) as the framework's economic base, and a non-tradable output that is perfectly elastic and determined solely by local demand (production by the rural non-farm sector). Haggblade et al. (1991) show that this model is more practical for our purposes as compared to more sophisticated models. That is particularly important given the shortage of reliable data.

Data for the variables discussed in the preceding chapter are inserted into an Excel spreadsheet and the impact of various assumptions tested. This is another

Electronic Supplementary Material: The online version of this article (https://doi. org/10.1007/978-3-319-65259-7_3) contains supplementary material, a spreadsheet for the calculations in the various tables, which is available to authorized users.

J.W. Mellor, *Agricultural Development and Economic Transformation*, Palgrave Studies in Agricultural Economics and Food Policy, https://doi.org/10.1007/978-3-319-65259-7_3

advantage to this methodology. It focuses on a small number of key variables that can be managed in a simple spreadsheet that in turn facilitates changing the coefficients as better data become available and testing for sensitivity. The spreadsheet is available, which is important given the current paucity of data and the expectation that this book will stimulate more empirical analysis of these variables. Mellor and Malik (2017) explain in detail the derivation of the Excel spreadsheet facilitating its reproduction and further use. Annex provides more detail on the construction of Tables 3.1, 3.2, 3.3, 3.4, 3.5, 3.6, and 3.7.

Each of the following sections present two tables covering a six percent and a three percent agricultural growth rate. The six percent growth rate is the carefully derived CAADP recommendation for Sub-Saharan Africa, and one used throughout this book, and is somewhat slower than that actually achieved in Ethiopia over the past 20 years. The three percent rate, as described in the preceding chapter, is what a traditional agriculture might achieve in the context of high population growth rates. That is faster than the actual agricultural growth rate in a substantial number of low- and middle-income countries. The growth rate for the urban sector is assumed at a high eight percent.

Six Percent Agricultural Growth Rate for Ethiopia

Ethiopia in its overall economic structure and proportions of the major rural household classes is broadly representative of other low-income countries (see Mellor and Malik 2017 and Jayne et al. 2006 for Africa). Ethiopia is of course exceptional in its continuous long-term success in achieving a high agricultural growth rate.

Ethiopia's urban production sector is large, but not dominant, at 42 percent of national income and 20 percent of national employment (Table 3.1). The rural sector comprises 58 percent of income with 19 percentage points of that being rural and small town-based industry and services and 39 percentage points being for agriculture. The rural non-farm sector measured by income is nearly half as large as the total urban sector.

Comparing rural and urban sectors, the household distribution is quite different to the income distribution, reflecting quite different levels of labor productivity and underemployment. The rural non-farm sector has 80 percent more households than its share of production, while the urban sector has 50 percent less. The differences in productivity, in a substantial part, reflect differences in capital and land per person. It also reflects underemployment of labor, considerable in the rural non-farm sector, substantial in parts of the small commercial farm sector, and relatively small in the urban sector (for empirical data on this see the careful analysis by McCullough 2016).

Assuming a six percent agricultural and eight percent urban growth rate, the employment growth rate is 3.7 percent, 50 percent higher than the population growth rate (Table 3.1). That brings rapid decline in poverty consistent with the World Bank poverty data (World Bank 2014). The high 5.1 percent employment

Table 3.1 Sectorial employment and income growth rates with a 6.0 percent rate of growth of the agricultural sector, Ethiopia

Sector	Base employment (%)	Base GDP (%)	Growth GDP (%)	Employment elasticity	Employment growth (%)	Incremental employment (%)	Incremental GDP (%)
Small commercial farming households	37	30	6	0.3	1.8	18	28
Rural non-farming households	43	24	5.7	0.9	5.1	60	22
Large commercial farming households	Less than 1	4	6	0.3	1.8	Less than 1	4
Rural households, total	80	58	5.5	0.6	3.6	78	54
Urban households, total	20	42	8	0.5	4.0	22	46
Total/Average	100	100	6.4	0.6	3.7	100	100

growth rate for the rural non-farm sector means a very rapid decline in poverty in that poverty dominated sector. That also explains why rural labor markets in rapid-growth agricultural, low-income countries so often tighten, with rising real wages, much earlier in development than had been expected.

The high employment elasticity for the rural non-farm sector and the large expenditure by the small commercial farmers in that sector are the major reasons for the large employment impact of agricultural growth. Note that 78 percent of the employment growth occurs in the rural sector, and 73 percent of the non-agricultural employment growth (rural plus urban) is in the rural sector. Employment grows in the two farming sectors at a slow 1.8 percent rate. With rapid agricultural growth, agriculture dominates the economic transformation. The faster agriculture grows the faster its *relative* importance declines.

The six percent growth rate for agriculture, assumed for comparative purposes, is somewhat slower than the actual rate Ethiopia maintained for the past 20 years. Ethiopia did better than shown in Table 3.1. A small number of other African countries are taking up the CAADP strategy and are showing initial signs of accelerating their agricultural sectors. Unfortunately, there have been short periods in the past that showed good agricultural growth, often simply a period of recovery from a previous setback, and then a slip back into the traditional growth rate.

A comprehensive analysis of Ethiopia by the World Bank showed that from 1994 to 2014 poverty dropped from the initially very high level of a little over 50 percent of the rural population to a little over 25 percent (World Bank 2014). The earlier number is typical of low-income countries. The latter is lower than some middle-income countries such as Pakistan. As is usual when the agricultural growth rate accelerates it has a larger impact on employment than on income.

It should be noted that the assumptions in all these tables are conservative so actual employment and growth rates will be faster than shown.

THREE PERCENT AGRICULTURAL GROWTH RATE FOR ETHIOPIA

Table 3.2 shows the disastrous impact in a low-income country of the traditional three percent agricultural growth rate. Typically, Sub-Saharan African countries have been averaging less than three percent agricultural growth rates.

The employment growth rate drops to 2.2 percent, well below the population growth rate.

Poverty will increase, even while the GDP growth rate moves along at 4.7 percent well above the population growth rate. The overall employment growth rate in the rural sector is 1.8 percent, two-thirds of the population growth rate. The poverty-dominated rural non-farm sector has a growth rate of 2.6 percent right at the population growth rate so there is little chance of poverty decline in that sector.

Even with such a slow agricultural growth rate, the rural sector still accounts for 64 percent of incremental employment. Thirty-six percent of employment

Table 3.2 Sectorial employment and income growth rates with a 3.0 percent rate of growth of the agricultural sector, Ethiopia

Sector	Base employment (%)	Base GDP (%)	Growth GDP (%)	Employment elasticity	Employment growth (%)	Incremental employment (%)	Incremental GDP (%)
Small commercial farming households	37	30	3.0	0.3	0.9	15	19
Rural non-farming households	43	24	2.9	0.9	2.6	49	15
Large commercial farming households	Less than 1	4	3.0	0.3	0.9	Less than 1	2
Rural Households, Total	80	58	2.7	0.6	1.8	64	36
Urban Households, Total	20	42	8	0.5	4.0	36	64
Total/Average	100	100	4.7	0.6	2.2	100	100

growth and 64 percent of GDP growth occurs in the urban sector. It is at such a high percentage because of the poor performance in agriculture.

As we will see in Chap. 4, the declining incomes in the rural sector will push the smaller small commercial farms into the rural non-farm sector as their size of farm decreases with increased numbers of children and the underemployed labor force grows. Poverty then increases. Migration to the cities will also increase in a desperate job search but with very slow job expansion unemployment will increase there as well. People keep coming to, in effect, stand in line for urban jobs. The larger the income differential, including any urban benefits, the larger the pool of urban unemployed (see Todaro and Smith 2011).

Increasing rural poverty, increasing rural underemployment, and increasing urban unemployment have been the standard story in most African countries over the past few decades. The neglect of agriculture lies behind that sad story.

Measuring Agriculture's Impact on the Economic Transformation: Middle-Income Countries

Middle-income countries have transformed to having far larger urban sectors than low-income countries. In order to achieve that, many countries had at least a period of rapid growth in agriculture. They may also have utilized other natural resources and foreign aid to provide additional resources to expand the urban sector. Punjab and Sindh Provinces of Pakistan are both middle-income, with Punjab being broadly representative of the situation of a period of rapid agricultural growth that ended prematurely and Sindh having the additional characteristic of a large feudal farming sector.

Six Percent Agricultural Growth Rate for Punjab, Pakistan

The agriculture of Punjab is dominated by excellent, largely irrigated, agricultural resources, and had a period during the 1970s and 1980s of rapid agricultural growth, which brought considerable economic transformation including a substantial rural non-farm sector. Subsequent to that period, most agricultural growth institutions failed to grow or deteriorated, with the exception of the agricultural university, and agricultural growth slowed to below the traditional rate averaging 2.2 percent for several years. As a result of the latter, rural poverty increased as farms divided with the smaller ones dropping into the rural non-farm category and underemployment in that sector increasing greatly.

Assuming the same rapid growth rates as for Ethiopia in each of the three exogenous sectors, Punjab shows a 14 percent faster GDP growth rate than Ethiopia (Table 3.3 compared to 3.1). That is largely due to the much higher proportion of the economy in the faster-growing urban sector.

In the fast agricultural growth scenario, overall GDP grows at a rapid 7.2 percent rate. Employment grows at 3.9 percent, which is 56 percent faster than the population growth rate and represents a rapid decline in rural and overall

Table 3.3 Sectorial employment and income growth rates with a 6.0 percent rate of growth of the agricultural sector, Punjab

Sector	Base employment (%)	Base GDP (%)	Growth GDP (%)	Employment elasticity	Employment growth (%)	Incremental employment (%)	Incremental GDP (%)
Small commercial farming households	8	15	6.0	0.3	1.8	4	12
Rural non-farming households	32	12	4.7	0.9	4.2	34	8
Large commercial farming households	Less than 1	4	6.0	0.3	1.8	Less than 1	3
Rural households, total	40	31	5.5	0.8	3.7	38	23
Urban households, total	60	69	8.0	0.5	4.0	62	77
Total/Average	100	100	7.2	0.6	3.9	100.00	100.00

poverty. It also accelerates the economic transformation due to the rapid growth of employment in the rural non-farm sector. The rural non-farm sector, increasingly located in market towns, grows at 4.2 percent. The rural non-farm sector accounts for 34 percent of the total increments to employment. That is nearly half as large as the additions to urban employment. Thus we see substantial growth in the market towns and hence geographic dispersal of urbanization. This of course is what would have happened if Pakistan provided for rapid agricultural growth. What actually happened is even worse than that depicted next.

Three Percent Agricultural Growth Rate for Punjab, Pakistan

The importance of agriculture to economic transformation, employment, and poverty reduction shows dramatically when the impact of a three percent agricultural growth rate is measured (Table 3.4). Actually, the Pakistan agricultural growth rate declined to 2.2 percent. The urban growth rate is maintained at eight percent to focus on the impact of the two different agricultural growth rates.

The overall GDP growth rate declines by 19 percent. The employment growth rate declines by 21 percent: from 3.9 percent to 3.1 percent. The urban sector provides 87 percent of GDP growth and the rural sector only 13 percent. The urban sector provides 77 percent of employment growth and the rural non-farm sector only 21 percent. However, the apparent rise of the urban sector simply reflects the decline of the rural sector.

Thus, even with rapid urban growth rural underemployment increases, the economic transformation slows, and what economic transformation occurs is concentrated in the major cities, most likely the one or two largest cities rather than being dispersed in market towns.

Sindh, Pakistan

Sindh has a similar distribution to Punjab of GDP and employment between agriculture and urban sectors. It differs in having a large feudal farm sector. That results in a much smaller, small commercial farm sector both in employment and in share of GDP.

There is a difference between the large commercial farms of the Punjab and the feudal holdings in the Sindh. That difference will be general wherever feudal holdings exist, although most countries with feudal systems have converted them through land reforms to small commercial farms, using "land to the tiller" programs or have evolved into large commercial farms as in parts of Latin America.

A feudal holding manages the land by dividing it into small holdings, usually considerably smaller than the small commercial farms, and manages them on a sharecropping basis. However, there is normally a substantial difference in size of tenant farms, with a portion comprised of moderately prosperous larger tenants.

Table 3.4 Sectorial employment and income growth rates with a 3.0 percent rate of growth of the agricultural sector, Punjab

Sector	Base employment (%)	Base GDP (%)	Growth GDP (%)	Employment elasticity	Employment growth (%)	Incremental employment (%)	Incremental GDP (%)
Small commercial farming households	8	15	3.0	0.3	0.9	2	7
Rural non-farming households	32	12	2.4	0.9	2.1	21	4
Large commercial farming households	Less than 1	4	3.0	0.3	0.9	Less than 1	2
Rural households, total	40	31	2.8	0.8	1.8	23	13
Urban households, total	60	69	8.0	0.5	4.0	77	87
Total/Average	100	100	6.4	0.6	3.1	100.00	100.00

That is probably the least management-intensive approach for maintaining control. The system suffers low productivity.

Commercial farmers both small and large prefer cash rents as that allows them to provide good management and reap the benefits of that. Thus in Pakistan, all the sharecropped land is counted as large feudal holdings and the tenants are counted as rural non-farm since they keep only half the income from the farm, have poor incentives to increase production, and only small holdings that leave them very poor.

With those definitions, compared to Punjab, Sindh has only half as high a proportion of small commercial farmers (Table 3.2 and 3.5). In Punjab the rural non-farm sector is substantially smaller than the small commercial farm sector, while in Sindh it is substantially larger. The expenditure of the small commercial farmers on the rural non-farm sector is spread over a larger number of households and so the impact of the small commercial farmer on poverty reduction is less in Sindh compared to Punjab.

The result is a 40 percent slower growth of the rural non-farm sector employment in Sindh and 3.4 percent growth rate in overall employment compared to 3.9 percent in Punjab. In this fast agricultural growth scenario 28 percent of the incremental employment is in the rural households in Sindh compared to 38 percent in Punjab. Thus both poverty reduction and the economic transformation proceeds more slowly in Sindh even with the same growth rates in each of the sectors.

Dropping the Sindh's agricultural growth rate to three percent reduces the rate of growth of employment from 3.4 percent to 2.9 percent (Table 3.6). That is a little above the population growth rate. The employment growth is mostly in the urban sector: 83 percent. Of course that is a high share of a very low rate of employment growth. The impact of the slow agricultural growth is even worse on employment in Sindh than in Punjab.

CONVERTING SHARECROPPING TO SMALL COMMERCIAL FARMS

Converting sharecroppers to small commercial farmers has two major effects on poverty reduction. In time, sharecroppers with new incentives should take up more productive farming methods. Second, they will take on the expenditure pattern of small commercial farmers. The income transfer is from expenditure on capital and import-intensive goods and services in the urban sector to labor-intensive rural non-farm producers in the rural sector. That has an important effect on rural poverty. The following focuses on the latter impact. These were the land tenure reforms of Japan, Taiwan, China, India, and Ethiopia. Most of the literature focuses on the effect on farm productivity, but the effect on poverty through the linkages described in this book is substantial.

Because the incomes of tenants are relatively low it is difficult to show how they can pay for the land in a land reform. Therefore, it is not surprising that most

Table 3.5 Sectorial employment and income growth rates with a 6.0 percent rate of growth of the agricultural sector, Sindh

Sector	Base employment (%)	Base GDP (%)	Growth GDP (%)	Employment elasticity	Employment growth (%)	Incremental employment (%)	Incremental GDP (%)
Small commercial households	4	9	6.0	0.3	1.8	2	7
Rural non-farm households	36	12	2.8	0.9	2.5	26	5
Large commercial/feudal households	Less than 1	6	6.0	0.3	1.8	Less than 1	5
Rural total	40	27	4.6	0.8	2.4	28	17
Urban	60	73	8.0	0.5	4.0	72	83
Total/Average	100	100	7.1	0.6	3.4	100.00	100.00

Table 3.6 Sectorial employment and income growth rates with a 3.0 percent rate of growth of the agricultural sector, Sindh

Sector	Base employment (%)	Base GDP (%)	Growth GDP (%)	Employment elasticity	Employment growth (%)	Incremental employment (%)	Incremental GDP (%)
Small commercial farming households	4	9	3.0	0.3	0.9	1	4
Rural non-farming households	36	12	1.4	0.9	1.3	16	3
Large commercial farming households	0	5	3.0	0.3	0.9	Less than 1	3
Rural households, total	40	27	2.3	0.8	1.2	17	10
Urban households, total	60	73	8.0	0.5	4.0	83	90
Total/Average	100	100	6.5	0.6	2.9	100.00	100.00

feudal land reforms are radical reforms brought about by major changes in government. The feudal landowners are obviously a major part of the power systems and hence if those power systems are overthrown land gets confiscated.

Table 3.7 shows the effect of converting sharecroppers into small commercial farms through redistributing land from feudal owners to sharecroppers so that the farming household keeps the entire income from farming. The focus is on the multiplier effects on rural employment assuming the same level of productivity. We do not calculate the multiplier resulting from the reduced income of the feudal landholders. However, we assume that this multiplier would be small due to the capital and import intensity of high-income urban expenditure patterns.

Table 3.7 takes Table 3.5, for the six percent growth rate in the Sindh, and keeps the assumptions in that table the same except to convert the sharecropping farms into small commercial farms. Recall that in the base situation, sharecropping households and half of sharecropped income are identified under the rural non-farm sector, with the remaining half of sharecropped income allocated to the large-scale feudal sub-sector. In our new scenario, both sets of income are transferred to the small commercial farm sector as are the households operating the sharecropped farms.

Thus, the base employment shares of the small commercial farm sector increases from 4.0 to 22 percent and the share of income increases from 9 to 19 percent. An important effect of these changes is the greatly increased size of the small commercial farm sector relative to the rural non-farm sector: a ratio increase from 0.75 to 1.6. As a result, a given percentage increase in income and expenditure from the small commercial farmer sector has a far greater percentage impact on the rural non-farm sector. In turn, the relative importance of the rural non-farm sector increases greatly as a share of employment and income growth.

This set of changes increases the rate of growth of employment from 3.4 percent to 3.7 percent, virtually the same as in Punjab. The overall annual increment to employment increases by 9.4 percent per year. The share of the rural sectors in employment creation increases from 29 percent to 36 percent. There is an immense reduction in rural poverty quite aside from directly lifting the sharecroppers out of poverty.

There is also an initial increase in total agricultural income from the transfer from sharecropping to small commercial farming. That is because of the large increase in the rural non-farm sector. The result is that the rural sector as a whole increases by 4.1 percent of total income. That is a real addition to national income.

The feudal sector's dominance is the cause of a significantly lower base level of rural income, a lower income growth rate, and a much lower employment growth rate. Converting feudal holdings to large commercial farms would have much less of an impact on employment, income levels, and likely reductions in poverty than converting to small commercial farms.

Table 3.7 Conversion of sharecropped households to small commercial farm households, Sindh

Sector	Base employment (%)	Base GDP (%)	Growth GDP (%)	Employment elasticity	Employment growth (%)	Incremental employment (%)	Incremental GDP (%)
Small commercial farming households	22	19	6.0	0.3	1.8	11	15
Rural non-farming households	18	12	5.8	0.9	5.2	25	9
Large commercial farming households	0	0.0	6.0	0.3	1.8	0.00	0
Rural households, total	40	31	5.9	0.6	3.3	36	24
Urban households, total	60	73	8.0	0.5	4.0	64	76
Total/Average	100	104	7.4	0.5	3.7	100	100

CONCLUSION

Rapid agricultural growth has a dominant impact on employment growth in the largely-poor rural non-farm sector. By impacting that non-agricultural sector, it hastens the economic transformation. Conversely, even with rapid urban industrial and service sector growth, poverty increases when the agricultural growth rate drops to three percent. We see these effects in low- and middle-income Punjab compared to low-income Ethiopia. The effect is greatly muted by substitution of a feudal system for much of the small commercial farmer sector. However, if the feudal system is converted through expropriation to a small commercial farmer system, the impact on poverty reduction climbs back close to that of Punjab.

ANNEX

Simplifying Assumptions to Accommodate Date Sources

(1) Area of farm is a proxy for agricultural income. (2) Households are a proxy for employment. (3) A perfectly elastic supply of labor, due to underemployment as above. Mellor and Ranade (2006) model assumptions of rising wage rate, reducing the employment effect, but still leaving a large effect on employment.

Determinant Calculations

The determinant calculations are for the rural non-farm sector, specifically the size of the sector, column 2, and the rate of growth of income in the sector, column 3. They are determined as follows:

Calculate the rural non-farm base income and growth rate of rural non-farm income which are central to our conclusions, using the formula:

$$Ire = (Ia) + (Inf) \tag{3.1}$$

where Ir is the base income of the rural non-farm class; Ia is agricultural income; and Inf is rural non-farm income.

$$Inf = (Is)(0.5)(1.25) \tag{3.2}$$

and

$$Irg = (Isg)(0.5)(Is/Ir)(1.25) \tag{3.3}$$

where Irg is the average growth rate of income for the rural non-farm sector; Isg is the average income growth rate for small commercial farmers; and $Is/$

Ir is the base ratio of average small commercial farmer income to average rural non-farm income. For an explanation of the latter see the text.

The coefficient of 1.25 is an estimate of the multiplier on spending (20 percent) by the rural non-farm sector, calculated as being spent on itself and iterated until it stabilizes in about five years (1.25).

Summary of Data Sources and Calculations by Column

Column 1. Base employment—The Rural and Urban sectors are reported in National Income Statistics. The division of rural into the three household sectors is according to the definitions in the text of Chap. 1. Rural non-farm calculated as above. Table 1.2 provides the data for Punjab, Sindh, and Ethiopia.

Column 2. Base income—Agriculture and non-agriculture are reported in National Income Statistics. For rural non-farm see above.

Column 3. Growth rate income—Exogenously determined except for rural non-farm, see above.

Column 4. Employment elasticity—Exogenously determined.

Column 5. Growth rate employment—Growth rate of income times the employment elasticity.

Column 7. Percent incremental employment—Growth rate of employment times the base employment and calculate each sector's percent of the total.

Column 9. Percent incremental income—Same as above but for income.

Table 3.8 The spread sheet for calculating Tables 3.1, 3.2, 3.3, 3.4, 3.5, 3.6, and 3.7

Sector	Base employment (%)	Base GDP (%)	Growth GDP (%)	Employment elasticity	Employment growth (%)	Employment 000,000	Incremental employment (%)	GDP	Incremental GDP (%)
SCF	8	15	6.0	0.3	1.8	14.4	3.72	88.2	12.17
RNF	31	12	4.7	0.9	4.2	131.4	33.90	55.1	7.61
LCF	1	4	6.0	0.3	1.8	1.8	0.46	22.7	3.13
rural total	40	30	5.5	0.8	3.7	147.6	38.08	166.0	22.91
urban	60	70	8.0	0.5	4.0	240.0	61.92	558.5	77.09
Total/ Average	100	100	7.2	0.6	3.9	387.6	100.00	724.5	100.00

Sources and calculations for Tables 3.1, 3.2, 3.3, 3.4, 3.5, 3.6, and 3.7

Presented in a generalized form to fit various countries. For detailed exposition specific to Punjab, Sindh, and Ethiopia see Mellor and Malik (2017)

REFERENCES

Haggblade, S., Hammer, J., & Hazell, P. (1991). Modeling agricultural growth multipliers. *American Journal of Agricultural Economics, 73*(2), 361–374.

Jayne, T. S., Mather, D., & Mghenyi, E. (2006). *Smallholder farming under increasingly difficult circumstances: Policy and public investment priorities for Africa* (MSU international development working paper no. 86). East Lansing: Michigan State University.

McCullough, E. B. (2016). Labor productivity and employment gaps in sub-Saharan Africa. *Food Policy, 67*, 133–152.

Mellor, J. W., & Malik, S. J. (2017). The impact of growth in small commercial farm productivity on rural poverty reduction. *World Development, 91*, 1–10.

Mellor, J. W., & Ranade, C. (2006). Why does agricultural growth dominate poverty reduction in low and middle-income countries? *The Pakistan Development Review, 45*(2), 221–240.

Todaro, M. P., & Smith, S. C. (2011). *Economic development* (10th ed.). New York: Prentice Hall/Addison-Wesley.

World Bank Group. (2014). *Ethiopia poverty assessment* (Report No. AUS6744). Washington, DC: World Bank Group.

CHAPTER 4

Poverty, Food Security, and Nutrition

The preceding chapter quantified rapid agricultural growth as the dominant means of reducing poverty. This chapter focuses on categories of the poor who tend not to benefit from rapid agricultural growth. They represent a more difficult context for poverty reduction. As poverty is reduced, food security increases and the focus can shift to the complex problem of improving nutrition quality.

There are substantial geographic areas that have a high proportion of their population in poverty but which are not suitable for the application of the improved technologies that drive agricultural income growth and its transfer to the poor. Those tend to be areas of relatively low population density so they are larger in geographic area than in share of population. More amenable to solution are classes that may not fully participate in poverty reduction even though they are in in areas suitable for rapid technological advance: female-headed households, subsistence farmers, high proportions of rural non-farm households, and disadvantageous tenure conditions.

The focus is largely on extreme poverty—an income of less than one dollar per day in 1996 prices as established by the World Bank (e.g., World Development Report – Agriculture 2008). Overall, extreme poverty has declined from 1.9 billion people in 1981 to 1.4 billion in 2005 (World Bank 2008) and according to UNDP to 1.3 billion in 2012. However, most of that decline has been in China. China registered a low 19 percent of its population in poverty, a decline from well over 50 percent prior to the start of rapid agricultural growth. Subsequently, rural poverty has declined further. The rest of the world decreased marginally from 1.3 billion in 1981 to 1.2 billion in 2005. Extreme poverty is now concentrated in South Asia and Sub-Saharan Africa.

© The Author(s) 2017
J.W. Mellor, *Agricultural Development and Economic Transformation*,
Palgrave Studies in Agricultural Economics and Food Policy,
https://doi.org/10.1007/978-3-319-65259-7_4

Famines are the result of a widespread decrease in the ability of the poor to command sufficient income to provide the minimum food to sustain human life (Mellor and Gavian 1987). Famines are now rare, mainly because of the highly developed response of the World Food Program (WFP) of the United Nations and bilateral programs such as USAID. They have become proficient at spotting famine conditions sufficiently early to move a large quantity of food to the famine locations. Also, famines now are largely political in origin.

The World Development Report (2008) states that 67 percent of those in poverty are in rural areas. Hence the relevance of the focus in this book on rural poverty. Low-income countries tend to range from 50 to 80 percent of the population rural and 40 to 70 percent of the rural population poor, while middle-income countries range from 40 to 60 percent of the population rural and 20 to 50 percent of the rural population poor.

The next section explains why some geographic areas are unresponsive to rapid growth-increasing modern technology and how their poverty incidence may be reduced. That is followed by a focus on classes that may be left out of poverty reduction in the rapid agricultural growth areas. Improvement in nutrition is then discussed and finally a brief treatment of rural urban income disparities is provided.

Poverty Reduction in Circumstances Inimical to Rapid Agricultural Growth

Poverty reducing, agricultural yield increasing technology does not work in some geographic areas and consequently the poor in those areas seem to be stuck in poverty. That is not uncommon and is most likely because of low and uncertain rainfall not subject to irrigation, or poor soil structure. Relatively unresponsive areas may be large in area but normally with low population densities and so while important they rarely comprise a large proportion of the total rural population. Poverty in such areas tends to be relatively uniform—most families are close to the poverty line.

Figures 4.1 and 4.2, both on the same scale, illustrate the effect of the difference in physical conditions on farm income levels. In areas of low productivity and potential the production function of output to increased labor input slopes up gradually and reaches a peak at a low level of yield (Fig. 4.1). The slope typically is roughly that required to provide a relatively low income. The average product at its peak is at a low income level, perhaps at a subsistence level. That means there is not enough margin of output to support hired labor, sharecropping, accumulation of large holdings, or a large rural non-farm population. Thus, the bulk of the population is farmers with modest-sized holdings who are relatively poor.

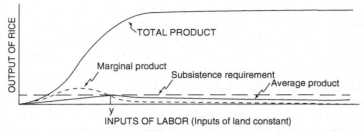

Source: John W. Mellor, and Robert D. Stevens, "The Average and Marginal Product of Farm Labor in Underdeveloped Economics," *Journal of farm Economics*, XXXVIII, no. 3 (Aug. 1956), 22–23.

Fig. 4.1 Hypothetical labor production function, low productivity soils (Source: Authors Construction)

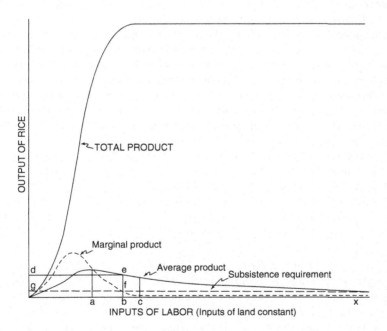

Fig. 4.2 Hypothetical labor production function, high productivity soils (Source: Same as Fig. 4.1)

The provision of modern technology tends to simply extend the function upwards at about the same slope or does not work at all. Thus the incentive to apply improved technology is low. In such areas there is usually a significant area of land that is only suitable for pasture and so there is often scope to increase livestock numbers. That will tend to be the basis for some farmers becoming less poor than their neighbors. These are areas in which much of the land will eventually be abandoned agriculturally. That is, the long-term poverty solution lies with outward migration with serious intermediate-term problems of a rapidly aging, low-income population.

In high productivity areas (Fig. 4.2) the production function relating labor input to output slopes up steeply, continues that slope to a much higher level than in Fig. 4.1, and is further extended with a steep slope by yield increasing technological change. Unlike in the low-productivity situation the average product is always well above the subsistence requirement. In that situation there is strong incentive and capability to accumulate larger holdings.

As population grows and land becomes more scarce some farmers may accumulate land and others, perhaps not as competent or encountering bad luck such as illness, lose land by sale or manipulation and gradually a landless and near landless class is formed. These are the rural non-farm households described earlier. It is not unusual for the process to proceed to large feudal holdings, some becoming managed in sharecropping systems. During the past century the tendency in Asia and in Ethiopia was for much of this land to be redistributed to tenants through radical land reforms. In other countries the more prosperous farmers are small commercial farmers.

The more prosperous farmers can support a larger and larger rural non-farm population. However, that population may grow faster through population growth than the means to support it, with a consequent increase in underemployment and poverty.

To return to the poverty issue, what can be done for those areas left out of modernizing technology change? The dominant solution for these disadvantaged areas is outward migration. If national policy facilitates the rapid growth of agricultural production in the large, responsive to technology, areas then outward migration from those areas largely stops. That leaves the urban jobs previously taken in substantial part by those in the more productive areas for those in disadvantaged areas. The rapidly growing market towns are also able to absorb migrants from the disadvantaged areas. That is particularly important if the disadvantaged area is geographically close to the advantaged areas. Thus migration becomes much easier for those in disadvantaged areas.

The outward migration eventually makes possible enlargement of farm size and the possibility of a sparse population on larger farms. That is more likely in the somewhat dry areas where livestock farming on a prosperous scale may develop. It is less likely on the poor soils since farming more land of low productivity often will not add up to a higher income. Those areas will eventually be abandoned from agriculture.

Migration can be encouraged by ensuring education in the requirements for the transition to urban jobs. Education in disadvantaged areas should be emphasized and usually it is not. The intractable problem, solved by time, is the aging of the remaining population with associated social and economic problems.

A more complex issue is investment in physical infrastructure. National politics will undoubtedly ensure connecting the administrative centers of disadvantaged areas. Connecting disadvantaged rural areas is logically a lower priority than having well-operating communications in those areas that respond well to agricultural technology. Indeed, investing in infrastructure in areas with agricultural growth potential may be of greater assistance to the disadvantaged areas than infrastructure in those areas. Infrastructure investment in the agriculturally responsive areas fosters even faster growth in those areas with increased job opportunities for those in the less responsive areas as described earlier in this section. The same investment in the less responsive areas of course provides at best small returns to those farmers because of the unresponsiveness of their land resource. Steady investment in improving infrastructure between the towns and with other areas makes economic and political sense and will proceed.

It is notable that in the early and mid-twentieth century when this issue was important in the United States, for example in New York State, careful mapping studies were carried out in the state agricultural research system to delineate areas with poor potential for agricultural growth. These were concentrated in the southern tier of counties where widespread farming had developed on the poorer upland soils of the Appalachian plateau. These areas came into farming earlier because they were easier to clear than the denser forests on the better lowland soils. The land use maps were used to avoid making road and other infrastructure improvements in those disadvantaged areas. That of course hastened these areas inevitable demise. Populations declined, age distributions moved more towards older people, and incomes were low. Now these areas are all effectively abandoned not only from agriculture but from human habitation. The next generation to those who left are indiscernible from other families in the areas to which they migrated.

It is useful to make an aside about the environmental issue of natural habitat. Agriculture inevitably contracts in areas not responsive to improved technology. That presents the solution of large, often contiguous, areas that can revert to their original habitat. Policy should consider ensuring those processes and connecting areas under such conditions to make large linked areas suitable for the full range of natural habitat (Mellor 2002b). It is striking, for example, now to fly over the northeastern states of the United States and see virtually continuous forest cover, even in populated areas. It is said that in the state of Vermont the forested area has now reverted to roughly the same size as prior to European settlement. One can see stone walls built through forests of huge fully mature trees showing that the process began in the mid-nineteenth century as the productive technology-responsive lands of the west opened and is still continuing. Those processes will inevitably take over in parts of Asia and Africa as land not suitable to modern high-productivity agriculture is agriculturally abandoned.

HIGH PROPORTION OF POVERTY COMPARED TO HIGH DENSITY OF POVERTY

As stated above, areas of naturally low agricultural productivity tend to have a high proportion of the population in poverty. They are poor areas. It is tempting to think of focusing poverty efforts in those areas. However, in a traditional agriculture the density of the poor, their numbers per unit area of land, is highest in the high-productivity areas that overall tend towards a dense rural population. Thus, initially the most cost effective way to reduce poverty is through rapid agricultural growth in the high-productivity areas. However, with modernization that changes. The rapidly rising incomes of the small commercial farmer bring a rapid increase in employment for the poor and not only the proportion of poor but the absolute number per unit area drops. These areas cease to be areas of concentrated poverty.

CIRCUMSTANCES THAT REDUCE THE IMPACT OF AGRICULTURAL GROWTH ON POVERTY REDUCTION

Even in areas that respond well to improved technology with poverty-reducing benefits flowing to the rural non-farm population, there will be groups that do not participate or are very slow in participation.

Female-Headed Households

Although often comprising five to ten percent of rural households, female-headed households are usually lower income than average and many fall below the poverty line. Two situations are differentiated: those with sufficient land to be classified as small commercial farmers and those who are part of the rural non-farm population.

Female small commercial farmers tend to have poor access to extension services that are normally molded to the time constraints of men rather than the often more-restricted time constraints of women. Extension should be accessible to farmers' wives and concurrently to female-headed households. Focus groups tend to show female-headed households as having poorer access and a greater need for credit unless they fall at the lower end of the small commercial farm size range and qualify for micro-credit. These problems require attention in the context of expanding credit for small commercial farmers.

The problem for the rural non-farm female-headed households is best solved in the context of the micro-credit organizations that concurrently solve a credit and an organizational problem for women. Expanding these agencies and keeping them focused on the poor is important.

Women participate in rural non-farm activities disproportionately to men so the strong impact of rapid agricultural growth is particularly helpful to them. Micro-credit is helpful in assisting the more disadvantaged, particularly women, to gain the leverage of group action and to finance small trading activities that can lead eventually to higher incomes. Larger credit is desirable for those who are entrepreneurial and see opportunities to expand beyond the local market. The scope for that increases over time. As highly entrepreneurial women rise, training in accounting and other business practices will be helpful.

Special Problem of Allocation of Food Within the Household

Gender issues in some societies have men eating prior to women with a consequence that if there is a shortage of food the women (and girls) obtain a lesser share. That outcome seems to be mainly in situations in which poverty does not allow an adequate diet for all and a tendency to imperfectly allocate food to those doing the most physical work in bringing in the basic income. That problem is solved in principle and in time by the development strategy that drives this book: increased agricultural production will of course help reduce inequities of this type.

Farms Just Below to Substantially Below Subsistence Level

These farms have a problem in that they are substantially involved in farming but have inadequate resources to reach significantly above the poverty level. However, their farming activities tend to exclude them from the growing rural non-farm market. Because they are close to the margin of survival they lack capital and risk-bearing capability, so it is difficult for them to move into the new technologies.

What can be done? Micro-credit is useful. Their credit needs are modest, group guaranteed loans are a reasonable possibility, and grouping to obtain extension and other services is desirable. These farms could benefit from extension activities. If they obtain half their income from farming and if technology can double that income they obtain a 25 percent increase in income. That would lift most of them above the poverty line. However, unless they are grouped, extension to a half-hectare farmer requires as much effort as to a two-hectare farmer with one-quarter of the impact. They also need somewhat different extension advice to that for the small commercial farmer – more in tune with low-input agriculture. That calls for special training programs for the extension workers. All that is expensive and tends not to get done.

It is argued that moving these smaller farmers into high-value commodities such as horticulture would move them into a much higher income bracket. However, they are ill-equipped to take the risks involved in putting most of their land into horticulture and a small fraction does little good. Intensifying livestock is a better possibility, but requires technical assistance and credit. Group micro-credit would be valuable. Intensive livestock has the advantage of involving farmers' wives more actively, for which the extension system needs to take note.

Of course, in the long run, many of these subsistence households will shift full-time to non-farm activities, often in market towns. At that point, an active land rental market would be helpful. They need to have surety of ownership and may need extension advice on rental arrangements. Sale of land is rarely preferred because the security of land ownership is large even for small-holdings so improved rental arrangements are important. Extension assistance could ensure the risk reduction.

High Proportion of Rural Non-farm Relative to Small Commercial Farmers

The larger the rural non-farm population relative to the small commercial farmers the less will be the impact of agricultural growth on poverty reduction. Once death rates decline the rural non-farm population will grow rapidly and the smaller of the small commercial farms will tend to drop into the rural non-farm population due to increased family size and consequent division of farms. As that occurs it is urgent that the processes of agricultural modernization be underway. That will raise income all around, accelerate the shift to lower birth rates, facilitate non-farm jobs for many of the children of farmers, and prevent division of farms into smaller units.

Pakistan is an excellent example of a country that neglected its agriculture after an initial spurt of success with the result that the rural non-farm population has grown to a very large size, but is distinguished more by underemployment than by employment stimulated by what is now a stagnant agriculture.

The total number of farms in Pakistan has increased by 70 percent over the past 55 years, with half of that increase occurring in the 20 years from 1990 to 2010 (Mellor and Malik 2017). Notably, the number of farms with less than five acres of land increased by over 33 percent – from a little less than half to two-thirds of the total number of farms. In contrast, small commercial farms decreased by about 30 percent from half to one-third of the total number of farms. Rapid population growth without rapid growth in income of the small commercial farmer and hence of the rural non-farm population creates massive poverty.

This retrogressive process is now proceeding in African countries where the rural non-farm populations are growing in the context of stagnant agricultures and similarly in the several laggard Asian countries.

High Proportion of Feudal Sharecropping

This has become a rare situation, Sindh Province, Pakistan being an important exception. The conceptually simplistic approach is expropriation without compensation. Because the tenant farms tend to be smaller than the average of small commercial farmers and pay half their net incomes in rent they are very poor and have little time for rural non-farm activities. There is little that can be done for them other than expropriation. Their incomes could be marginally increased by shifting to fixed rent (unfortunately increasing a risk they are ill-prepared to manage) and then increasing yields rapidly with the help of credit and extension. In theory they could shift to the types of sharecropping (including the same split of input costs as output) but in feudal systems this is apt to be seen as reducing the owners' control.

High Proportion of Land in Large-Scale Farms

This problem rarely arises in most of Africa and Asia because of the normally low proportion of land in such holdings. Where they dominate there is little potential for an environment favorable to the rural non-farm population development of the market towns. The policy implication is clear: do not artificially encourage them. Where they continue to exist they should not be discouraged from self-financed growth.

FLUCTUATIONS IN THE NUMBERS OF THE POOR: TRANSITORY POVERTY

Substantial numbers of the poor rotate in and out of poverty. This is often called transitory poverty. The largest cause of those fluctuations is weather, primarily because the poverty line we are using is close to the basic requirement for survival. Households cannot survive if they are much below that line. A high proportion of the poor are, by definition, fairly close to the line. As a result, fluctuations in weather that raise crop yields substantially, and hence the income and expenditure of the small commercial farmer, will raise a significant portion of the poor above the poverty line, only to drop below it when the weather reverts to normal or worse (see Chapter 7 in Haggblade et al. 2007). Those poor who have some land also experience a direct decrease in income and food supplies.

Illness and other unfortunate events will have the same effect as weather. The poor are particularly subject to such events, depending very much on their labor for survival and when they cannot work they drop further into poverty. Being near the poverty line is very unstable, risky, and unpleasant.

If the total supply of food is inadequate the shortage will be most pronounced in the period most distant from the previous harvest. The poor, however, do stretch their incomes and food supplies and generally experience modest seasonality in consumption. The solution of course is to increase agricultural production and the income of the rural poor, as discussed throughout this book.

When farm incomes decline and consequently spending by the small commercial farmer drops drastically, the poor have various coping measures, all of which create serious long-term problems. Those with assets, such as livestock, may reduce the assets to maintain consumption. That only shifts the problem into the future. The privation then continues as they attempt to rebuild assets ready for the next bad episode. Those with few assets may preserve a minimum of those assets to maintain future income and further reduce consumption. Reduced consumption means an inadequate quantity of food—they and their children become hungry and malnourished The poor may take on debt, which further increases future poverty due to interest payments. Whatever they do, the impact on health and food security is large. The poor suffer immensely from instability. To say they have coping mechanisms is not to say that is a good situation. Coping primarily pushes part of the problem into the next period.

There is a rich literature (e.g., Dercon and Christiaensen 2011; Karlan et al. 2012) that notes options of insurance, savings, and loans as a means of dealing with adversity. That literature emphasizes the value of insurance and notes a parallel literature on experiments with crop insurance. Recent efforts at tying crop insurance to local indices of rainfall have lowered the cost of crop insurance. However, all the studies are clear that nowhere are farmers willing to pay the commercial cost of insurance. The poor are notably unwilling. That is not a problem in the United States where huge farmer price subsidies are being converted to crop insurance but it is a barrier when, as in low-income countries, the opportunity cost of insurance subsidies is foregone public investment in rapid agricultural growth.

The insurance literature is not explicit about the small commercial farmer but is implicitly oriented towards those close to subsistence and poverty, the poor and near poor. The small commercial farmer does have informal insurance in the form of help in times of stress from extended families, their own savings, rescheduling of loans and drawing down on their storage of food crops. The latter even serves as modest insurance to the rural poor since it allows expenditure in their sector to be somewhat smoother The poor should be able to reschedule micro credit but otherwise lack these coping mechanism, and particularly informal insurance.

Foreign aid, particularly in the form of food aid, normally increases in the face of severe drought thereby reducing the added privation of the poor. The World Food Program, financed by multiple donors, has the greatest in-house expertise in dealing with these situations. The United States also has substantial capacity in this area. In low-income countries such aid is rarely sufficient to lift significant numbers out of poverty but it does, in effect, serve as a moderately effective insurance against bad weather.

The critical issue for foreign aid in dealing with bad weather is seeing the problem sufficiently early to get timely supplies when needed. There are horror stories of foreign food to lessen a drought situation arriving just as the next bumper crop comes in. That of course then further depresses prices that are already heading down. Fortunately, that is not the norm of foreign aid for food security. The impact of drought comes well after the preceding harvest, so it is predictable sufficiently far ahead to allow for shipping time.

SAFETY NETS

Provision of a safety net of income payments to those below the poverty line or provision of food through food for work or similar programs can lift households out of poverty or at least prevent them from falling further under the poverty line. In general, studies show that providing cash to poor households instead of direct provision of food is efficient in that the poor do in fact spend income as the providers think best; that is, for improving their food intake. And to survive they do need to make some non-food expenditures. The World Food Program, to some extent recipient countries, and to some extent bilateral donors have become efficient at targeting those around or below the poverty line.

Safety nets come in a wide variety of forms. School lunch programs are common and have a positive interaction with the benefits of education. A wide range of rural public works and employment guarantee schemes are a potentially effective means of obtaining infrastructures and other benefits that foster long-term growth as well as rationing the programs to the poor who are more willing to work for additional income. To be effective in generating productive assets requires a substantial complement of non-food/labor resources (e.g. culverts for roads). Their absence results in ineffective asset production. IFPRI has conducted considerable research into the relative efficiency of these programs noting that many are poorly targeted at the poor, thus greatly reducing efficiency in achieving the target of a safety net for the poor.

POVERTY TRAPS

There is a large body of research about poverty traps. They are defined as "arising when poverty becomes self reinforcing due to equilibrium behavior that perpetuates a low standard of living" (Barrett et al. 2016). This severe and concentrated poverty is seen as confined largely to Sub-Saharan Africa and parts of South Asia (Barrett et al. 2016). By this narrow definition, that emphasizes self-reinforcing, it is likely to be limited to remote and otherwise disadvantaged areas.

Stated more broadly, poverty traps arise when "people, communities and even entire nations remain moored in grinding poverty, while others enjoy improvement in their standard of living" (Barrett et al. 2016). However, that avoids the more specific question as to why nations do not choose to accelerate agricultural production and achieve economic transformation and poverty decline.

Most study of poverty traps is conducted in countries that are not experiencing high agricultural growth rates. Therefore, they tend to ignore the growth approach and to see poverty as long standing with no apparent prospects for decline. That leads to an inflated view of the incidence of poverty traps. Note the confluence of generally agriculture neglecting Sub-Saharan Africa and the poverty trap discoveries.

FOOD SECURITY

Food security is assured supplies of food at a level defined by the poverty level. In practice it is seen as calorie adequacy and hence largely as the adequacy of cereals and other low-cost calorie sources. Chapter 11 presents data on the impact of agricultural production growth on the cereal intake of each of the household groups defined in this book. It shows that the poor reach food security rapidly in the context of small commercial farmer induced rapid growth in agricultural production.

IMPROVED NUTRITION

Engels law states that as income rises the proportion spent on food declines. Bennett's law states that as incomes rise the proportion spent on starchy staples declines versus other foods such as nutritionally higher-quality meat, diary products, fruits and vegetables. The market works to improve nutrition quality not just caloric intake.

However, the situation is somewhat more complex for nutrition. Analysis of expenditure patterns from an unpublished USAID study of Nepali farmers moving into higher-value products for sale shows that increasing livestock product consumption by small commercial farmers producing livestock is about what would be expected from the income effect. However, for those producing horticultural products the increase in home consumption is far larger than that. That result is most likely because of the greater perishability of horticultural products and hence their low price at the margin in households that produce for sale. That is a favorable finding for nutrition improvement.

Nutritionist Shubh Kumar makes the observation that there seems to be a breaking point when calorie consumption reaches 90 percent of the "required" level. Then further income increases begin to be spent on the more expensive, higher-quality sources of nutrients. Since from that point income allocation becomes increasingly discretionary, decisions could be improved with education programs. I remember how at home in Vermont in the 1930s the home economics extension agent influenced my mother to enlarge our home garden from largely potatoes to a wider range of vegetables. Very few low- and middle-income countries have such programs. They will work best where the incomes of the rural poor are rising.

An important element of agricultural research in the international research system (CGIAR— formerly the Consultative Group for International Agricultural Research) is increasing the nutrient content of basic food sources. An example is the striking success in increasing the vitamin A content of cereals. The CGIAR centers have a significant share of expenditure on such efforts, partly driven by foreign assistance donors' special emphasis on nutrition quality.

CLIMATE CHANGE AND QUALITY OF DIET

The attention paid to climate change brought with it a focus on the large contribution to greenhouse gas from livestock and an argument for reduced consumption of livestock products. It is rarely mentioned that the problem is quite different for low-income families in low- and middle-income countries. They consume essentially no livestock products and would benefit healthwise from an increase, particularly the children.

RURAL URBAN INCOME DISPARITIES

McCullough (2016) shows that rural urban labor productivity and income disparities are substantially overstated. That supports the core positons in this book. Nevertheless, they are real, although at a lower level than previously thought, and eventually become politically important.

Since net migration is consistently from farming to non-farming and from rural to urban there must be income differentials to provide the incentives for that movement. Since those who do not migrate also benefit from the migration through better employment in the rural non-farm sector this disparity tends not to be a problem in low-income countries. However, as middle-income status is reached and labor markets tighten there is increasing attention paid to the disparity between incomes of the small commercial farmers and urban workers. The problem becomes severe when advantage is not taken to constantly increase agricultural productivity.

In the early stages of the economic transformation, rapid agricultural growth allows the incomes of small commercial farmers to keep pace with rising urban incomes. Productivity is rising and farm prices tend not to be declining, for the reasons stated earlier. A problem arises when the initial impetus for increasing productivity in cereals runs down, with a failure to shift into the high-value livestock and horticulture for which demand is rapidly increasing. Most middle-income countries have failed to follow cereal productivity increases with an increase in the high-value commodities. As a result, small commercial farmers' incomes stagnate. And the income gap between this group and urban area dwellers becomes more apparent.

The solution to that problem is research and extension and other activities to encourage a wide entry of the small commercial farmer into high-value commodities, including exports. That would keep farmers' incomes growing in pace with urban productivity gains. That transition is complex and requires explicit government programs to assist the small commercial farmer in meeting modern urban and export requirements. As that potential also runs down, the remaining solution is to accelerate the outward migration of farmers allowing size of farm to increase with mechanization.

Eventually, the size of the small commercial farmer sector diminishes in relative size so that direct subsidies to income or to environmentally desired outcomes take only a small portion of income from the rest of the economy and one has the subsidy situation of high-income countries.

REFERENCES

Barrett, C. B., Garg, T., & McBride, L. (2016). Well-being dynamics and poverty traps. *Annual Review of Resource Economics, 8,* 303–327.

Dercon, S., & Christiaensen, L. (2011). Consumption risk, technology adoption and poverty traps: Evidence from Ethiopia. *Journal of Development Economics, 96*(2), 159–173.

Haggblade, S., Hazell, P. B., & Dorosh, P. A. (2007). Sectoral growth linkages between agriculture and the rural nonfarm economy. In S. Haggblade, P. B. Hazell, & T. Reardon (Eds.), *Transforming the rural nonfarm economy: Opportunities and threats in the developing world* (pp. 141–182). Baltimore: Published for the International Food Policy Research Institute by Johns Hopkins University Press.

Karlan, D., Osei-Akoto, R., & Udry, C. (2012). *Agricultural decision after relaxing credit and risk constraints* (NBER working paper series no. 18463). Cambridge, MA: National Bureau of Economic Research.

McCullough, E. B. (2016). Labor productivity and employment gaps in sub-Saharan Africa. *Food Policy, 67,* 133–152.

Mellor, J. W. (2002a). *How much employment can rapid agricultural growth generate? Sectoral policies for maximum impact in Rwanda* (Occasional Paper No. 19).

Bethesda: Prepared for United States Agency for International Development by Abt Associates Inc.

Mellor, J. W. (2002b). *Poverty reduction and biodiversity conservation: The complex role for intensifying agriculture. A viewpoint series on poverty and environment.* Washington, DC: WWF Macroeconomics Program Office.

Mellor, J. W., & Gavian, S. (1987). Famine: Causes, prevention and relief. *Science, 235,* 539–546.

Mellor, J. W., & Malik, S. J. (2017). The impact of growth in small commercial farm productivity on rural poverty reduction. *World Development, 91,* 1–10.

World Bank Group. (2008). *World development report 2008: Agriculture for development.* Washington, DC: World Bank Group.

CHAPTER 5

Capital Formation and the Exchange Rate

This chapter explains why capital transfers from the agricultural to the non-agricultural sector can be valuable not only to overall growth but to agricultural households as well. A case study of Taiwan describes how a wide variety of mechanisms for inter-sectoral capital transfer from agriculture played a substantial role in the development of the urban industrial sector. The chapter closes with a comparative statement of the role of trade in a rapid agricultural growth strategy.

Long-term rapid growth and prosperity of agriculture requires demand from a large and growing urban sector. Also, farmers want jobs for some of their children in the urban sector and educating their children is a response to that need. They may similarly benefit from additional capital transfers to urban production growth.

Massive capital inflows are required for the economic transformation of the urban sector. At the very least the urban sector requires capital to productively absorb large populations from the less-technologically responsive rural areas. Agriculture providing the food to support labor transfer has been widely discussed in the literature. There is, however, a question of how the food transfer is to be financed. There is also a large capital requirement complementary to that labor transfer.

Agriculture can speed economic transformation by assisting in financing capital for the urban sector. Some countries have extracted massively from agriculture in the context of little or no agricultural growth. The result has been reduced income in agriculture and even massive starvation. There is a large literature analysing overvalued exchange rates as a means of extracting from agriculture, often emphasizing an unfavorable effect on agricultural growth. A contribution from agriculture has quite a different impact when agricultural productivity is growing rapidly through technological change.

© The Author(s) 2017
J.W. Mellor, *Agricultural Development and Economic Transformation*,
Palgrave Studies in Agricultural Economics and Food Policy,
https://doi.org/10.1007/978-3-319-65259-7_5

Agriculture's Requirements of the Urban Sector

Rural sector prosperity requires that the urban sector absorb large quantities of underemployed rural labor. In the context of rapid agricultural growth, the substantial geographic areas not participating in that growth must turn to the urban sector for labor absorption. Much of the early literature on development, most importantly W. Arthur Lewis's (1954) seminal writing, emphasized agriculture's major contribution to urban sector growth as increasing labor productivity and thereby releasing labor to the urban sector.

Lewis probably did not have in mind the existence of a substantial rural non-farm sector with considerable underemployment in that sector. As already emphasized, even with rapid output growth, employment directly in agriculture grows only slowly because of the land constraint on overall growth and the increased labor productivity accompanying yield-increasing technology. From the beginning, even rapidly growing agriculture has difficulty generating enough employment to absorb the underemployment typical of the rural non-farm population in high-potential agricultural areas plus the surplus labor in low-potential areas. Initially it helps growth if some of the underemployed labor can be absorbed in the urban sector and as development proceeds that need will increase.

To put it simply, the small commercial farmer expects her eldest son to take over the farm and hopes the others will find a good urban job. That is so even in high-growth areas. In such cases, local job growth is left largely to the less-educated rural non-farm households. She makes a capital contribution by getting education for those sons who are expected to leave. Then there is the increasingly relevant question of employment for her daughters. Many young women will be absorbed in a rapidly growing rural non-farm sector at low capital per worker; some will marry into a small commercial farm; but others will go to the major urban centers.

Although not important initially, when agriculture is heavily concentrated in basic food production, in the longer-run growth in agriculture depends on rapidly growing urban markets for high-value livestock and horticultural output. The urban demand for these goods will be income elastic—demand will grow quickly creating a potential for rapid growth in output. The demand is also price elastic so somewhat higher prices may occur but not dramatically higher.

Thus, if agriculture can help break the capital scarcity bottleneck to urban expansion, it can itself benefit in the longer run. The following sections explore various means by which that may happen.

Squeezing Agriculture for Capital

Historically, Russia, China, colonial governments, and to some extent several contemporary African countries, have squeezed a technologically stagnant agriculture for resources for the urban sector. Particularly in the cases of Russia and China, a stagnant agriculture was taxed by various devices, most obviously by simply commandeering huge quantities of agricultural output to finance labor costs for building capital goods. In both cases, at least for a short period, the extent of levies on farms reduced remaining food supplies to below starvation levels and huge rural famines resulted.

In China, this effort in the 1960s was called the great leap forward. The concept was to pull resources from agriculture in large quantity and use that for a great leap forward (upward) in growth of production capacity, particularly of capital goods, in the urban sector (Bachman 2006). In a sense, what was done was consistent with Lewis's view of pulling resources, food, from agriculture, although Lewis always saw this happening in the context of increased labor productivity in agriculture. However, the underlying concept is similar.

Colonial governments taxed agriculture, to some extent at the farm level as in India, in other cases, as in parts of West Africa, by taxing export commodities, such as cocoa, at the point of export. The latter was done through marketing boards (Lele 1991). In effect they were systems for serving as the only buyer of export commodities, paying low prices to the farmer and selling at greatly increased prices on the international market. They were heavily taxing agriculture and transferring the revenues out of agriculture, mostly to the colonial power. That incidentally gave marketing boards a bad name, which made it difficult in the post-colonial period to develop them for the positive development of agricultural export sectors. The colonial governments, at least to some extent, pursued policies for increasing production and productivity of the agricultural export sectors. The extraction rate was still heavy.

A subtler means of squeezing agriculture is to foster an overvalued exchange rate. There is a large literature quantifying this effect under a wide range of conditions (Anderson 2010; Krueger et al. 1988). Protective tariffs insulate domestic manufacturing from international prices, while agriculture produces for export at international prices but receives a low domestic price because of the overvalued exchange rate, or even sustains net imports through foreign food aid and even commercial imports. The result is a change in the terms of trade internally that makes agricultural output cheaper relative to industrial goods. That is, in effect, a substantial subsidy (cheaper wage goods) to the industrial sector and a tax on agriculture.

Krueger et al. (1988) emphasize and measure the effect on agricultural incentives and show a substantial disincentive effect over a wide range of countries. Anderson (2010) shows that the effect has been greatly reduced since that early article. The Krueger et al. paper was probably influential in bringing about those changes since they entered into the World Bank's conditioning of assistance to policy reform.

The argument in this book is quite different. It is that these incentive effects of overvalued exchange rates are less important than a foregone opportunity for large-scale cost-reducing technological change in agriculture. In the context of a stagnant agriculture they represent a substantial transfer of resources from agriculture and a reduction of real agricultural incomes, and a negative incentive to produce. However, in the context of major cost reducing technological change they appear as one more means of sharing that increase in income to accelerate growth in other sectors. The latter benefits agriculture as well as other sectors of the economy.

THE ALTERATIVE OF PRODUCTIVITY INCREASING AGRICULTURE

The thrust of this book is that the bulk of agriculture in every low- and middle-income country has the potential for a lengthy period of rapid "catch-up" growth. It is part of the argument that the rate of return on the investment required is very high if that investment is effectively grounded in major flows of yield-increasing technology. That provides the basis for withdrawing a portion of that increased productivity to partially finance growth in the urban sector that will then absorb a portion of the excess rural population, foster accelerated urban growth, and eventually provide increased markets for high-value agricultural output.

Of course the productivity increase must be substantial and attention must be paid to the disincentive involved in the extraction of resources. The golden goose should not be killed. The following sections of this chapter explore the various mechanisms that play a role in transferring resources from agriculture to a rapidly growing urban sector and describes a case study, Taiwan, where substantial resource transfers were made in the context of agricultural growth.

Low Capital Job Creation in Agriculture

A prime objective of resource transfers to the urban sector is to increase non-farm job formation. Chapter 3 documents the massive job creation in the rural non-farm sector, with those job holders gravitating to the market towns and eventually gaining a life separate from agriculture. Especially in the early stages of agricultural growth those jobs are created with very little capital combined with labor: they are labor intensive. So the first task of providing capital to non-agriculture is to create a large number of jobs for the labor-intensive rural non-farm production systems and fostering the growth of market towns.

The jobs created by rising farm incomes are in general low-wage jobs—that is why they are so competitive for farmer expenditures. That is sometimes seen as disadvantageous, but obviously for the rural underemployed more employment at a low existing wage is desirable compared to the alternative of underemployment. For many, if not most, of the rural non-farm population, employment in the local rural and small town environment is a desirable outcome. Eventually, and it is surprisingly sooner than later (surprising given the extent of underemployment) wages will begin to rise. That will slow the growth in employment but only modestly (Mellor and Ranade (2006) model this relationship). The low capital cost means of increasing labor productivity are ubiquitous (e.g., simple tools, better deployment of clerks).

Four features of this type of job creation are notable.

First, the usual comparison is simply of the much greater output per worker in the urban industrial sector compared to the rural non-farm jobs.

McCullough (2016) documents that the disparity in output per hour worked is much less than that per worker. In any case, a substantial proportion of that higher level of output per urban worker is due to the much larger amount of capital invested per worker in the urban industrial sector. That high output is allocable substantially to capital not to labor.

Second, the cost of living for labor is much lower in rural areas. That derives from three sources. One, the rural areas have a substantial existing stock of housing that can be expanded at much lower cost than in urban areas. Two, food is much cheaper since very little marketing cost is involved and some higher-quality food (e.g., horticulture and livestock products) do not have the high losses in transport and storage. Three, labor is much cheaper and hence many of the services are much cheaper. Of course, one wants economic transformation, but rural and market town absorption of underemployed labor should be seen as a positive contribution to the transformation.

Third, historically the transition from rural employment to major city employment is via intermediate jobs in the rural non-farm sector and then in small towns. The more dynamic those sectors the more rapid the transition to the urban centers. On the way, the discipline of urban jobs is learned, as are other skills needed for adaptation. That transition path was particularly marked in the literature on the southern United States when it was making its transition, but it is observed in contemporary low-income countries as well.

Fourth, the opportunity cost of the required capital tends to be low. Rapid agricultural growth areas exhibit high marginal savings rates—that is rapid capital accumulation. Note the net outflow of resources from rural areas from agricultural finance institutions in low- and middle-income countries (Desai and Mellor 1993).

Capital Transfer Mechanisms

W. Arthur Lewis focused on the expanding labor force for the industrial sector as not only coming from agriculture but bringing its own support. That is, the food which comprised the bulk of the wage rate was provided to the urban sector to sustain the enlarging urban labor force. The following discussion will consider the several mechanisms by which that "wages good" could be supplied by the agricultural sector. The Chinese and Russian examples, in a sense, followed Lewis's approach by physically transferring food from the rural to the urban sector.

The economists behind the early Indian five-year plans in the middle of the previous century, including Noble Laureate Amartya Sen and a cohort of prominent economists from the Massachusetts Institute of Technology, who worked in India under US foreign aid programs, saw the need for rapid growth in the urban capital supply for the industrial growth they saw as central to economic growth. Central planning would allocate resources to the industries producing capital goods and thereby put capital goods production in an accelerating path of growth. Eventually the share of capital goods would become large. The resources were from government revenues from taxes and foreign aid. Agriculture was largely ignored in these conceptualizations.

The four principal mechanisms for transfer of resources, capital, from the small commercial farmer to urban investment are: change in relative prices against the agricultural sector; an overvalued exchange rate; the banking system; and direct investment by large farm households. Contemporary low- and middle-income countries rarely tax agriculture significantly, in part because heavy taxation in the colonial period gave it a bad name. It should be noted that each of these transfer mechanisms, especially the first two, have a large literature documenting the amounts and generally taking a negative view of them as negative incentives to production. But that negative view is usually in the context of a lack of large, cost-reducing, technological changes in agriculture.

Relative Prices

Wage rates in labor surplus economies are very responsive to changes in the cost of food. Thus, if agricultural production grows more rapidly than demand the price of food will decline relative to other commodities. That decrease in the price of food will allow a decline in nominal wages which will make the output of labor-intensive industries lower cost and hence more competitive both domestically and for international markets. That is the standard mechanism discussed in the literature on economic development (see the modeling of this in Lele and Mellor (1981)).

Lower real food prices, or stable prices in the face of rapid employment growth, is the logical extension of Lewis's view of agriculture contributing to the growth of the urban labor force. In practice, as will be shown in Chap. 11, small commercial farmer induced rapid agricultural growth tends not to be accompanied by a decline in relative food prices. That is because the increased, rural, non-farm employment generates an increased demand of about 90 percent of the increased supply; and feed, seed, and waste more than accounts for the remainder. However, maintaining stable food prices, which are not increasing or decreasing, is itself a substantial contribution to assisting rapid growth in urban employment. That ensures an elastic supply of labor.

If, in a middle-income country, urban employment is growing in the context of a stagnant agriculture there is likely to be steady upward pressure on agricultural prices because, while the growth in demand in the rural area will be slow, the urban growth in demand is faster than the supply growth. In such a situation, there will be a tendency to import food in order to keep the urban population politically quiescent. Of course, such imports in place of domestic production require foreign exchange that could otherwise be used to import capital goods not producible domestically. Domestic agriculture stepping in to fill that gap illustrates agriculture contributing to capital formation in the urban sector.

Foreign Exchange Rates

A low-income country inevitably faces a dual constraint of lack of capital to generate employment for a large underemployed labor force and of foreign exchange to pay for the wide range of imported capital goods and raw materials essential to investment and job formation (see Chenery and Strout 1966). In low-income countries the foreign exchange constraint is often the greater of the two and they are not perfect substitutes. The result is upwards pressure on the foreign exchange price. That makes imports more expensive and drives up domestic agricultural prices. Both of which are unfortunate events from the point of view of a government's interest in economic transformation.

Governments then tend to ration the supply of foreign exchange, and so its price is constrained below what would be the free market price. That makes imports cheaper, including agricultural imports, and therefore tends to depress domestic agricultural prices. There is a large literature documenting the size of this reduction in domestic agricultural prices and the disincentive to domestic production (see the review by Anderson (2010) and the earlier paper by Krueger et al. (1988)). However, these studies are normally in the context of stagnant agriculture.

The effect of the higher-priced foreign exchange is that imports, such as fertilizer, become expensive relative to the domestic price of agricultural output. That is often described as being disadvantageous to agricultural growth. Which it is, but perhaps not large relative to the cost reductions from technological change. In any case, this has the same effect of agriculture assisting growth of the urban sector as the price changes described in the preceding section.

The literature documents large exchange rate distortions and the high costs to agriculture. These studies take the equilibrium exchange rate under the ruling conditions, which are government ones for growth purposes, ensuring that imports are far greater than would otherwise be the case. That it is the exchange rate that makes imports more expensive is due to the government's policies. In that context, having agriculture absorb the costs of artificially reducing that exchange rate (making buying foreign currencies cheaper than otherwise) might be seen as a reasonable contribution from agriculture.

It is also sometimes argued that the availability of cheap food both from food aid programs and from an overvalued exchange rate is an explanation of the failure to emphasize agriculture. The failure, however, is to not recognize the major additions to real national income from technologically-based agricultural growth and proceeding from that to how those benefits are best allocated.

The Banking System

Chapter 14 will document the importance of a financial system to meet the special needs of the small commercial farmer. It will be argued that that institution should not only lend to farmers, but it should also collect deposits. In that chapter, the argument for deposits is to assist in achieving scale economies in the context of a high density of branches. Here the point is made that receiving deposits may lead to resource (capital) transfers from agriculture to speed the economic transformation.

The perhaps surprising finding in studies of propensities to save, is that farmers in the context of technological change, in aggregate save and deposit more than they borrow (Desai and Mellor 1993). The net funds are then transferred out of agriculture by the banking system, to the growing urban sectors. This is a potentially important source of capital for the urban sector.

That net transfers out of agriculture may occur does not mean that credit is not needed. Not all farmers innovate concurrently and hence, at any one time, only a portion of farmers is borrowing to invest. Other farmers are saving. The net of all those force, over time, is for saving to be larger than borrowing. It is likely that whole regions innovate rapidly relative to other regions and some of those regions will be net borrowers at any given point in time and others net savers. The purpose of a national financial system is to make transfers across regions and time.

Direct Investment by Wealthy Large and Feudal Farmers

Those few countries with a substantial share of feudal holdings, for example Pakistan, may transfer substantial resources from agriculture in the form of sharecropping rent and investment in the urban sector. No doubt some of Pakistan's urban industrial investment came from this source, but more likely is expenditure on conspicuous consumption.

However, even if a substantial share of rental payments is invested it is at the expense of the very-low capital to labor ratio of investment in the rural non-farm sector. It is a sub-optimal allocation of resources compared to converting the sharecroppers into small commercial farmers.

Large commercial farmers do invest in their own large farms. But, compared to what is optimal with given, rural, capital-labor relationships, they invest too heavily in capital-intensive machinery. They may also invest somewhat in the urban industrial sector and that is a positive investment from agriculture to the urban industrial sector. In any case, the size of the large-scale farm sector is usually small and therefore a minor source of capital transfer.

A Detailed Account of Capital Transfers from Agriculture to the Urban Sector: Taiwan

A unique detailed account of capital flows from agriculture to the non-agricultural sectors has been provided by Teng-hui Lee for Taiwan. He collected detailed data for years in Taiwan and then wrote a comprehensive PhD thesis that won the American Agricultural Economics Association award for best PhD thesis that was then published by Cornell University Press (Teng-hui Lee 1971; Mellor 1973). Teng-hui Lee later became the first native Taiwanese President of Taiwan and is credited with bringing democracy to Taiwan. So we can learn from a book by an extraordinarily knowledgeable and accomplished person.

Taiwan has an unusually successful economic growth record and unlike Korea rapid agricultural growth played a major role in achieving that success. A success that provides the opportunity to examine the relationship between rapid agricultural growth and the even more rapid growth of other sectors.

Teng-hui Lee laboriously and meticulously assembled a set of accounts to describe the growth and net flows of resources and income between agriculture and other sectors. He relates these flows to the process of agricultural development, describes the mechanisms, and measures the flow of resources among sectors. He is particularly meticulous in handling the difficult empirical relations on the role of agricultural prices in these processes. The bulk of the statistical series used in this analysis was actually developed by Teng-hui Lee and his staff, giving a special authority to this work.

The key points from Teng-hui Lee's analysis is that agricultural development proceeded throughout the period studied (1895–1960), that large public investment was made in agriculture, that net capital outflows to other sectors continued throughout the period, and the transfer mechanisms changed considerably from time to time according to changing political circumstances.

The net capital outflow from agriculture slowly increased from 1895 to 1940 and tended to decline after 1950. In the prewar period, the principal mechanisms of transfer were rent payments under the old land tenure system and government taxes after the land reforms. Changes in price relationships were not important in the earlier period. In the postwar period, it was farmers' savings and a relative decline in agricultural prices that provided the transfers. Thus, all the mechanisms discussed in this chapter played a role at one time or another.

Throughout, there was never any evidence that the capital transfers held back increased production, productivity or technological change in agriculture. In fact, at an important stage of agricultural growth very large investments were made in irrigation, and throughout there was a large investment by government in rural infrastructure, agricultural research, and extension. Agricultural productivity grew throughout the period analysed as did farm wages and net farm income.

At the time of his analysis there was a view that any net outflow of resources from agriculture required deceleration in the rate of growth of population. The Taiwan data show clearly that a net outflow of resources occurred at a time of high rate of growth of the agricultural population and labor force. That was in the context of a high growth rate in agricultural production. Of course, reducing the population growth rate is helpful to this process even though it is not essential. It also shows that even with a high rate of growth of the urban sector the agricultural labor force will continue to grow throughout the early stages of the economic transformation. This is a point emphasized in my writings with Bruce Johnston (Johnston and Mellor 1961, 1984).

It should be noted that in the colonial period the net outflow of resources was heavily for the growth of Japan's colonial economy, not that of Taiwan's. In the post World War II period the outflow was for the Taiwanese economy.

Teng-hui Lee also shows, consistent with an overriding principle in this book, that the share of labor in the agriculture sector's output declines over time while the share of labor in the non-agricultural sector increases. The latter is consistent with the point made in this book: that the elasticity of employment in technological change-based agricultural production is very low. The rural non-farm sector is, of course, a part of the non-agricultural sector and its high labor share undoubtedly substantially explains the increasing labor share in the non-agricultural sector.

The conclusions Teng-hui Lee draws about the basic agricultural strategy are as follows: (1) basic agricultural investment must be accompanied by technological improvement (hence our emphasis throughout on research and extension as central to agricultural growth); (2) an appropriate investment program with large labor input and less input of capital goods should be selected; and (3) a capital transfer mechanism should be selected. The relative importance of these components changes with changes in the conditions in which they are applied. The key to all this is a technologically dynamic agriculture.

OVERVIEW OF TRADE ISSUES

Most treatments of the economic development of low- and middle-income countries place international market pricing and open trading regimes as central to rapid growth. That is, they see resource endowments of low- and middle-income countries as very different to those of high-income countries with consequent large gains from trade.

It is correct that with a rapid growth in agriculture the role of trade is smaller than in expositions dominated by rapid growth in the industrial sector. The import content of rapid agricultural growth is modest—largely comprised of chemical fertilizers. A substantial portion of the non-agricultural growth stimulated by agricultural growth is in non-tradables and these will, therefore, represent a significant and growing portion of the economy. Most countries have a sufficiently diverse set of agricultural resources that the bulk of domestic agricultural consumption will be domestically produced.

Many low- and middle-income countries have substantial agricultural resources with a comparative advantage in export commodities. Obviously such a comparative advantage should be fully exploited, but is compromised by trade restrictions including an overvalued exchange rate. This chapter discusses using an overvalued exchange rate as a means of taxing the agriculture sector to provide capital for the non-agricultural sector, but it does so in the context of cost-reducing technological change.

Chapter 11 makes the case for protecting domestic agriculture in a low- or middle-income country from international prices when those prices are driven by weather factors that differ greatly from that of the country under analysis.

References

Anderson, K. (2010). *Krueger, Schiff, and Valdes revisited: Agricultural price and trade policy reform in developing countries since 1960* (Policy research working paper no. 5165). Washington, DC: World Bank Group.

Bachman, D. (2006). *Bureaucracy, economy, and leadership in China: The institutional origins of the great leap forward.* Cambridge: Cambridge University Press.

Chenery, H., & Strout, A. (1966). Foreign assistance and economic development. *The American Economic Review, 56*(4), 679–733.

Desai, B. M., & Mellor, J. W. (1993). *Institutional finance for agricultural development. An analytical survey of critical issues and food policy review* (1st ed.). Washington, DC: International Food Policy Research Institute.

Johnston, B. F., & Mellor, J. W. (1961). The role of agriculture in economic development. *The American Economic Review, 51*(4), 566–593.

Johnston, B. F., & Mellor, J. W. (1984). The world food equation: Interrelations among development, employment, and food consumption. *Journal of Economic Literature, 22,* 531–574.

Krueger, A. O., Schiff, M., & Valdés, A. (1988). Agricultural incentives in developing countries: Measuring the effect of sectoral and economywide policies. *World Bank Economic Review, 2*(3), 255–272.

Lee, T. H. (1971). *Inter-sectoral capital flows in the economic development of Taiwan, 1895–1960.* Ithaca: Cornell University Press.

Lele, U., & Mellor, J. W. (1981). Technological change, distributive bias and labor transfer in a two sector economy. *Oxford Economic Papers, 33*(3), 426–441.

Lele, U. (1991). *Aid to African agriculture. Lessons from two decades of donors' experience.* Baltimore: Johns Hopkins University Press.

Lewis, W. A. (1954). Economic development with unlimited supplies of labour. *The Manchester School, 22*(2), 139–191.

McCullough, E. B. (2016). Labor productivity and employment gaps in sub-Saharan Africa. *Food Policy, 67,* 133–152.

Mellor, J. W. (1973). Accelerated growth in agricultural production and the intersectoral transfer of resources. *Economic Development and Cultural Change, 22*(1), 1–16.

Mellor, J. W., & Ranade, C. (2006). Why does agricultural growth dominate poverty reduction in low and middle income countries? *The Pakistan Development Review, 45* (2), 221–240.

PART II

Traditional Agriculture: The Base for Modernization

CHAPTER 6

The Farm, the Farmer, and Labor Supply

Rapid agricultural growth with all its benefits is possible because of potential for the small commercial farmer to change from low-productivity underutilization of resources in traditional agriculture to high-productivity greater use of resources in a modernizing agriculture. The conditions of traditional agriculture provide the base for modernization, influencing how it proceeds, and its impact.

Traditional agriculture is locally self-contained. Farmers may well innovate but innovation is generated locally from local practices and is innately slower paced than that from modern research institutions. It is not embodied in purchased inputs. Traditional agriculture tends to grow at about the population growth rate. It is still important in much of Sub-Saharan Africa and in a sprinkling of countries in Asia, such as Nepal and Burma.

Traditional farms in high-productivity areas compared to low-productivity areas will differ considerably in size of farm distribution, net income, and land and labor intensity, even when land quality is the same. Those in low-productivity areas will be much more uniform.

In some countries, modernizing has proceeded for some time with considerable economic transformation; then the institutions of modernization stagnated or deteriorated and agricultural growth slowed to the rate of traditional agriculture or even lower. It is more useful to see these farms as modernizing but in a state of abeyance with the policy issue of how to restart somewhat different from that of building the institutions from the beginning.

The next section describes the small commercial farm in traditional agriculture. That is followed by exposition of the nature of the labor/leisure choices of the small commercial farmer in traditional agriculture, why they may differ considerably, and provide the basis for quite different outcomes in a variety of situations. These relationships provide the basis, as modernization proceeds, for a large increase in labor input from the small commercial farm family. The final section discusses policies for increasing production in traditional agriculture. That will show why continuous rapid growth does not occur in traditional agriculture.

© The Author(s) 2017
J.W. Mellor, *Agricultural Development and Economic Transformation,*
Palgrave Studies in Agricultural Economics and Food Policy,
https://doi.org/10.1007/978-3-319-65259-7_6

Chapter 7 will examine the nature and role of land and land tenure in traditional agriculture. That will complete preparation for Part 3 detailing the many requirements for modernizing traditional agriculture.

CHARACTERISTICS OF THE SMALL COMMERCIAL FARMER IN TRADITIONAL AGRICULTURE

In modernization, labor productivity increases as does total labor input. Because of the management intensiveness of modernization that labor must come largely from the farm operator. There is no evidence that the relatively prosperous farmers in the small commercial farmer class are pushing their marginal labor product to zero and still have a substantial stock of unused labor. In any case, many of them employ hired labor and have similar yields to those who do not. This chapter explains where the added labor for modernization comes from, and why it can be mobilized.

Poor But Efficient

It is important when understanding labor use to understand that the traditional small commercial farmer is a rational decision maker. It was once widely believed by urban oriented policy makers that these farmers were tradition bound, inefficient decision makers. I remember innumerable informal discussions with Indian government officials who patiently said that I must understand that my village research would not go well because I was dealing with uneducated people who would not be able to understand my questions about agriculture. I would not encounter such views now. The reality for me was sitting in fields, clumsily smoking a hookah, and intelligently discussing topics from farming in the United States to politics and how to make my questionnaire relevant to their realities.

Nobel laureate T.W. Schultz (1964) took hold of field research in India by W. David Hopper and others and showed that farmers in traditional agriculture were poor but efficient. They made sensible decisions. In a later paper (Schultz 1975) he put this view in a more complex context, as does this exposition. Way back in 1929–1933, J. Lossing Buck (1937) in a classic survey, still widely quoted in the China literature, covering 38,000 farmers and 22 Provinces in China similarly showed that production was, from what is defined here as, small commercial farmers and that they made generally sensible decisions. He also showed the immense variability among traditional farmers on a wide range of variables.

One should not exaggerate the degree of efficiency in traditional agriculture because that leads away from several critical needs for modernizing agriculture. In a traditional context, decisions are of course made in a changing environment so there needs to be adaptation. However, the situation is far more dynamic in a modernizing agriculture. Technology changes quickly, price relationships are more complex if for no other reason than the greater range of commodity choices. In traditional agriculture with relatively static levels of technology, physical conditions, and factor costs, farmers gradually evolve efficient farms. That is assisted by observation by less analytical farmers of their more analytical neighbors.

Great Variability in Yields (and Income)

There is considerable variability in crop yields, intensity of labor use, and income among small commercial farmers.[1] That variability among farmers tends to be greater than in modernized agriculture—that is it declines with modernization.

In high-productivity areas, to be emphasized in fast-growth strategies, land area tends to be quite homogeneous with a relatively flat topography, productive soil structure, and well-controlled water either through irrigation or adequate reliable rainfall. In that situation, differences in yields among farmers are largely due to differences in labor input. Despite this commonality in the resource base, there are large yield differences among those with the larger holdings. Although to a somewhat lesser extent there are also substantial yield differences among those with smallholdings as well.

In the examples later in this chapter, the highest yields are three times the lowest yields on a homogeneous land quality. Better timing of operations, so important in weather influenced agriculture, requires priority to working on the farm over social activities. More careful weeding, more careful sowing, much labor carrying huge quantities of green manure (made on the farm) to the fields and on and on. All these are labor based, the farmer has to be there doing that. Why do some farmers work so much harder than others at farming? And why is it so much more varied in traditional agriculture than modern agriculture? The likely explanation will be discussed in a later section of this chapter.

Risk

Risk for the small commercial farmer in traditional agriculture on highly productive resources from occasionally unfavorable weather, or eventually from technology, is quite small, predictable, and comes with coping mechanisms. In contrast, serious illness or death of the head of the household is a huge problem very difficult to manage financially. Life expectancies are shorter and more unpredictable than in high-income countries and illness is more frequent and more severe. Another risk is loss of land in litigation (and government commandeering of land). Even though one bad weather year is manageable, two or three bad crop years in a row can be a disaster for an otherwise prosperous small commercial farmer. These risks are an important background to farming decisions that determine modernization. In high-income countries many of these events, while less disastrous and far less frequent, are also insured against, usually at the greatly subsidized rates a low-income country can ill afford.

The nature of these risks explains much of the staying power of the joint family as an institution which serves to insure spreading of the risk of disaster over the full breadth of large families. Note that the joint family tends to be much stronger and larger for those who have substantial assets. It protects those assets.

Labor Leisure Choices in Traditional Agriculture

The basic argument is that in traditional agriculture the combination of relatively low productivity of labor and poor access to modern consumption goods leads to substantial variability in farm operator labor input among farms and in a substantial stock of unemployed family labor (Mellor 1963, 1966; Mellor and Stevens 1956). That stock of unemployed labor is available for application in the context of modernizations that provides increased returns to farm operator labor and a very different utility schedule for leisure. Application of that labor not only increases output directly but also indirectly through bringing previously uncultivated land into production.

This argument and details that follow are consistent with the following observations about traditional agriculture (see footnote 1 and the case studies in this chapter).

1. The income to farm operator labor is much lower than in modernizing agriculture. In terms of the labor/leisure choice literature this is the result of differences in production functions of output to labor and the labor leisure utility schedules.
2. Crop yields are, in the context of relatively homogenous, high-yielding areas that facilitate such comparisons, much more variable than in modernizing agriculture. This is an outcome of diverse labor/leisure choices.
3. Farm operators hire more labor, relative to size of farm and operator income than in comparable situations in modernizing agriculture. This is also an outcome of the labor/leisure choices. However, the cost of hired labor tends to rise as the quantity used increases—mainly because of the mounting costs of supervision.
4. Potentially productive land that has some costs for initiating cultivation is brought into agricultural production as modernization proceeds. This could be entirely due to change in the production function but it requires labor to bring it into cultivation and labor to farm it, and so is due at least in part to the change in labor/leisure utility functions (for a full exposition see Mellor 1966).

The extent to which farmers use their own and family labor for productive employment is a function of the net utility derived from the fruits of employment and the disutility of that employment (or the utility of leisure use of time). Leisure is of course a broad term covering all activities other than rest/sleep including traveling to and interacting in market towns, and interacting with friends and associates. Further complicating the context is the potential for hiring labor to displace family labor. The cost of that labor, its productivity and the cost of management become additional variables in that determination. These relationships are discussed here in the context of traditional agriculture. The shift to modernization will change each of these variables markedly, often resulting in quite different decisions about labor mobilization and use.

Farmers with a very small amount of land and no other source of income have a very high utility from work in order to provide biological subsistence; that is, the minimum food, clothing, shelter and other essentials for maintaining human life on a replacement basis. That is in essence the World Bank poverty line. The utility of increments of money income up to the provision of a biological subsistence level is bound to be high and so labor input and yields will be in the order of the maximum the available technology will permit. This is the high-yield small farm, often described in the literature. There is a large literature on this inverse relationship between size of farm and yields that emphasizes a wide range of forces at work, for example, Barrett (1996), Barrett et al. (2008), and Barrett et al. (2010). The emphasis in this book is on the labor/leisure differences that will change most radically with modernization and the causes of variability within size of farm bands.

Beyond the biological subsistence level, a culturally defined subsistence level may be defined, again pushing for high yields. But not all small farms will choose these high yields. For example, if a farmer with a small amount of land has urban income, perhaps from resident relatives, he may choose more leisure and lower yields. Farmers with larger holdings will have a wider range of choices. Some will choose the higher income from intensive use of labor, including even hired labor with the operator's considerable labor cost of supervision (for a full treatment of the complexities of hired labor in Asia see Hirashima 1977). Thus as size of farm increases, yields may drop or not depending on the respective utility schedules. A further variable in the labor leisure utility function is the attitude towards farm work. Some farmers get direct pleasure from working in the fields compared to social occasions; similarly they may obtain pleasure from being regarded as excellent farmers. All these and perhaps more affect the labor leisure choice, provide varying amounts of labor withheld from farming and offer opportunity for change with modernization.

The critical change in the labor/leisure choice with modernization is the increased access, in a sense the sharp reduction in cost, and greater attraction of modern consumption goods. Modernization brings radical change in rural physical infrastructure (roads and electrification) and what of the world view (formal education and eventually exposure to public media)? Some of what becomes available with modernization is services. For example, all studies of consumption show for rural people a high elasticity of expenditure on travel. For rural people that is largely bus travel, but local taxis also have increased in use.

In a traditional agriculture, the bulk of return to leisure is in the amount of social contacts: how much time in the fields is spent talking in groups, how much time in the market town associating with a range of friends, how much time with family, how much time in formal social occasions. Some of this increases a return to work paying for social occasions as well as a return to leisure. But these are largely leisure activities and time is the major requirement. They likely have lower utility than modern consumption goods. They desire leisure because there are so few alternatives and the returns to work are quite low given the traditional agriculture production functions.

The argument is that with modernization the increased expenditure on modern consumer goods and services increases the utility of work and because of their variety serve to decrease the variability amongst households of the same income level on the work/leisure choice. Crop yields will be somewhat less variable within a given farm size. This is another reason why yields will tend to be less variable with modernization. De Janvry et al. (1991) provide a formal exposition of the full range of variables and place that discussion in a context of market failure. As stated above, our exposition places a heavier emphasis on the labor/leisure choices and the change in the context of those choices with modernization.

EXAMPLES OF DIVERSITY IN LABOR INPUT

Six case studies have been chosen to provide practical examples of the complexity of the relationships described in the preceding text (see Mellor 1966). Three of the cases demonstrate a high utility to increased farm income and consequent high yields, and they illustrate this for a small, medium, and large size of farm. The other three cases illustrate a low utility of increased farm income and low yields, and cover two large farms and one medium-size farm. The illustrations are purposefully in a traditional agriculture and since they are for India they must be from several decades ago. In this case, only one farmer used commercial fertilizer and that at a low level. I also wanted an area on which the green revolution has had a tremendous impact. Those two criteria resulted in western Uttar Pradesh, India, in the Indo-Gangetic Plain. This had the further advantage in that I was intimately connected with this area and its farmers. These farmers were selected from a sample for which detailed data were collected over a more than one-year period involving weekly, close contact with the farmers, and much hookah smoking.

The cases illustrate the primary importance of yields per acre and of acres per full-time worker in determining farm family earnings in traditional agriculture. They also show a quite different readiness for modernization.

1. Lotan: smallholding, high yields, hard work, high income

With 7.9 acres, Lotan had one of the smallest operating units in the village. The labor force consisted of the operator and his 15-year-old son. The operator's wife worked on the farm more than is typical of the women in this area. Despite the small size of this farm, farm family earnings were high and the earnings per full-time family worker were the second highest in a substantial random sample of farmers. In the sample, the earnings were exceeded only by Chatursal, who had three times as much land per permanent farm worker.

The success of this farm lies with crop yields. Lotan had the highest yield index and had the top yield in every crop but one. His wheat yield was 27 bushels per acre. He operated at an only slightly higher than average intensity of Rabi cropping and a slightly higher than average proportion of the land in the Kharif-harvested crop. Nevertheless, the value of production per acre was almost twice the sample average. Note how low all these yields are compared to contemporary US yields—less than one-fifth.

This farmer's high yields are accounted for largely by substantial application of labor in support of good husbandry. He used largely traditional methods: no commercial fertilizer was used, seed was home produced, no improved implements were used, and no green manuring was practiced. Heavy manuring with farmyard manure was practiced. Apparently, traditional operations on this farm were performed well and on time. The fact of a few acres per full-time worker and per bullock team facilitated this. Despite the fact that in regard to these two factors this farmer ranked near the bottom in this study, and he was nearly always interviewed in the fields while working rather than at home. Casual observation suggests that this man put in more time in the fields than most of the farmers with considerably more land.

The success of this farmer, using largely traditional methods, is not an argument against improved methods. Rather, it indicates the scope for improvement of yields within the confines of traditional husbandry. In all likelihood this farmer with his superior husbandry would get a much greater absolute response from improved practices, particularly seed and fertilizer, than other farmers in the sample. (He did!) Thus the case also suggests the importance to many farmers of raising the standard of husbandry if innovation is to be fully effective.

2. Charan Singh: medium-sized holding, high yields, hard work, good income

Charan Singh had an operating unit only slightly smaller in size than the village average. Farming with his brother, who lived in a separate household, and his 22-year-old son, this farmer had well below the average number of acres per full-time worker. In this respect, his operation was similar to Lotan's. However, the larger total size of operation gave fuller use of the bullocks, at 6 acres per bullock.

As on Lotan's farm, the strong point in this business was high crop yields. With an index of 82, Charan Singh averaged the second highest in the sample. His wheat yields were 20 bushels per acre. Total value of crop production was $48 per acre, which is about 40 percent above the average. The second strong point on this farm was the low level of variable expenses per acre, explained largely by the fact that this family hired very little temporary hired labor. Charan Singh made a point of stating that he preferred to do the work himself as much as possible.

From a moderate-sized holding, he earned a farm income of $461. Despite the small number of acres per worker, this came to $154 per full-time worker. Charan Singh is an intelligent, forward-looking man who previously served as a schoolmaster. He found farming a personally satisfying occupation and more rewarding financially than teaching in school.

He used home-produced seed but has used commercial fertilizer and was pleased with the results. His use of commercial fertilizer will probably increase relatively rapidly. (It did!) As in the case of Lotan, the basic explanation of high yields lies with his skill and diligence as a farmer rather than with technological innovation.

3. Ram Singh: large holding, high yields, high income

Ram Singh had a larger than average unit, at 20 acres. With a three-man family labor force and three bullocks, he had only slightly more than the average amount of land per man and per bullock. The permanent farm labor force consisted of the operator, his brother, and a 15-year old son. He had higher than average farm family earnings and earnings per permanent worker. The sources of this lie in a combination of adequate land per person and per bullock by the technological standards of the area and better than average crop yields.

This farmer was a diligent, hard-working man who was frequently found in his fields. He hired more temporary labor than the average despite the low cropping intensity, but evidence indicates that he supervised his hired labor closely. Ram Singh used indigenous seeds, no commercial fertilizer, and no green manuring. Again, he built a substantial income largely from good husbandry within the confines of traditional methods.

4. Beni Ram: small farm, low yields, low farm income, substantial off-farm income from relatives living with him

Beni Ram's situation exemplifies the consequences of low yields on a farm which has little land per worker. With an average number of acres per full-time family worker and with yields well down in the bottom third, the farm income per full-time family worker was only $38. In addition to one son working on the farm, Beni Ram had two other sons who worked in urban jobs; these sons' families lived in the father's household, and the sons sent money home for family support. Off-farm income resulted in low yields given his labor/leisure choices.

5. Chatursal: very large holding, low yields, high income

Chatursal had the largest holding in this sample, 33 acres. He and his 15-year-old brother had one full-time hired man, so that they had nearly twice as many acres as the average per full-time worker. This farmer only hired the average amount of temporary labor per acre.

Crop yields on this farm were well down in the lowest third in the study. The wheat yield was about ten bushels per acre. The land of this farmer appears at least as good as that of the higher yielding farms. No unusual natural calamities affected this farmer. Thus the low yields are due to a low standard of husbandry. Despite the low level of yields, Chatursal made a substantial farm income. Because of high cropping intensity and efficient labor utilization, he was able to make one of the highest incomes per full-time worker. An intelligent young man who was very receptive to new ideas he appeared to be a person who would respond well to technical advice. Some encouragement, plus greater availability of consumer goods, would increase his incentive to raise yield considerably. Doubling the farm income could be a minimum short-term goal to set for this farm. With the green revolution, just a few years later, he experienced a massive increase in income with a radical change in consumption. When asked what he thought of the changes in farming he facetiously said, "really bad, my wife spends all her time traveling to Agra (nearby city) and spending money and I have to work harder." His wife laughed.

6. Dharm Singh: large farm, very low yields, good income

Dharm Singh had the next to the largest unit in the cohort. It illustrates how a large farm may still make only a small return per full-time worker. The major causes of failure were low yields (in the bottom third) plus very high hired-labor expenses. Note that Dharm Singh had slightly less land per full-time worker and operated at lower cropping intensity than Chatursal, and yet he spent nearly three time as much on temporary hired labor. This probably indicates two problems on this farm: unusually high labor cost and insufficient supervision of hired labor.

The high-yielding, fertilizer-responsive varieties hit this village six year later. When I visited four years after that, all six of these farmers were using the new varieties and heavy applications of fertilizer. Their yields had closed in although the order of yields remained similar. That is small farmer Lotan still had the highest yields but Chatursal was close. Of course the income gap between them increased greatly.

POLICY TO INCREASE AGRICULTURAL PRODUCTION THROUGH INCREASED LABOR INPUT

The wide range in crop yields characteristic of traditional agriculture and the associated wide range in labor input suggest a potential for a substantial increase in production. Unlike the continuous growth from modernizing agriculture it is a once and for all increase. However, the analysis of labor/leisure choices suggest that these differences are due to household decisions based on production and consumption possibilities that are the product of the complex changes in modernization, specifically rural infrastructure, education and technical change. Nevertheless, there are policies that may increase sales and perhaps production in the context of traditional agriculture. We consider two: taxes and prices.

Taxation

There is a substantial literature on taxation, much of it referencing smallholder traditional agriculture as in colonial countries, and examining the effects of various market failures, with labor/leisure choices prominent, as in this chapter, as is a distinction between food crops and commercial crops (e.g., de Janvry et al. 1991). Taxes removing a portion of farm income, often through a program of forced provision to the government, decrease income and increase the value of work relative to leisure. Farmers will then be encouraged to move further out on their given production possibility curves, thereby providing higher yields per acre and greater total production. This was presumably part of the rationale of the heavy taxes imposed in Russia and China.

A progressive land tax, imposing higher rates on the larger holdings, would have a particular advantage. It could be constructed so as to place little or no burden on those with smallholdings who are already operating at very low marginal productivities of labor and who would not be further stimulated by such a tax. It would bear most heavily on those with the large-size holdings, forcing a higher level of output in order to maintain a given standard of living.

Raising Agricultural Prices

Raising agricultural prices may cause either an increase or a decrease in labor input and agricultural production. A change in agricultural prices will influence the point of operation on the utility surface through its influence on income, and will also affect the production possibilities by increasing the value of items produced from additional work. These two effects (one an income effect, the other a substitution effect) are in opposition to each other. Increasing prices by raising the marginal value product of labor will encourage greater labor input; but, by raising income, it will decrease the marginal utility of material goods income and encourage a withdrawal of labor. The more sharply utility from goods and services declines with an increase in income, the more likely that the income effect will overwhelm the substitution effect. That is more likely in traditional agriculture than in modernizing agriculture.

GENDER

Three points stand out with respect to gender. First, the gradual loss in family decision making of the farmer's wife. Second, the poor access of female-headed households to technical advice. Third, the great importance of rural non-farm income generation to rural women, including farmer's wives, and hence the importance of business development support to women.

There is considerable variation in the extent to which women do the physical work in farming. Palacios-Lopez et al. (2017), for Sub-Saharan Africa, place the proportion much lower than previous studies but at a still large 40 percent. See also World Bank (2012), FAO (2011), and Kumar (1987). In general, in South Asia the proportion of work in the fields by women is much less than in Sub-Saharan Africa. Physical work in the fields is in general considered onerous and as incomes rise women withdraw from such work. It is important to understand, although talked about a lot as a source of importance, that doing the physical work is not the most important source of women's influence. Access to information, as in the rest of the world, is a more important source of influence.

Although female-headed households are a small proportion of the total, they tend to lose on two grounds. They tend to have smaller than average holdings, compounded by poorer access to outside information, especially on technical improvements in farming.

Women in traditional agriculture, and even more with modernization, tend to play a much larger role in rural non-farm activities than directly in farming. That is true on the small commercial farms as well as in the rural non-farm sector. Modern credit institutions often are less open to women than men. That is particularly disadvantageous for women in the rural non-farm sector. It is important that situation be rectified. Micro-credit is more successful in assisting women than traditional loan sources.

NOTE

1. I make these and later observations on the basis of decades of observing rural areas in various stages of development and from perusing a wide literature, particularly including: the field surveys at IFPRI while I was the Director; and J. Lossing Buck's (1937) massive China field studies. The latter was of a traditional agriculture and is an unusually detailed source. It shows a high degree of variability throughout the country, with greatest variability in the higher productivity areas; Mellor (1963, 1966; Mellor and Stevens 1956) provides that detail for one area in India, representative of the Indo-Gangetic Plain; Jayne and his colleagues at Michigan State University have published numerous papers that describe a similar agriculture in Sub-Saharan Africa with great variability within similar areas; the large rural household surveys published in numerous World Bank papers for many countries in Asia and Africa and include areas still dominated by traditional agriculture and showing similar variability.

REFERENCES

Barrett, C. B. (1996). On price risk and the inverse farm size-productivity relationship. *Journal of Development Economics, 51*(2), 193–215.

Barrett, C. B., Sherlund, S. M., & Adesina, A. A. (2008). Shadow wages, allocative inefficiency, and labor supply in smallholder agriculture. *Agricultural Economics, 38* (1), 21–34.

Barrett, C. B., Bellemare, M. F., & Hou, J. Y. (2010). Reconsidering conventional explanations of the inverse productivity–size relationship. *World Development, 38*(1), 88–97.

Buck, J. L. (1937). *Land utilization in China: A study of 16,786 farms in 168 localities, and 38,256 farm families in twenty-two province in China, 1929–1933.* Shanghai: University of Nanking.

De Janvry, A., Fafchamps, M., & Sadoulet, E. (1991). Peasant household behaviour with missing markets: Some paradoxes explained. *The Economic Journal, 101*(409), 1400–1417.

Food and Agriculture Organization. (2011). *The state of food and agriculture: Women in agriculture, closing the gender gap for development.* Rome: Food and Agriculture Organization.

Hirashima, S. (1977). Zamindars and kammees in the Punjab: An economic analysis of non-farm households in the Pakistan Punjab. In S. Hirashima (Ed.), *Hired labor in rural Asia*. Tokyo: Institute of Developing Economies.

Kumar, S. K. (1987). Women's role and agricultural technology. In J. W. Mellor, C. L. Delgado, & M. J. Blackie (Eds.), *Accelerating food production in sub-Saharan Africa* (pp. 135–147). Baltimore: Johns Hopkins University Press.

Mellor, J. W. (1963). The use and productivity of farm family labor in early stages of agricultural development. *Journal of Farm Economics, 45*(3), 517–534.

Mellor, J. W. (1966). *The economics of agricultural development*. Ithaca: Cornell University Press.

Mellor, J. W., & Stevens, R. D. (1956). The average and marginal product of farm labor in underdeveloped economies. *Journal of Farm Economics, 38*(3), 780–791.

Palacios-Lopez, A., Christiaensen, L., & Kilic, T. (2017). How much of the labor in African agriculture is provided by women? *Food Policy, 67*, 52–63.

Schultz, T. W. (1964). *Transforming traditional agriculture*. New Haven: Yale University Press.

Schultz, T. W. (1975). The value of the ability to deal with disequilibria. *Journal of Economic Literature, 13*(3), 827–846.

World Bank Group. (2012). *World development report 2012: Gender equality in development*. Washington, DC: World Bank Group.

Land and Land Tenure

In both traditional and modernizing agriculture, area and quality of land farmed is the principal determinant of income potential. The essence of modernization is a large sustained increase in crop yields. That potential is influenced by the characteristics of land in traditional agriculture. This chapter provides the background for Part 3, modernization of agriculture, by describing (1) the characteristics of land, (2) the systems of land tenure, (3) the potentials to increase land area, and (4) sustainability and environmental issues in land preservation (for a full discussion of land markets in development starting from traditional agriculture see Hirashima (2008)).

CHARACTERISTICS OF LAND IMPORTANT TO PRODUCTIVITY AND MODERNIZATION

Land Productivity

In traditional agriculture, land productivity is highly variable around a low average. Rooted in low-productivity production functions and labor leisure choices it will change only slowly in the traditional context. With modernization and its impact on production possibilities and labor leisure choices, the low initial level of yield offers the opportunity for a large increase in productivity and income. As those processes proceed, inter-farm variability in yields will also decline. The divergence in yield and income between initially high-productivity areas and low-productivity areas will increase.

Fragmentation of Farms

There is a common problem of farm fragmentation—a division into many small segments often quite distant from each other. That arises partly from the

J.W. Mellor, *Agricultural Development and Economic Transformation*,
Palgrave Studies in Agricultural Economics and Food Policy,
https://doi.org/10.1007/978-3-319-65259-7_7

complexity of generations of inheritance, and occasionally from small purchases. In a traditional agriculture, fragmentation has the advantage of diversifying risk—cutting across different soil and even rainfall regimes.

However, with modernization, especially the tapping of ground water on a small scale, and to some extent with machinery and for marketing purposes, consolidating land holdings has a major advantage. The process is socially costly and therefore is not likely to succeed unless the economic benefits are substantial. Even then, government intervention may be necessary to reconcile local differences on whether and how to proceed. When the appropriate time comes, costs can be contained by the appointment of outside staff to adjudicate the marshaling of local knowledge about land ownership and the relative values for exchange as consolidation takes place. As modernization proceeds, consolidation rises on the scale of important changes.

Land Registration

In a traditional agriculture, land ownership is commonly legitimized by tradition rather than legal registration and documentation. Everyone knows, including the village leader, that "this has been our land for generations." As modernization proceeds it becomes desirable to have well-working land markets with land registration (see Feder and Nishio (1998) for a full exposition).

In a traditional agriculture and in early stages of modernization, premature registration of land and consequent formal title may simply strengthen those who would like to dispossess weaker members of the community. In a situation of domination by a tribal chief, the less scrupulous may allocate land to themselves and seal the transfer with registration. It may also strengthen corrupt elements in government who could seize land and register it in their own names before the weaker members in the community can respond.

In the early stages of modernization, the benefits of land registration are minimal. Land should not be used as collateral for working capital or intermediate term loans, although banks may attempt to demand this. In high-income countries, land is used as collateral primarily for the transfer of land, common when generations change, but this transaction is much less common in low- and middle-income countries. In low-income countries, a land sale is more likely to be a distress sale than in high-income countries.

Given the importance of land as a storehouse of wealth in low- and middle-income countries, it is better to develop open, well-operating, rental markets than markets for sales. Increasingly, those with very small land holdings will migrate to urban areas and with a well-operating rental market they can rent their land to those with larger holdings and thereby preserve one of the few means of holding assets open to them. The most important feature of a well-functioning rental market is security of ownership in the face of land being operated for years by another, more politically powerful family.

CREDIT IN TRADITIONAL SYSTEMS

Credit in traditional agricultural systems is usually required for social events, such as marriages, and to deal with crises of the smaller of the small commercial farmers in the context of successive years of bad weather, death, and illness. Since those needing credit are those near the margin of subsistence they have difficulty in repaying loans. The lending agencies are normally family, for which some reasonable repayment scheme may be developed, and village money lenders who supervise repayments closely, obtain them even under very difficult conditions, and are prepared to possess the borrower's land if debts accumulate—as they are likely to do. It is an unpleasant system, hence the bad reputation of money lending in a traditional rural society.

It follows that these institutions have difficulty adjusting to the very different regime of borrowing for income increasing modernization. They may still serve a purpose but in competition with new institutions that cater for rising incomes, technological change, and the more prosperous of the small commercial farmers.

LAND TENURE

The small commercial farmer is the focus of this book, both for increased agricultural production and the principal instrument of rural poverty reduction. Feudal systems once dominated large parts of Asia and Ethiopia. Large commercial farms and plantations are important in a few low- and middle-income countries and are seen as important components of agricultural growth by some analysts.

Small Commercial Farms

Most low- and middle-income countries' agriculture is dominated by small commercial farms. There is considerable inequality within the small commercial farm and subsistence sectors, with rural Gini coefficients, a measure of inequality, at quite a high level—in the range of 50. There is little or no evidence of political processes that would reduce that inequality or distribute land to those with little or no land. This book argues that such efforts would be counter-productive in the context of growth and poverty reduction.

Large-Scale Farms and Plantations

Small areas in South East Asia, and somewhat larger areas in parts of Africa, are devoted to large commercial farms and plantations. Plantations are simply large-scale commercial farms producing tropical export commodities. These were mainly the product of colonial systems that were reinforced by the special conditions of tropical export commodities, particularly the need for quality control and conglomeration for export, and the high level of profitability for colonial owners. Large commercial farms do not support the local, rural, non-farm population's activities and hence do not transfer income to that group to reduce poverty. This is a critical issue in judging the value of large commercial farms.

Large-scale farms, including plantations, tend to be managed at a high level of technical competence. They have a scale advantage in access to modern technology and inputs even if the national government is not ensuring access to small commercial farmers. Deininger and Byerlee (2012) provide a broad survey of the increase in number of large farms in what they term land abundant countries. Consistent with the positon in this book, they find them generally productive. However, our analysis covers their low indirect contributions to poverty reduction and raises an important question about the opportunity cost of government assistance to them.

It is sometimes proposed that large commercial farms and plantations could serve as centers for providing the surrounding small commercial farmers with research results, an extension service, input supplies, and marketing services. There are three questions linked to this approach. First, why is the government not providing these services? Second, why would a large-scale farm provide resources to its surrounding small commercial farms? Third, in response to providing a monopoly over marketing and the input supply, why would the larger operation not exploit that power to extract additional returns from the small commercial farmers? The argument for a large-scale operations serving as a development nucleus is largely based on the refusal of governments to provide, in the order of ten percent of their budgets, support for the key conditions for modernization of the small commercial farmer.

Land reform discussions may suggest dividing large commercial farms into small commercial farms. In practice, this rarely if ever happens, partly for political reasons but there is also a practical issue. The physical infrastructures such as irrigation are set up to support large farms. It is normally expensive and even impossible to reestablish these institutional and social structures around a large number of small farmers.

A good case in point is Guatemala where the very large farms on the Pacific Coast have large-scale irrigation systems that are very expensive to convert to smallholdings' use. The situation in the Union of South Africa is even more difficult. Essentially, all the high-quality land is in large holdings with all the institutional structures keyed to them.

In the contrasting case of Zimbabwe, a substantial portion of the better land is in the hands of small commercial farmers. However, the government has refused to develop the key institutions to support the small commercial farmer even though those institutions had the potential to do so and could have been oriented to the small commercial farmer. Thus little progress has been made on rural poverty reduction. When the large farms were nationalized, instead of breaking them up into smallholdings they were kept as large units and handed out as political favors. Obviously the quality of farming declined.

Given their staying power, large-scale farms should continue to be productive, benefiting from public resources in research and other activities but not competing with small commercial farmers for government support.

There has been concern expressed, Johnston and Mellor (1984) and Johnston and Kilby (1978), that the concurrent presence of large-scale farms and small commercial farms will result in the greater political weight of the large-scale farms channeling scarce resources towards them rather than the public institutions serving the small commercial farmer. This is referred to in the literature as a bi-modal situation. The point being, as in this book, that the optimal farming decisions come from the small commercial farmer. Public resources need to be steered to the poverty-reducing small commercial farmer.

FEUDAL SYSTEMS AND RADICAL REFORM

Morris Birkback in 1814 caught the essence of feudal land tenure systems and radical land reform: "I ask for the wretched peasantry of whom I have heard so much; but I am always referred to the revolution. It seems they vanished then" (*Financial Times* 2016).

At one time, large feudal holdings dominated much of India, China, Taiwan, Ethiopia, and Latin America. These were largely in the more productive areas. Radical land reforms in the first four were in the context of major political change, from an occupying power in India and Taiwan and domestic revolutions in China and Ethiopia (for a full discussion of land reforms in economic development see De Janvry 1981; for a more recent discussion see Binswanger-Mkhize et al. 2009).

The postindependence land reforms in India were basically land to the tiller (tenant) movements that converted from feudal holdings to small commercial farms. Land reforms, largely confiscatory, converted feudal holdings in China first to communal holdings and then some decades later to small commercial farms. In Ethiopia there was a two-decade lag between land reform, largely land to the tiller, and the institution of government policies for rapid modernization. In the interim little growth occurred. In Latin America, the feudal holdings evolved towards large-scale commercial farms or in some more radical political changes into small commercial farms. Pakistan is a remaining country with large feudal holdings.

The typical feudal system in Sindh Pakistan is described and analysed in Chap. 3. The incentive for good husbandry is modest at best. The incentive to take up modernization is also modest although eventually systems are developed, such as cost sharing, to encourage commercial fertilizer and to some extent improved seed use. Sharecropping in high-income countries is increasing rapidly and is an entirely different system with very different power bases, demonstrating that sharecropping can be a highly productive system.

POTENTIAL TO INCREASE LAND AREA AS A SOURCE OF GROWTH

Perhaps surprisingly, increased cultivated land area normally accounts for a significant portion of production increase in the early stages of modernization. There are two quite divergent trends: many small but widespread additions in already high population density areas; and, occasionally, large tracts of underutilized land in low population density areas.

Additions in High Population Density Areas

In high population density rural areas, it appears to the casual observer that there is no unused potentially agricultural land. However, in India in the immediate postindependence period, increased land area was more important than yield increases in achieving a substantial growth rate (Mellor et al. 1968). In densely populated Ethiopia, for more than 20 years, increased land accounted for about 40 percent of the rapid agricultural growth rate (Mellor 2017).

Of course an increase in area farmed follows periods of disruption, when land was abandoned from farming. But in these and other examples the increase in area cultivated went beyond the period when all previously abandoned land was brought back into cultivation. The source of new cultivated land was pasture, road sides, and edges of cultivated fields.

The logic is clear. Technological change brings increased returns to land, covering the costs of bringing additional land into cultivation. Concurrently, a change in attitudes and availability of attractive consumer goods increases the value of the output of labor relative to leisure. Land is of course limited and so increased land area will add to the growth for a limited period, as shown by India and Ethiopia, perhaps for a decade or somewhat more.

Additions in Low Population Density Areas

The situation in low population density areas is very different to that in high population density areas. It is common for such areas to be dry and inhabited sparsely by semi-nomadic families relying on cattle herding for the bulk of their income. In other cases, disease may have restricted use, as in some areas of West Africa. Such land may have high potential productivity but it tends to require substantial investment in roads and irrigation systems, although developing it may be highly profitable. That is thought to be particularly so in East Africa. If so, it should cover all its costs, leaving public investment for the high-potential, densely populated areas.

It has been tempting for governments to respond to these opportunities by encouraging purchase by foreign investors, including those from the rich Gulf countries concerned about ensuring future food supplies (see the full discussion of these issues in Deininger and Byerlee 2012). There is also a tendency for investors to see the valuation of such land as moving counter to the valuation of other assets, encouraging further investment in such areas as a means of reducing risk. However, there are two major issues about developing such land.

First is the issue of who will make the infrastructure investment and this should be considered in view of the investment made by those who will farm the land. That decision is in the context of small commercial farm areas with the potential for large increases in productivity but requiring large public investment in infrastructure—the same kind of infrastructure as is required in the new land areas. On the economic side, it is likely that such investment in high population density areas will have just as large or a larger impact on productivity as in the low population areas, and will have large externalities from small commercial farmers' expenditure as a result of increased income, greatly reducing poverty in the rural non-farm sector. There will also be an infrastructure impact on groups other than farmers.

Second, is the irrigation issue. Returns from investment in irrigation are likely to be higher in existing areas that could benefit from an additional crop and ensuring production in the main cropping season, often with lower-cost water sources. As for infrastructure, it should be paid for by those who benefit from farming that land.

There is a remaining issue of providing for the low population density indigenous people. It is likely that labor intensity, even with substantial mechanization as is likely with large-scale farms, would absorb much of the low population density population. There may still be a special cost to these people and at the very least they should not be worse off than in their previous condition. However, the usual practice is to largely ignore them and consequently they suffer not only a change in lifestyle but a substantial reduction in income.

A further option is bringing new land into cultivation and dividing into plots in, say, the mid-range of small commercial farmers. That decision might best be made by calculating the benefits from those necessary investments compared to making the same investments in the high population density areas with their attendant strong employment multipliers—multipliers that are lacking in resettled areas without the rural non-farm population. Those calculations will rarely show new land settlement as a more profitable choice. Land settlement programs of this type have been common, for example, in Indonesia, and have in general not been cost effective.

Conversion of large natural forests into agriculture such as oil palm is a notable issue in Indonesia and potentially in some African countries. It is important to view all the costs of converting natural forest into commercial tree crops such as oil palm. The negative externalities may require measures to force them to be taken into account, for example, by government taxes. That may not occur if the negative externalities fall substantially outside the country, for example through climate change.

There is occasional discussion about displacing small commercial farmers to allow massing their land into a few large-scale holdings, but that is of course a highly uneconomic investment. The shifts is from appropriate labor:machinery ratios to highly inappropriate ones given the relative cost structures. The discussion arises largely because of the urban-based belief, with no supporting evidence, that small commercial farmers are not capable of profitably applying the elements of modern high-yield agriculture. It also ignores the impact of small commercial farmer income growth on the rural non-farm sector.

The upshot of this discussion is that in a low- or middle-income country with substantial underinvestment in high population density agriculture, public investment should concentrate on those areas. If it pays private investors to invest in new land when all costs are covered then it is economically logical that they should be allowed to do so.

Large-Scale Farms

There is a prominent literature favorable to large-scale commercial farms. That literature falls into two categories.

The first, summarized by Deininger and Byerlee (2012), reviews the evidence geographically and over time for the establishment of large-scale farms. It is a generally positive approach concerned with how to maximize the benefits from such investment, but does not treat the question of public investment or the aggregate importance of such farms. It points to ample failures and states how such failures might be avoided. None of that is in contradiction to the position in this book.

The second, epitomized by Collier and Dercon (2014), states that "smallholders are not up" to the requirements for agriculture over the next 35 years. In a somewhat vague manner, they espouse large-scale farms but never define either smallholders or large-scale farms. There are three problems with their viewpoint.

First, they are clearly unaware of the small commercial farmer, who is able to modernize and fulfill the functions Collier and Dercon have in mind and is clearly doing so (in the Punjab region of India, Ethiopia, most of China, etc.) where public institutional resources are available. Their "smallholder" is obviously the poor non-commercial average of the small commercial farmer and the rural non-farmer who produces only a small proportion of agricultural output.

Second, they seem to have in mind conversion of the land from "smallholders" to large-scale farms. They do not give a clue as to how they are going to get from here to there.

Third, in dispersed agriculture, hired labor is difficult to manage. Collier and Dercon must have in mind farms mechanized far beyond that consistent with current capital labor costs and non-farm job opportunities. Let the market operate and mechanization happens modestly on small commercial farms where it breaks seasonal bottlenecks and allows increased not decreased employment. As the economic transformation proceeds, perhaps ten or 20 years down the road all the children will leave some farms for urban employment, and farms will gradually double in size and continue to slowly grow from there. But this is apparently not the size Collier and Dercon have in mind.

Irrigation as a Source of Increased Land Area

Irrigation will be discussed more fully in the context of modernization and new forms of inputs. Suffice to say in this context that irrigation investment tends to be high cost, its rate of return greatly increased by the modernization discussed in the chapters of Part 3, and therefore a questionable investment without that modernization. Having said that, vast areas of Asia (e.g., in India and Pakistan) have been irrigated, long before modern yield-increasing technologies were on the horizon. Presumably that investment paid off, at least where the underlying resource was dry. Of course modernization has greatly increased returns to that irrigation investment.

SUSTAINABILITY AND ENVIRONMENTAL ISSUES

Society's interests and the sustainability of farmers in that society tend to be broadly congruent. Lack of short-run congruence is often due to income pressures on farmers that are substantially mitigated by modernization of agriculture. That is, rapid agricultural growth through technological change is largely positive for the environment. Conversely, rapid population growth in the context of traditional agriculture is destructive of the environment.

Land Degradation, Nature Reserves, and Biodiversity Preservation

FAO (Faostat 2015) estimates that 30 percent of the global cropped area is subject to severe degradation (see also Johnson and Lewis 2007). These studies likely have an upward bias as the strong negatives make a more publishable story. Also much of that land may not have a long-term future in agriculture.

Farmers understand that their land is their most valuable asset, that it is vulnerable to degradation, and that good husbandry is in their best interests. The FAO data show that severe degradation is much greater on land operated by those below the poverty line. That is a reflection of the pressure of population against limited land resources—farms getting smaller with each generation and pushing onto land that is vulnerable to degradation.

The modernization process raises yield and profitability to higher levels on the already more productive land and makes it unnecessary and indeed unprofitable to farm the more vulnerable land (Mellor 2002). Land abandonment from agriculture is an inevitable accompaniment of yield-increasing technology. A major environmental benefit from land abandonment as it occurs in the context of modernization is the potential development of such land as areas of biodiversity. This should be seen as an opportunity to be hastened (Mellor 2002).

There is an argument that increased crop yields from modern technology make it profitable to bring marginal land into cultivation but that is rarely the case. The lower productivity land responds less well to innovation and therefore tends not to be able to cover the incremental costs of more intensive farming. The pressure then is to take land out of cultivation.

As a significant exception, tropical forests are often on land that becomes profitable owing to tree crops such as oil palm, with increasing yields resulting from the conversion of tropical forest into more intensive use. The loss is in biodiversity and other benefits of tropical forests. Governments need to recognize those externalities and legislate to prevent such use.

We see that wherever modernization has occurred low productivity land is removed from cultivation. The extreme of that is in the northeastern United States where the reverting of land to forest has taken forest cover back to where it was when Europeans first settled. It is striking to walk in New England's back country and see stone walls, marking previously cultivated fields, in the middle of mature forest. The twin impacts of farming more productive land, more responsive to modern technology, in the mid-West and the increased productivity and profitability of the small amounts of responsive land in new England both had their effect. Those processes are barely underway in most low- and middle-income countries but they have started and will accelerate. The problem for these abandoned fields is not so much lower prices as inability to provide a modern level of living and returns to labor.

An apparent exception to this rule is the case of soils with good structure but very low in nutrients, for example, somewhat sandy soils. The reduced costs of purchased nutrients make it profitable to bring such soils into cultivation. These cases rarely lead to degradation. Related to this, some soils under traditional cultivation already suffer depletion of nutrients as crops are harvested without fertilizer being added. That can eventually lead to physical degradation through erosion.

A serious problem is loss of irrigated land through waterlogging from excess use of water and poor drainage. This is partly a problem of poor initial drainage design as occurred in the United States at one time. In general, that problem is being rectified elsewhere. It is also a problem that users near an unmetered water source are prone to overusing water, creating waterlogging problems as well as unnecessary scarcity for downstream users. This is also a problem in high-income countries where initial users obtained rights over later users. Water is a problem that is rarely solved because of the strength of vested interests so the end result is poor use of water.

Excess Use of Inputs

The remaining environmental issue is that of damage from the processes of modernization. Two issues are paramount: nitrogen and phosphate pollution and collateral damage from chemical pesticides. Agriculture typically provides close to half the excess run-off of these nutrients and the cost of mitigation tends to be lower in agriculture than for other sources.

Ground water pollution from nitrogen and phosphorus run-off into water tables and nearby bodies of water is an important issue. The most important point is that farmers do not want to spend money on fertilizer that ends up in the ground water table or as run-off. Hence there will be cooperation in principle from farmers and there are two approaches.

First, is extension education to induce farmers to follow known practices that minimize nutrient run-off. Unfortunately, this is in a context in which governments greatly underinvest in extension. Concern for the environment means a substantially larger extension force than normal, intensive training of extension agents and demonstrations of best practices. Many of these practices will be profitable and hence the environment for extending them is favorable. The problem in low- and middle-income countries is less one of overuse and more of poor application practices which are amenable to extension efforts. As will be discussed in later chapters, farmers do respond to a national vision and hence, among sensible environmental practices, a national priority will help in gaining full acceptance.

In high-income countries there is a serious problem of livestock raised in intensely crowded conditions, that seems objectionable on moral grounds, and requires massive use of antibiotics with a heavy cost in developing resistant strains of pathogens. This is a classic problem of the commons. It would seem sensible for low- and middle-income countries to prevent such development—perhaps by banning antibiotic use for animals, at least for preventive use—and encouraging smallholder livestock is a preferred solution. The solid economic and poverty reduction arguments are reinforced by the environmental features.

Second, research needs to be intensified on fertilizer practices that increase plant up-take, reduce run-off and increase fertilizer efficiency, i.e. decrease the amount of nutrients used per unit of economic output. There are already technical means of reducing fertilizer run-off and increasing the percentage that is taken up by plants. Pesticides are more amenable to research that obviates their use and plants can be bred to resist disease.

Pesticide use in low- and middle-income countries poses severe health hazards for users and environmental damage. Research has great scope for developing biological alternatives and as that is pursued the standard research and extension pushes need to be encouraged as for fertilizers.

CLIMATE CHANGE

The consensus view (Rosegrant et al. 2008) is that the impact of climate change on agriculture will be greater in tropical than temperate latitudes and hence greater for low- and middle-income countries than for high-income ones. Consequently, the burden on the poor is seen as particularly great. Agriculture in low- and middle-income countries contributes about 13 percent of climate change with 37 percent of that from livestock and 37 percent from fertilizer (Rosegrant et al. 2008).

For low- and middle-income countries the core adaptation to climate change is to accelerate the pursuit of modernization processes. In high productivity conditions they will give a high rate of return with impacts on both growth rates and poverty, and will provide some insurance against any lowering of yields from climate change.

In the context of climate change two areas merit special attention. The research effort must be larger than otherwise (keeping in mind that it is always grossly underfunded relative to marginal costs and returns) to cover research on dealing with higher temperatures, perhaps more variable rainfall, and other possible effects of climate change. That should involve breeding of existing crops for the expected new conditions, and testing alternative crops, all subject to profitability calculations with unbiased price regimes. Throughout it must be kept in mind that climate change is a slow long-term process.

Irrigation should be pursued at levels higher than merited without climate change. In monsoonal areas the greater strength of the wet and dry monsoons should lead to greater emphasis on ground water storage during the wet seasons, including appropriate drainage schemes, and ground water development during dry seasons and during dry periods in the wet season. In the context of modernization, irrigation is often underinvested, in particular small-scale schemes that supplement rainfall. With climate change these changes need to accelerate.

Low-lying areas connected to the great oceans will have more flooding and mapping is needed of the areas that will go out of agriculture in the near future and those that may suffer more waterlogging but stay in agriculture. This is a serious problem for many low-income countries (e.g., Bangladesh).

It is quite possible that some areas will benefit from climate change. That increased future productivity should be built into research systems to take full advantage of such improved situations. Including the greater potential to recharge water tables, some monsoonal areas could be major beneficiaries. Such speculation needs to be monitored and special emphasis given to climate change research to confirm (or otherwise) such potential.

References

Binswanger-Mkhize, H. P., Bourguignon, C., & Van Den Brink, R. J. (2009). *Agricultural land redistribution: Toward greater consensus.* Washington, DC: World Bank Publications.

Collier, P., & Dercon, S. (2014). African agriculture in 50 years: Smallholders in a rapidly changing world. *World Development, 63,* 92–101.

De Janvry, A. (1981). The role of land reforms in economic development: Policies and politics. *American Journal of Agricultural Economics, 63,* 384–392.

Deininger, K., & Byerlee, D. (2012). The rise of large farms in land abundant countries: Do they have a future? *World Development, 40*(4), 701–714.

FAOSTAT. (2015). *Food and Agriculture Organization* (various years).

Feder, G., & Nishio, A. (1998). The benefits of land registration and titling: Economic and social perspectives. *Land Use Policy, 15*(1), 25–43.

Financial Times. (2016, April).

Hirashima, S. (2008). The land market in development: A case study of Punjab in Pakistan and India. *Economic and Political Weekly, 43*(42), 41–47.

Johnston, B. F., & Mellor, J. W. (1961). The role of agriculture in economic development. *The American Economic Review, 51*(4), 566–593.

Johnston, B. F., & Kilby, P. (1978). *Agriculture and structural transformation: Economic strategies in late developing countries.* New York: Oxford University Press.

Johnston, B. F., & Mellor, J. W. (1984). The world food equation: Interrelations among development, employment, and food consumption. *Journal of Economic Literature, 22*, 531–574.

Johnson, D. L., & Lewis, L. A. (2007). *Land degradation: Creation and destruction.* Lanham: Rowman & Littlefield.

Mellor, J. W. (2002). *How much employment can rapid agricultural growth generate? Sectoral policies for maximum impact in Rwanda* (Occasional Paper No. 19). Bethesda: Prepared for United States Agency for International Development by Abt Associates Inc.

Mellor, J. W. (2017). *Ethiopia: An African land productivity success story.* Under review by John Mellor Associates.

Mellor, J. W., Weaver, T. F., & Lele, U. (1968). *Developing rural India: Plan and practice.* Ithaca: Cornell University Press.

Rosegrant, M. W., Ewing, M., Yohe, G., Burton, I., Huq, S., & Valmonte-Santos, R. (2008). *Climate change and agriculture: Threats and opportunities.* Eschborn: GTZ.

PART III

Modernization of the Small Commercial Farm

CHAPTER 8

Government and the Institutions of Modernization

One of the two major thrusts of this book is the large essential role of government if agricultural modernization is to succeed. Part 3 states the essential public institutional structures for modernization of agriculture, what they are to accomplish, how they interact with the dominant private sector, and key issues in their development.

Modernization shifts agricultural production from tradition-based, relatively static management of land and labor to continuous, dynamic processes of science and purchased, input-based innovation. That requires active building of new government and quasi-government institutions and the modification of old institutions. Chapters 9, 10, 11, 12, 13, 14 and 15 spell this out for each of the major functional areas to be covered.

Douglass North (1987) presents an all-encompassing view of institutions in economic development. A different approach is developed in Hayami and Ruttan (1985), in essence a market-oriented approach, in which differences in factor proportions, e.g. land to labor ratios, drive a market determination of institutional choices and future factor proportions. They explain the very different growth paths of agriculture in the United States and Japan. This book focuses on the specific public institutions for modernizing agriculture and the explicit public sector decisions required.

The first section of this chapter discusses farmers and private businesses whose incentive-based decisions determine the effect of government policies and institutions. The second section discusses key issues important in determining the long-run success of government programs for agricultural modernization. A third section discusses the critical issue of geographic concentration of government effort, before a final section outlines the interrelation between the succeeding chapters.

It will become clear that many governments perform poorly when facilitating agricultural modernization. Political scientists, for example, Bates (2014) and Bates and Block (2013) have written extensively on this issue and conclude that agriculture receives less unfavorable treatment in the context of representative

© The Author(s) 2017
J.W. Mellor, *Agricultural Development and Economic Transformation*,
Palgrave Studies in Agricultural Economics and Food Policy,
https://doi.org/10.1007/978-3-319-65259-7_8

electoral systems, i.e. those in which elections provide a strong voice for the population dominant rural people: "governments raided agriculture because they were not representative e.g. responding to the electorate." However, their analysis focuses largely on the more measurable actions, such as monetary transfers, through various forms of taxes and trade restrictions rather than on building appropriate institutions. Because of the strong technical assistance component in these institutions the following chapters also look at the fluctuating fashions in the foreign assistance donor community.

FARMER DECISION MAKING

Science and purchased, input-based, adaptive and adoptive decisions and their implementation by small commercial farmers are the essential final step in achieving modernization of agriculture. Those decisions are made in a complex context of factors affecting monetary profitability, the small commercial farmers' sense of self-esteem, community, and nation and their part in those, and a set of modern institutions that influence and manage that content and context. Government plays a leading role with respect to change in all of those processes. Part of modernizing is bringing greater equality among farmers in response to these background factors.

The profitability of production-oriented change is rarely certain and therefore farmers must discount the most likely profit. The discount rate will vary according to the nature of the change, from farmer to farmer, and from time to time. The more qualified the research and extension service, and the more efficient and respected government agencies are, the lower uncertainty will be.

Effective government policy requires input from farmers. Ideally farmers will organize to meet complex needs and farmers' organizations can be pyramided up from the lowest level to provide a mechanism for farmers to send feedback to the political process. Most high-income countries have politically powerful farmers' organizations, for example, the Farm Bureau in the United States. In low- and middle-income countries, large-scale farmers tend to be well organized, but small commercial farmers normally require some institutional assistance to organize.

PRIVATE BUSINESS NEEDS AND DECISIONS

Agricultural input supply and marketing are initially private sector, can expand rapidly, and should remain private sector. Having said that, it is important to recognize the extent to which private sector operations in a traditional, relatively stagnant context are deficient when playing an essential role in modernization.

In a traditional economy, small businesses serving agriculture are operated largely by traders. Their business is buying and selling and obtaining a margin. They are good at that—bargaining and spotting price differentials. They are not experienced in producing goods. For example, the move into seed production is a big jump for existing small businesses. Providing technical services, such as advice on fertilizer use, in a rapidly changing technical and price environment, is not something in which they are experienced. Hence, the government may temporarily fill these gaps. As private businesses inevitably grow more complex, modern accounting and other business practices are required. They ask for and should receive technical assistance in improving in these areas. Some changes will be dramatic, such as the rise of supermarkets, with assistance required if the small commercial farmer is to adapt.

Cooperatives

Cooperatives often play a major role in agricultural modernization by providing new critical services to small commercial farmers. The world over, cooperatives are relatively much more important in agriculture than in other sectors. Cooperatives normally operate in an environment of competing private sector businesses.

The greater importance of cooperatives in agriculture is probably because agriculture tends to be dominated by small commercial farmers who form a critical geographic concentration—they define geographic regions; those farmers are sufficiently homogenous that they are comfortable in the same organization. Whatever the reality, famers tend to view private traders as exploitative and therefore have a favorable view of cooperatives. Thus, cooperatives have an advantage in a loyal membership. In any case, in low-income countries, when effective cooperatives form they bring added competition and margins tend to decline.

Although the record of success of agricultural cooperatives is mixed there is a large literature dealing with the successes and how they were achieved. Verhofstadt and Maertens (2014) review literature dealing with success and point to cooperatives succeeding in improving price information and market participation, increasing the adoption of improved technology, and increased farmer income. It is noted, consistent with this analysis, that the lowest-income farmers tend not to participate. A Rwandan study notes that cooperative members have 50 percent more land than non-members, only two-thirds as many poor as in the non-member category, and have twice the income of non-members. In Ethiopia the bulk of cooperative members are small commercial farmers and subsistence farmers tend not to join. That membership composition of cooperatives is to be expected since they are commercially oriented.

Ortmann and King (2007), in analysing the reasons for cooperative failure, emphasizes lack of accountability of cooperative management to members as a principal reason for failure. That is to say, they fail when they are not true cooperatives. In low- and middle-income countries they are often started as a matter of government policy, run initially as government bureaucracies, and never make the transition to being farmer owned and managed. In the present day, high-income countries' cooperatives tend to start at the grassroots level so they were innately member owned and managed. However, the whole set of financial cooperatives in the United States was started by the government and initially operated by government officials, but very quickly moved to being farmer owned and managed. That transition has often been difficult or even non-existent in present day, low- and middle-income countries.

Nevertheless, organizing farmers into properly capitalized cooperatives with efficient management systems is difficult and government normally plays a role in facilitating their development. For cooperatives to be farmer run requires a primary cooperative with members who elect a board. To achieve essential scale economies, primary cooperatives must be organized into cooperative unions and those unions must escalate into what will normally be a national level apex body.

As the government plays its important organizational role, with government staffing, it is natural to use the cooperatives to fulfill other needs, including the nationally set social goals. However, those may not be the first priorities of the primary members and such actions lead to weak and often failing cooperatives.

It is important, as cooperative leadership develops, that the special insights of women, including female heads of households and farmers' wives, be drawn upon in leadership positions. Unfortunately, the strong position of women in family decision making in a traditional, inward, village-oriented context greatly weakens as the sources of critical information move outside the village. Women cannot obtain leadership positions in production cooperatives if they are not fully up to speed on the requisite outside knowledge. Changing that is a key component of accelerating modernization.

Non-governmental Organizations (NGOs)

NGOs are non-governmental agencies providing important services to agriculture and more broadly (for a detailed analysis of NGOs see Riddell and Robinson (1995)). They usually have relatively low-paid volunteer staff who are driven by an urge to contribute to reducing poverty. They rose into prominence in the context of a phase of foreign aid that de-emphasized the role of government, a positon particularly detrimental to the agricultural sector. NGOs can play an important role in testing new ideas and complementing and supplementing broad government actions. Finally, a national aggregate impact requires government institutions.

The Overarching Role of National Government

Four factors make the role of government essential to the small commercial farm fulfilling its promise in the economic transformation.

First is the need for a national vision and strategy with respect to the economic transformation with explicit reference to the critical role of agriculture. That contributes to motivating farmers in the national interest and guides the provision of government services. To be effective, government's role in agricultural modernization must be based on carefully defined priorities and evolve over time in response to the dynamics of technological change and growing private sector capabilities.

Second, to play its role in the economic transformation agriculture requires an infrastructure of education, roads, electricity, and computerization. The greater political power of the urban sector obtains those investments while agriculture and the rural sector tend to be neglected. The dispersed nature of agriculture makes the provision of these infrastructures more expensive per capita than in urban areas.

Third, agricultural growth is based on scientific advancements tailored to local conditions. That requires large-scale nationwide institutions not only to generate the steady stream of new science but to provide the essential complements for its full implementation.

Fourth, the small commercial farmers are small businesses and cannot provide those services on their own. Some of the services required by modernization of agriculture can be provided by the private sector, but some are largely provided by governments even in high-income countries with highly developed large-scale private firms.

In high-income countries that have completed the economic transformation these functions became institutionalized and the role of government remains substantial, while the private sector will have taken over a significant portion of the total. All high-income countries have a public sector system fostering production growth for agriculture that is disproportionately large compared to the economic size of agriculture.

Vision and Strategy from the Highest Level

Governments must provide a clear quantifiable vision and strategy fully publicized and committed to mobilize rural people and particularly small commercial farmers in support of the plan and to be motivated to search for and implement profitable means of increasing production.

Ethiopia began its economic transformation with Prime Minister Meles Zenawi stating a clear vision of becoming a middle-income country in 25 years. Given its place near the bottom of the list of low-income countries with respect to income and development institutions that was a challenging vision. The strategy was termed ADLI—Agricultural Development Led Industrialization (see Ethiopia 2010). It was clear that agriculture, meaning rural people and specifically small commercial farmers, was to play a central role in converting the country from one dominated by agriculture to one in which agriculture would still be important and modern but only one of several important sectors.

The vision and the strategy were widely and constantly publicized. That was particularly true for rural areas where it could be explained by an extension service of over 60,000 agents stationed at the lowest administrative level, the Kebela. Farmers felt part of a national effort to transform the economy.

The vision and strategy placed intense pressure on government agriculture staff to produce the eight percent growth rate that was stated as the target for realizing the vision. The result has been a constant examination by government staff of policies and institutional arrangements.

Government Responsiveness to the Small Commercial Farmer

As the sector strategy is unrolled constant interaction with farmers is required not only to ensure implementation, but even more importantly, to quickly discover errors in the process and rectify them. A variety of institutional structures may fill this need: extension agents; cooperatives; other forms of farmer organization; university and Ministry of Agriculture research programs; and regular and wide-spread field visits by government officials at all levels. One of the important functions of a large extension system is providing feedback on how technological change is proceeding and what needs to be done to improve on that. Of course, in a low-income country these efforts will be imperfectly pursued, but they must have a positive impact.

University and ministry, systematic, field survey-based research should be developed and monitored to provide regular information from the field from the general to very explicit study of specific aspects of the agricultural growth and poverty alleviation process.

Scarcity of Resources and Consequent Priorities

For low-income countries, agriculture's requirements from the government occur in a context of acute shortage of financial, human, and institutional resources. The financial constraint on public resources tends to be greater than the overall capital constraint, and that has two implications.

First, in making plans special focus must be given to maximizing the use of the private sector in providing essential services in a profitable pricing context. Often the government will have an important diagnostic role in ensuring that the private sector is fulfilling its functions.

Second, the plans must be realistic in terms of the share and absolute quantity of public resources to be made available. The African Union's ten percent of government expenditure allocated to agriculture is a sensible target. Many low- and middle-income countries fail to meet that target; and many miss it by more than half. Revealed preference states that those countries are not serious about modernizing agriculture to play an important role in the economic transformation.

Removing Government Presence

In the early stages of agricultural modernization some functions that are most efficient in the private sector do not have an initial base. Urgency in getting on with the job leads government agencies to initially having to fill that gap.

For example, production of hybrid seed is highly specialized and initially there will be few, if any, in the private sector with the necessary combination of technical and business management skills. The government, at least through its research system, has seed production capability and can readily expand. The private sector sooner or later must enter the market and the sooner the better. In

Africa, foreign assistance agencies and particularly Dutch foreign agencies and the Gates Foundation have made a valuable contribution to the training of private sector seed producers.

As the private sector builds competitive capacity, the management of government institutions is often reluctant to lose a commanding position and often restrictions are placed on private sector expansion. It is very easy for the public sector to price below cost and thereby keep out the private sector. The Minister of Agriculture must recognize the long timescale needed, build a regulatory system, foster competition, and withdraw as the private sector steps in.

Corruption

Given the importance of public institutions to rapid agricultural growth and poverty reduction, high levels of corruption are anathema to agricultural modernization. At its most obvious, corruption reduces the rate of return to public sector investment, perhaps to the point at which those investments are not economic. It has been widely publicized that cost per mile for the comparable highways from the port to the capital city cost twice as much in Kenya as in Ethiopia. That is due to differences in corruption levels. The result is that if the investment makes a 20 percent rate of return with Ethiopian costs it drops to ten percent under Kenyan circumstances. The former pays, the latter is doubtful.

Fink (2002) documents the many ways in which corruption impedes technological improvement, development of the credit system and corrupts the land markets. Anik et al. (2013) document the impact on food security of the poorer rural families as they too must make corruption payments and these out of an already inadequate income for achieving food security. There is a profound equity problem, as well as an agricultural growth problem.

Corruption has hidden losses in diverting the attention of government officials from effective operation of their departments and of course it leads to lack of confidence of ordinary people in their government, a serious problem when small commercial farmers need to be mobilized in pursuit of rapid agricultural growth. Corruption also turns government officials away from prioritizing agriculture, given that agricultural expenditure is less accommodating to large-scale corruption because of the nature of the investments. Corrupt officials prefer expenditure that facilitates corruption, leading away from an agricultural growth strategy except for large-scale irrigation. It follows that high levels of corruption rule out modernization of agriculture, to the great disadvantage of the poor and of many geographic regions.

Local Government

Strong local governments facilitate small commercial farmer oriented needs for infrastructure and other broad areas of government input. Historically, truly local government was seen as inimical to colonial interests. Local government was a colonial officer stationed at the local level. Unfortunately, that central-based top-down approach is still the norm. Partly as a result most low- and middle-income countries have weak rural local governments. That is in contrast to the early stage development situation in many high-income countries. Lack of taxation powers and hence control of a revenue source is the overriding problem in the development of contemporary local government; while lack of trained personnel at the local level is another major problem.

Foreign aid, as in most rural activities, has gone through cycles of emphasis and de-emphasis of local government. During the up phases it has provided valuable technical assistance to develop local government, but lack of consistency weakened efforts to build effective local government (Dickovick 2014).

Mgbenka et al. (2015) gives detail for Nigeria as an example of the worst of the local government effort. There local government expanded under pressure to develop from central government and foreign aid donors. But what transpired was a system without locally elected officials, filled with corruption of all kinds, an abysmal record in fostering infrastructure investment, and little or no technical impact on agriculture. In contrast, India has made a major effort to re-establish the traditional panchayats (village councils) as local government. They have developed somewhat as planned although are still not a strong element in accelerating technical change in agriculture.

GEOGRAPHIC CONCENTRATION

Given resource scarcity it is important that governments concentrate resources where the returns are the highest. Conventional wisdom (described by Fan and Hazell (2001) as they go on to make the opposing case), successful practice (Ethiopia 2010), and this book concentrate on already high productivity areas. Concentration refers particularly to infrastructure, roads and electrification, and research/extension. That is justified in terms of stylized production functions relating labor input to output (see Chap. 4). High potential areas have steeply sloping functions extending to high yields and providing scope for large surplus over labor input. In contrast, low potential areas have gently sloping functions that reach a maximum at low yields. Improved technology tends to extend the underlying function in high potential areas to higher levels with the same slope. Obviously returns to infrastructure and new technology are higher in the area of the function with a steep slope and rising to a high level of output. In practice, this is achieved by concentrating on rural areas of high rather than low population density.

In a complex multi-equation system Fan and Hazell (2001) estimate the returns on several types of investment and their impact on growth and poverty in irrigated, high-potential rain-fed and low-potential rain-fed areas in India and China. They consistently find the marginal impact on production and poverty reduction greater in the low-potential rain-fed areas compared to the irrigated areas. They conclude that policy needs to promote agricultural intensification for both high- and low-potential areas. This leaves no geographic priority. There are three concerns with this conclusion.

First, as this book consistently shows, returns in the high-potential areas have been declining because the development effort, particularly research and extension, have not evolved with development. The returns now are highest in horticulture, livestock, and exports, rather than the basic cereals. That would reflect the finding of currently low returns in the high-potential areas.

Second, perhaps the definitions of low-potential areas include substantial areas of high potential. The classification in this book is according to rural population density—broadly reflecting the carrying capacity per area of land, rather than irrigation and rainfall.

Third, in India the quality of the basic technology institutions has been declining (Tamboli and Nene 2011). As a result, the later arriving geographic areas could derive a high rate of return from the old recommendations while the more progressive areas run out of support.

On close examination the Fan and Hazell findings are consistent with the various geographic area findings in this book. The deterioration from a high level in the Indian higher agricultural education, research, and extension systems is consistent with the much larger decline in return on investment in irrigated areas in India compared to China.

For China the poverty level had by the later period declined to under two percent in the irrigated areas and under four percent in the high-potential rain-fed areas. Hence, essentially there is no scope for further decline in poverty in the high-potential areas. The low-potential areas still had significant poverty to be reduced.

The marketing chapter (Chap. 15) notes that as the scope for growth in cereals declines as middle-income status is reached there needs to be rapid growth in the livestock and horticulture sectors to match rapidly growing demand. The general failure for that to happen depressed returns on investing in the more advanced areas that are best suited to those activities.

The research chapter (Chap. 12) recommends a basic level of research and associated extension for the low potential areas. The infrastructure chapter (Chap. 9) notes approvingly that central infrastructure, between major towns, is progressed by the political system but later than for the high-potential areas, and likewise for electrification.

KEYS TO MODERNIZATION

The next seven chapters treat separately the keys to modernization. However, they each interact with and are dependent on the others. Government action is essential to each. Physical infrastructure, Chap. 9, notably roads then electrification, requires the most expenditure, is essential for the full set of incentives, is critical as social infrastructure and is a never-ending task. It enhances competition and returns to the other institutions. Education and health, Chap. 10, increase returns to innovation but also increase the incentive to labor input. Price policy, Chap. 11, affects returns to innovation and incentives but has a limited role because of the reverse effect on real incomes of the poor and the high opportunity cost of government expenditure on raising agricultural prices. Technological change is a better incentive than higher agricultural prices. Of course the core change required for modernizing is the steady stream of productivity increasing innovation, Chap. 12, which requires constant change in the providing institutions. Chapter 13 deals with the purchased inputs that are the normal embodiment of technical change. That leads to Chap. 14, finance, required for the optimal level of purchased inputs and many other aspects of technological change. Finance may come later than many of the requirements but is essential to the long-run process. Finally, the rise of cities and rapid change in marketing institutions, Chap. 15, puts special pressures on small commercial farmers requiring specialized assistance.

References

Anik, A. R., Manjunatha, A. V., & Bauer, S. (2013). Impact of farm level corruption on the food security of households in Bangladesh. *Food Security, 5*(4), 565–574.
Bates, R. H. (2014). *Markets and states in tropical Africa: The political basis of agricultural policies.* Berkeley/London: University of California Press.
Bates, R. H., & Block, S. A. (2013). Revisiting African agriculture: Institutional change and productivity growth. *The Journal of Politics, 75*(2), 372–384.
Dickovick, J. T. (2014). Foreign aid and decentralization: Limitations on impact in autonomy and responsiveness. *Public Administration and Development, 34*(3), 194–206.
Ethiopia. (2010). *Ethiopia's agriculture sector policy and investment framework: Ten year road map (2010–2020).* Addis Ababa: Fedral Democratic Republic of Ethiopia.
Fan, S., & Hazell, P. (2001). Returns to public investments in the less-favored areas of India and China. *American Journal of Agricultural Economics, 83*(5), 1217–1222.
Fink, R. (2002). *Corruption and the agricultural sector.* Washington, DC: Management Systems International.
Hayami, Y., & Ruttan, V. W. (1985). *Agricultural development: An international perspective* (2nd ed.). Baltimore: Johns Hopkins University Press.
Mgbenka, R., Bah, E., & Ezeano, C. (2015). The role of local government council in agricultural transformation in Nigeria: Need for review of policy. *Agricultural Engineering Research Journal, 5*(2), 27–32.
North, D. (1987). Institutions, transaction cost and economic growth. *Economic Enquiry, 25*(3), 419–428.
Ortmann, G. F., & King, R. P. (2007). Agricultural cooperatives I: History, theory and problems. *Agrekon, 46*(1), 18–46.
Riddell, R. C., & Robinson, R. (1995). *Non-governmental organizations and rural poverty alleviation.* Oxford: Oxford University Press.
Tamboli, P.M., & Nene, Y.L. (2011). Revitalizing higher agricultural education in India: Journey towards excellence. Secunderabad, India: Asian Agri-History Foundation.
Verhofstadt, E., & Maertens, M. (2014). *Can agricultural cooperatives reduce poverty? Heterogeneous impact of cooperative membership on farmers' welfare in Rwanda* (Bioeconomics working paper series no. 2). Leuven: Department of Earth and Environmental Sciences, University of Leuven.

CHAPTER 9

Physical Infrastructure

Agricultural modernization requires large-scale investment in rural physical infrastructure—roads, electrification, communications, computer access. It requires integrated markets over large areas. Moser et al. (2009) show decisively how impossible that is to achieve without reliable roads; conversely they show rapidly widening marketing margins as roads become worse or non-existent. Rural infrastructure is critical to rural social well-being, including the universal objectives of health and education systems and income generation in the rural non-farm sector. Equally important, infrastructure must be constantly upgraded: it is a never-ending task.

Governments vary tremendously in the extent to which they allocate resources to rural infrastructure. That is an important indicator of government concern or lack of concern for the people of rural areas and rapid agricultural growth.

Rural infrastructure has four principal components—rural roads tend to come first, followed by electrification. Increasingly cell phones will come first because of their low cost and great utility. The rural infrastructure for computers has historically received little attention in low- and middle-income countries. Computer infrastructure is important to much of rural development from accounting systems in cooperatives to sophisticated pricing comparisons.

Contrasts in Infrastructure Investment Among Countries

High-income countries have a comprehensive road network. In the three high-income country examples in Table 9.1, the range in road length per 1000 population is large, but it relates to population density. Low-density United States has twice the level of high-density Japan, and France stands exactly half way between those two. That source of disparity also applies to low- and middle-income countries. Nevertheless, the contrast of high-income countries with Asian and African countries is extraordinary, and underlines the immense task

© The Author(s) 2017
J.W. Mellor, *Agricultural Development and Economic Transformation*,
Palgrave Studies in Agricultural Economics and Food Policy,
https://doi.org/10.1007/978-3-319-65259-7_9

Table 9.1   Investment in infrastructure, selected countries

Country	Roads (km per 1000 people)	% of all roads rural	% of all roads paved	Rural electrification rate (% of all rural households with access to electricity)[a]	National electrification (% of all households with access to electricity)[a]	Cell-phone subscriptions (per 100 people)[b]
Bangladesh[c]	1.0	82	14	48	62	80.04
Pakistan[c]	1.7	52	60	62	73	73.33
India[c]	2.4	78	49	74	81	74.48
Indonesia[c]	1.5	79	54			128.78
China[c]	1.4	76	N/A	100	100	92.27
Ethiopia[d]	0.3		23	10	24	31.59
Rwanda[d]	1.5		23	5	21	64.02
Tanzania[d]	1.4		9	4	24	62.77
Ghana[d]	1.8		16	50	72	114.82
Nigeria[d]	0.8		32	37	45	77.84
Bolivia				74	88	96.34
United States	20.81					110.20
France	14.56					139.66
Japan	9.55					120.23

[a]IEA – International Energy Agency – Electricity access database (2016). Worldenergyoutlook.org
[b]ITU – International Technological University (2016)
[c]Donnges et al. (2007). (Asian countries) All road date (three columns)
[d]William et al. (2008). (African countries) All roads data (three columns)

facing low- and middle-income countries. They are typically one-tenth to one-quarter the level of Japan and of course twice that disparity with the United States. In terms of broad societal objectives and economic growth they have an immense amount of investment to make before they catch up. Unfortunately, many of them have hardly started the task. Very low-income Ethiopia, which is making large investments in roads shows how far back a truly low-income country is, being one-third the level of most other Asian and African countries. Most African countries are very low on electricity coverage, but cell phones are everywhere!

The Impact of Infrastructure on Economic and Social Indicators

Fan and Chan-Kang (2005) provide an in-depth analysis of road investment in China. Much of the road investment was made prior to the modern reform that brought rapid agricultural growth. The returns on road investment were low in that early period. However, when combined with the policy reforms and all the other government actions the returns on road became very high, in the order of 50 percent, ranking second only to research expenditure. The point is that rural road investment depends for its returns on rapid agricultural growth and for that many other requirements must also be met.

One of the most careful and detailed rural infrastructure studies was undertaken by IFPRI in Ethiopia (Stifel et al. 2016). That study is particularly relevant because it looks specifically at the impact of rural infrastructure in the context of a country implementing a fast agricultural growth strategy. The study divided the data into quintiles according to transport cost from different market levels.

From the least-cost quintile to the highest-cost, travel time to a major market increased by five times; the transport cost increased by three times. The median size of holding declined by almost half—holdings are larger in locations close to markets. The soils were poorer in the more distant locations. That means that higher priority was given to roads serving the better agricultural areas, which makes economic sense. Also cities have a tendency to grow around productive agricultural areas, providing better infrastructure to those nearby areas. Perhaps surprisingly the time to reach a school or health center did not increase with increasing transport costs, except for the highest quintile. But the data did not measure the extent or quality of the services. With low transport costs nearly all farmers, even the subsistence ones, used fertilizer of each type (N, P, K), while 79 percent in the higher transport cost situation used fertilizer. Presumably the levels of use were also higher in the low transport cost areas.

A host of studies in differing conditions all confirm the high returns on roads (e.g., Dorosh et al. 2012 for Sub-Saharan Africa; Gollin and Rogerson 2014 for subsistence agriculture). A study in Bangladesh (Khandker et al. 2009) found that rural road investments reduced poverty significantly through higher agricultural production, lower input and transportation costs, and higher agricultural output prices at local village markets. Rural road development also led to higher secondary school enrollment for boys and girls. In rural Kenya, areas devoted to cash crops are only located close to markets, a finding corroborated for Guatemala. A broad review of the literature found that falling transport costs increase the production of high-input crops which tend to be the high-value crops.

DIRECT IMPACT OF ROADS ON POVERTY

Focus group studies of the rural poor consistently show high priority to access to all-weather roads. That is partly because of the importance for access to health facilities, but it also reflects a recognition that employment increases rapidly in the context of all-weather roads and possibly recognition that good teachers and health workers come with good roads.

Several studies look at the relation between increased road density and poverty. For example, in Nepal, roads improved the welfare of the poor, but did not decrease inequality. A broad review of literature shows that rural road investments reduce poverty through their impact on increased agricultural production, higher wages, lower input costs, and higher output prices. Similarly, lowering transport costs reduced the probability of multi-dimensional poverty through improvements in health, education, and standard of living. These studies note that improved transport protects the poor from local bad crop years by facilitating the import of food, including through foreign aid programs.

A careful measurement found a major impact of increased road density on the most precise measure of child poverty (Blimpo et al. 2013). A standard deviation increase in kilometers of road per square kilometer reduced the number of stunted children by four times as much as a standard deviation increase in land for crops. In a sense, increasing road density is more valuable for that form of poverty reduction than increased land area. Several studies show that improving rural roads increases school attendance for both girls and boys.

One of the problems in making rural road decisions is not only to calculate the monetary benefits to the poor, but also the non-monetary benefits such as access to schools. Van de Walle (2002) provides a methodology for doing that, applying it to Vietnam.

Benefit Categories for Roads

Attracting Trained Personnel to Rural Areas

The reach of a modern nation's institutions is critical to agricultural growth. The faces of those institutions are highly trained staff who make the final link to small commercial farmers. The welfare of those families depends on ready access to schools and medical clinics. It is easy to construct buildings for these activities in isolated areas, but difficult to attract trained staff who want to live where the amenities are adequate. With poor rural infrastructure those places may be distant from the small commercial farmer clientele.

There is a widespread problem in rural areas of trained staff for schools and clinics not showing up for work—chronic absenteeism is rife. There are many explanations but an important one is that these trained people tend to live in a market town which has, at least, minimum urban amenities and access via bus to major urban centers. The commute to work in rural areas is often arduous and time consuming so the temptation to skip a day here and there is strong. Roads and later electrification and associated developments make it attractive to live in the smaller towns with a shorter commute. That applies to all the key personnel, such as extension workers, accountants, and managers for the cooperatives.

Increasing Incentives to Generate Income

Improved infrastructure including both roads and electrification also incentivize farmers and farmers' wives by increasing the range of exotic goods, widening their world view, and thereby increasing the incentive to take up income-increasing innovations. Small commercial farmers spend half their incremental income on the employment-intensive rural non-farm sector and one-quarter on improved quality of food consumption, still leaving one-quarter of incremental income for urban-based goods the attractiveness and accessibility of which increases with improved infrastructure.

Increased Production Incentives

Economists emphasize, often solely, increased production incentives. Marketing margins are often reduced by one-quarter as significant improvements in terms of trade and hence the incentive to increase output and to mobilize labor for that purpose result. Those forces then interact with improved technology of modernization to bring large increases in production, income, and indirectly, poverty reduction. The IFPRI study (Stifel et al. 2016), cited above, of the impact of improved infrastructure in Ethiopia documents the improvement in price relationships simply from the better connections between primary and secondary markets. The benefits become larger when including the improved connection between the farm and primary markets. Fertilizer becomes more readily available and more agents compete for business, further reducing margins and improving price relationships. Extension agents make more visits with more demonstrations.

Increased Competition

Moser et al. (2009) corroborate that good infrastructure leads to more traders in a given area and hence greater competition and lower margins leading to more favorable prices at the farm level.

Issues with Respect to Road Investment

Finance

The financial requirements for a high level of rural infrastructure are immense. Ideally, the bulk of the financing in the technology responsive areas would be local financing. Those areas are the big beneficiaries and so why should they not pay? That has the large advantage that local supervision will generally do a better job of locating roads and ensuring efficient construction and hence lower costs. There is, of course, some danger that local political officials will favor their own areas over others, but perhaps that will determine the order in which roads are done rather than the total effort.

For local financing, property taxes are a logical means of financing since the benefits will go disproportionately to owners of land that becomes more productive. Again, unfortunately, in most low- and middle-income countries rural property taxes are not a favored means of raising revenue. This situation has its roots in colonial systems which used land taxes heavily and in an exploitative manner.

In most contemporary low- and middle-income countries the development of local governments and particularly their revenue-raising authority is small relative to that in the early stages of development of contemporary high-income countries. In the former case the financing will be from national revenues. Unfortunately, it is often the national level governments that look askance at rural development.

Upgrading Infrastructure

Long standing IFPRI studies, particularly in Bangladesh (Ahmed and Hossain 1990), show that roads have a major impact on agricultural growth when they are upgraded to all-weather status, but not when they are closed off during the year due to rain and other factors. The Khandker et al. (2009) study of Bangladesh was entirely with respect to paved roads.

For all the benefits cited, infrastructure reliability is important. The teacher needs to get to school every day, likewise the clinician. Products must be marketed regularly, particularly as perishables such as livestock and horticulture become prominent. Extension agents must appear as scheduled. Thus, for roads to become inoperable in periods of heavy rain is unacceptable.

Roads must be seen as a never-ending task. First a track is laid out by choosing elevations carefully, then it is widened, then it is graveled and eventually it receives a permanent hard surface. Finally, it is widened. To the casual visitor, or even regular travelers, traveling on a gravel road seems fine, but this is illusory as repair bills are substantially higher for trucks working on gravel roads as compared to hard-surface roads. Thus road building must have a clear objective and time phasing for road upgrading. Flying over backward rural areas it is generally the case that the road network appears adequate, but it is only on the ground that the need for upgrading becomes evident and urgent.

Road Maintenance

The road story is full of horrors about road maintenance. For example, the World Bank has calculated that in 2003, for every mile of new road in Sub-Saharan Africa, three miles of old roads deteriorate to a barely usable state. The length of usable roads is declining! The usual explanation is that initial investment in new roads is largely made by foreign aid agencies with maintenance left to the receiving country. That in essence says that the country had little interest in its roads.

My enlightening experience on this view was in Nepal, observing a major market to market road in bad shape and asking a village elder about it. He said the foreign donor would not pay maintenance but if it deteriorated sufficiently, in only a few more years, it would build a new road on the old roadbed. A few years of higher costs due to deterioration was much cheaper than maintenance.

Maintenance is a separate issue from initial investment and one of importance but with substantial critical problems. First is financing. Obviously maintenance should be done by the local government, perhaps with private contractors. Local government is best placed to contain costs and to benefit from maintenance. The problem is that local governments lack taxing authority, so how will they pay?

A second problem is lack of institutional structure for maintenance. Often the road itself was built by foreign contractors with no provision for local capacity to take on the maintenance. The national government, even if it contracts foreign firms, should specify building in some local capacity so the local government or private contractors can provide the maintenance. Foreign donors should ensure that capacity for maintenance is allowed for as part of their initial loan.

RURAL EMPLOYMENT PROGRAMS AND ROAD BUILDING

Guaranteed employment programs, as in India, are a common means of providing income safety nets to deal with rural poverty. They have the advantage of self-selection to the poor since those with high-incomes do not want to do the physical work entailed in such programs, which are frequently used to build infrastructure including roads. To be successful the objective must be to provide a productive asset.

Once that is settled it becomes clear that a productive road requires much more than labor—surveying, engineering, culverts, and bridges are needed, requiring a substantial budget. The needs are for two objectives, each with its own financing but fully coordinated—employment and road construction (and maintenance!).

LOW-COST RURAL ROAD RESEARCH

In high-income countries it is recognized that rural roads are different to main highways and that local conditions vary. As a result, research is carried out, primarily in the US in land grant universities, as to how to reduce the cost of rural roads suited to local conditions. Just as low- and middle-income countries must have their own national systems of agricultural research so they should be carrying out research to reduce the cost and increase the effectiveness of an intricate system of low-cost roads and the priorities for developing them. Logically, such research would be closely associated with the agricultural research system, as in the United States, but integrated with the road building departments nationally and locally.

INFRASTRUCTURE FOR LOW-POTENTIAL RURAL AREAS

In general, rural infrastructure investment will have the greatest impact on both growth and poverty reduction in the high-potential agricultural areas. Eventually the lowest potential areas will be abandoned from agriculture, and much of the rural infrastructure wasted. The solution is outmigration in the context of increased opportunities provided by rapid growth in the high-potential areas, but the unfortunate results are an aging, low-income population. The political system will normally ensure roads and other infrastructure connecting the larger towns and then with the rest of the country. That should at least facilitate education and some possibility of low-wage businesses moving in.

RURAL ELECTRIFICATION

Justification for rural electrification for agricultural production tends to tell a limited story associated with irrigation and cold storage. These specific, high-return uses grossly understate the range of needs. Electrification as a consumption good is universally desired. It is the path to many consumer goods and consumption patterns which increase production incentives. The farmer's wife is equally and even more desirous of electrification than the male farmer, and likewise for those under the poverty line. As for roads, the investment required is immense.

High-income countries have close to 100 percent of families with electricity. Low- and middle-income countries have a high percentage of urban people with access to electricity, but the rural sector is very variable. More typically in Asia half to three-quarters of rural families have electricity (Table 9.1). In Africa the range is five to ten percent, except for a few countries in the range of one-third to one-half. Again the infrastructure investment problem facing African countries is immense.

However, several countries have had huge success in rural electrification. China has pushed rural electrification and essentially all rural households now have electricity. By the year 2005 Thailand had 90 percent of rural households with electricity and Costa Rica 95 percent.

In a broad review of success stories several features stand out (Barnes 2007). While government involvement was universal in the success stories, political interference with payments and priorities was very modest, but on the latter the opposite is true of the failures.

Subsidies have been universal in rural electrification, presumably because of higher distribution costs compared to urban areas. In the successful countries, subsidies take the form of a portion of the capital cost, particularly for distribution, with the operating costs covered by rates with high levels of payment. It is best to maintain our anti-subsidy position given the high rate of return on electricity and under-investment, and emphasize national borrowing at a high level with returns guaranteed by rates that are paid. However, that is not the norm.

The cost of renewable energy (e.g., solar panels) has been decreasing rapidly. To fill all the important functions rural electrification requires low cost, as for urban areas. Perhaps renewables now provide a solution to access for remote areas (Urmee et al. 2009).

Private, public, and cooperative forms were each represented in success stories and so no generalization can be made about the institutional form. It was common to recognize low levels of use per rural household and thus to pursue low capital cost systems. It was notable that operating subsidies tend to be associated with low reliability of service as the distribution institution tried to reduce the problem of non-payment.

As urban populations and incomes rise the market for livestock producers and horticulture expands rapidly. Maintaining a high growth rate requires taking advantage of those new markets. Cold storage, requiring electrification, is critical to many of those activities. Minten et al. (2014) give a dramatic example of the impact of cold storage rapidly affecting substantial areas of low-income Bihar, India, reaching farmers in all size classes and facilitating a large increase in potato production, incomes, and poverty reduction.

CELL PHONES

The speed with which cell phones have spread, even in rural areas of low-income countries, is truly astounding (Table 9.1). Even in Africa, two-thirds of all households are covered and soon it will be virtually all. The IFPRI Ethiopian study (Stifel et al. 2016) found a major impact of cell phones on increased agricultural marketing efficiency. There is a substantial literature dealing with various aspects of mobile phone interaction with credit, and banking more generally (e.g. Jack and Suri 2011). But it is important to keep in mind the critical importance of day-to-day direct contact between the loan officer and the borrowers to ensure sound loans and full repayment. The cell phone can shift the accounting burden off the agent and increase direct contact between clients and the home office on a range of activities but it is not a substitute for personal service in this context.

There is also a major impact in access to social services. Remember the women in the isolated village in Nepal who desperately wanted to be able to talk to a distant doctor in a childbirth emergency? They now have a cell phone. Next to come is their trade via cell phone of their high-value crops providing them with the assurance of a market.

REFERENCES

Ahmed, R., & Hossain, M. (1990). *Developmental impact of rural infrastructure in Bangladesh* (Vol. 83). Washington, DC: International Food Policy Research Institute.

Barnes, D. F. (2007). *The challenge of rural electrification: Strategies for developing countries.* Washington, DC: Resources for the Future Press.

Blimpo, M. P., Harding, R., & Wantchekon, L. (2013). Public investment in rural infrastructure: Some political economy considerations. *Journal of African Economies, 22*(2), ii57–ii83.

Donnges, C., Edmonds, G., & Johannessen, B. (2007). *Rural road maintenance – Sustaining the benefits of improved access.* Bangkok: International Labour Organization (ILO).

Dorosh, P., Wang, H. G., You, L., & Schmidt, E. (2012). Road connectivity, population and crop production in sub-Saharan Africa. *Agricultural Economics, 43*(1), 89–103.

Fan, S., & Chan-Kang, C. (2005). *Road development, economic growth, and poverty reduction in China* (Vol. 12). Washington, DC: International Food Policy Research Institute.

Gollin, D., & Rogerson, R. (2014). Productivity, transport costs and subsistence agriculture. *Journal of Development Economics, 107*, 38–48.

International Energy Agency. (2016). World energy outlook 2016 – Electricity access database. Retrieved from http://www.worldenergyoutlook.org/media/weowebsite/2015/WEO2016Electricity.xlsx

International Technological University. (2016). Statistics: ICT facts & figures, mobile phone subscriptions. Retrieved from www.itu.int/ict

Jack, W., & Suri, T. (2011). *Mobile money: The economics of M-Pesa* (NBER Working Paper Series No. 16721). Cambridge, MA: National Bureau of Economic Research.

Khandker, S. R., Bakht, Z., & Koolwal, G. B. (2009). The poverty impact of rural roads: Evidence from Bangladesh. *Economic Development and Cultural Change, 57*(4), 685–722.

Minten, B., Reardon, T., Singh, K., & Sutradhar, R. (2014). The new and changing roles of cold storages in the potato supply chain in Bihar. *Economic and Political Weekly, 49*(52), 98–108.

Moser, C., Barrett, C., & Minten, B. (2009). Spatial integration at multiple scales: Rice markets in Madagascar. *Agricultural Economics, 40*(3), 281–294.

Stifel, D., Minten, B., & Koru, B. (2016). Economic benefits of rural feeder roads: Evidence from Ethiopia. *The Journal of Development Studies, 52*(9), 1335–1356.

Urmee, T., Harries, D., & Schlapfer, A. (2009). Issues related to rural electrification using renewable energy in developing countries of Asia and Pacific. *Renewable Energy, 34*(2), 354–357.

Van de Walle, D. (2002). Choosing rural road investments to help reduce poverty. *World Development, 30*(4), 575–589.

William, G. K., Foster, V., Archondo-Callao, R., Briceño-Garmendia, C., Nogales, A., & Sethi, K. (2008). *The burden of maintenance: Roads in sub-Saharan Africa* (AICD Background Paper No. 14). Washington, DC: World Bank Group.

CHAPTER 10

Rural Education and Health

Increased employment and income of the rural poor derived from rapid agricultural growth creates an improved context for increasing school attendance and improved health. Concurrently, greater participation in education and improved health increase the response by small commercial farmers to productivity-increasing modernization.

Rural education and health have much in common with physical infrastructure. They require large public sector investments. Those investments never end—they need to keep growing over time. They are as important to universal social objectives as to agricultural growth and so the cost should be seen as being substantially for the former. Perhaps most important, farmers consistently state that schools and health clinics are what they most want from government, with roads following close behind.

Schools and clinics require physical infrastructure if they are to be fully cost effective. And, like physical infrastructure they are more dispersed and hence more expensive per capita than urban expenditure for the same purpose and quality. Rural areas fare much worse on both quantity and quality compared to urban areas.

Given that education is of critical importance to agricultural growth and requires substantial resources for its provision, it is indeed fortunate that growth in education is directly consistent with the ultimate human objectives of the development process—direct satisfaction of rural people from being educated and the broad preparation of people for greater individual freedom of action and greater choices.

All levels of education are essential to agricultural modernization. Primary education must be universal so everyone has the basic skills of literacy and numeracy. Secondary education must be achieved by a rapidly increasing portion of the population as modernization demands those skills and for selection to higher education. Higher education is essential for rapidly increasing qualified staff for public and private institutions serving a modernizing agriculture.

© The Author(s) 2017   123
J.W. Mellor, *Agricultural Development and Economic Transformation*,
Palgrave Studies in Agricultural Economics and Food Policy,
https://doi.org/10.1007/978-3-319-65259-7_10

THE RATE OF RETURN TO PUBLIC EXPENDITURE ON RURAL EDUCATION

There is a large literature on rates of return to education under a wide range of circumstances and conditions. The World Bank analysis by Montenegro and Patrinos (2014) summarizes much of that literature from which Table 10.1 is reproduced below.

The rate of return to education is highest for Sub-Saharan African countries at 12.4 percent. That is 24 percent higher than the high-income countries and 60 percent higher than other low-income country regions. That is somewhat surprising given the less attractive growth environment but is consistent with the much fewer years of schooling in Sub-Saharan Africa compared to other regions. Primary education tends generally, but not always, to show higher rates of return than secondary education.

It is notable and consistent with many similar studies, that returns to female education are markedly higher than for male education. That is most substantial for Sub-Saharan Africa at 28 percent higher than for males.

Time series data show the returns to education declining modestly over time. That probably reflects an effort to catch up on the provision of schools and hence the supply of educated people increasing somewhat faster than demand. That is not only unsurprising but what should happen. If the returns are high, there should be more investment and that should lower the returns.

Studies commonly show somewhat lower rates of return to rural education than urban. However, when the data are controlled for income, that disparity disappears for boys but remains for girls. Thus, much of the rural disparity for girls is due to factors other than lower rural incomes—presumably discrimination against girls' education. School attendance in rural areas is generally lower than urban areas. Worldwide studies show only 18 percent of urban children are out of school compared to 30 percent of rural children.

Table 10.1   Average returns to schooling (latest period for each country)

Region	Average returns to schooling			Average years of schooling		
	Total	Male	Female	Total	Male	Female
High-income economies	10.0	9.5	11.1	12.9	12.7	13.1
East Asia & Pacific	9.4	9.2	10.1	10.4	10.2	10.7
Europe & Central Asia	7.4	6.9	9.4	12.4	12.2	12.7
Latin America & Caribbean	9.2	8.8	10.7	10.1	9.5	10.9
Middle East & North Africa	7.3	6.5	11.1	9.4	9.2	11.0
South Asia	7.7	6.9	10.2	6.5	6.5	6.4
Sub-Saharan Africa	12.4	11.3	14.5	8.0	8.1	8.1
All economies	9.7	9.1	11.4	10.4	10.2	10.8

Source: Montenegro and Patrinos (2014)

Consistently, poor children are greatly underrepresented in school. That is due to an inability to cover the substantial cost of school attendance (clothing, books, fees, travel) and the higher opportunity cost of their labor to the family (they are needed for household and farming tasks). However, in countries such as Sierra Leone that have expanded schools rapidly the rural–urban disparity has declined markedly.

Rural school attendance increases rapidly with improved infrastructure. In India from 2003 to 2010 the proportion of schools within one kilometer of a paved road increased from 69 percent to 78 percent and schools with electricity increased from 20 percent to 45 percent.

ATTENDANCE RATES

From a sample of low-, middle-, and high-income countries and several regions attendance in primary and secondary schools, and of girls and boys in high-income countries is roughly the same and close to universal (Table 10.2). In contrast in low- and middle-income countries the rates are far lower in secondary school than in primary. The record is mixed for girls compared to boys: for both primary and secondary school three of the 11 low- and middle-income countries had higher enrollment rates for girls than boys at the secondary school level and six of 11 at the primary level.

From the same source (Montenegro and Patrinos 2014) the percentage of rural children out of school in low- and middle-income countries is far higher in rural than urban areas. Bangladesh is a striking exception at a low 13 percent and 14 percent respectively. Bangladesh also has a lower percentage of girls than boys

Table 10.2 School enrollment, by girls and boys, selected countries

Country	Gross enrollment ratio of boys in primary school	Gross enrollment ratio of girls in primary school	Gross enrollment ratio of boys in secondary school	Gross enrollment ratio of girls in secondary school
Bangladesh	111	118	50	57
Pakistan	98	86	44	32
India	113	116	73	69
Indonesia	109	109	84	82
China	126	127	99	100
Ghana	109	109	64	58
Nigeria	88	81	46	41
Bolivia	92	90	80	80
Guatemala	106	102	68	62
Mexico	105	105	84	91
Egypt	116	113	90	88
United States	98	97	94	94
France	108	107	108	110
Japan	102	102	102	102

Source: Montenegro and Patrinos (2014)

out of school. The Bangladesh record shows that low attendance in rural areas and for girls can be eliminated by political will and appropriate policy.

BENEFITS OF INCREASED EDUCATION AND IMPROVED HEALTH

Education affects in many ways the pace of modernization and production growth: it broadens horizons about consumption and therefore the incentives to increase production; it increases the vocabulary for understanding technical issues; it facilitates computation of economic returns; and it opens the mind to contributions from outsiders including educated extension workers or researchers. The slow emulation of progressive farmers is fine in slowly changing traditional agriculture, but modernization moves rapidly and the leaders and followers will move more rapidly with a formal education.

Of great importance is the requirement that education expands the goods and services produced by the rural non-farm population under the stimulus of rising expenditure from small commercial farmers. It is not just small commercial farmers who need a formal education. Surveys of expenditure patterns show that for all rural households increased travel is one of the most rapid changes with rising incomes. Bus drivers and conductors are needed, along with ticket sellers and mechanics. Houses are then expanded, requiring skilled trades people. The demand for educated people as employment accelerates in rural areas is elastic with respect to the overall employment growth rate. Hence one should expect higher growth rates for educated people than that shown for overall employment in Chap. 2.

It is notable that in the United States the agricultural research systems did not have much impact on farm productivity until the 1920s, long after the Land Grant Act of 1862, when rural people, namely farmers' children, began to graduate from institutors of higher education and to staff the agricultural universities and research systems. The same is true of contemporary low- and middle-income countries. There is the need in agricultural servicing institutions and government employment for farmers' children who have contacts in the countryside and knowledge of how things work in a smallholder agriculture to obtain higher education and blend those two sources of knowledge.

The benefits of education come earlier as children receive a formal education and grow up, and are able to give helpful explanations to their parents. It is also important that girls participate, interacting with the mother who is the principal point of contact and influence on the head of the household.

There has been a tendency, as higher education expands rapidly, for some of the educated to be unemployed. However, the demand for higher education to support agricultural modernization is immense and will be a major employer of those with higher education skills.

By the standards of high-income countries, the incidence of farmer illness is immense and is one of the largest risks facing small commercial farmers. It greatly impacts formal education both by causing teacher absences but crucially also student absences—partly from students' own illnesses but even more from having to fill in for ill parents. Improving health is important to the pursuit of agricultural modernization and benefits of course from higher incomes.

THE SPECIAL IMPORTANCE OF GIRLS' EDUCATION

Specifically, in terms of the thrust of this book, girls' education is of special importance. Some small commercial farm households are headed by women, women are important participants in household farming decisions, women's leadership is needed in the full range of institutions serving agriculture, and they have a specific impact on decisions that affect the rate of population growth. Consistent with that logic, data are clear that returns on girls' education are higher than for boys. That differential may well be larger in rural areas than urban areas. While overall girls' attendance rates are comparable to boys, attendance in rural areas is poorer for girls. The social returns to girls' education over that of boys may be even higher in rural as compared to urban areas.

Education reduces birth rates (Martin 1995). The impact of a reduction in birth rates works off a higher underlying birth rate in rural areas compared to urban areas. Education interacts with other variables including modernization of agriculture and its influence may change over time and vary from place to place. That so many variables are most usefully expressed in per capita terms suggests a very high social rate of return on girls' education—perhaps even by girls in a subtle way influencing their mothers.

Previous chapters have noted the decline in the farmer's wife's influence in family decisions including farming decisions because of the shift of the knowledge base from within the village to outside. Girls' education will increase their access to outside knowledge and strengthen the role of wives in family decision making.

Women need to bring their perspectives to the running of rural institutions. They cannot contribute those important perceptions without formal education and understanding of the rapidly growing scientific bases for farming and community decisions. Tapping only the women from upper-class rural households is not enough. There is a vast pool of intelligence lower down the income scale that needs to be accessed.

In many societies, girls and boys must be educated in separate institutions. There are empirical studies that show that such separation has advantages for girls. However, that tends to widen the geographic space between schools and increase costs, particularly in rural areas. It should not be a cause for lowering girls' school attendance.

As incomes increase with modernization the scope for improved nutritional status through improving the quality of diet increases with measures within the reach of low- income families. Girls' education will hasten that process of improving nutrition and will, more broadly, improve health. That may have some impact on the current generation and will be very important in the next generation, interacting with rising income levels. The short-run scope for improvements in nutrition are greater in rural areas.

Huisman and Smits (2009) show a wide range of interacting factors affecting parents' decisions about their children attending school, but distance to the school features large and the percentage of women teachers is important with respect to girls' attendance. We saw elsewhere that female teachers improve girls' enrollment and by implication their learning experience. Decreasing the distance to school in rural areas is shown to be important: so more schools need to be built.

Given all the above, the case is clear that social benefits from girls' education are vastly greater than individual family benefits. Girls' education should be subsidized, contrary to this book's position on agricultural subsidies. Subsidization has been important to the great success of girls' education in Bangladesh. As a compromise on cost, the preceding exposition builds a case for priority to be given to subsidizing rural girls relative to their urban counterparts.

VOCATIONAL EDUCATION

It is sometimes argued that education in rural areas should emphasize training in agriculture. Perhaps some education along those lines, or emphasizing farming examples, makes sense. However, there are strong arguments for primary schools just emphasizing the basic literacy and numeracy skills.

First, the schools are not very good. Better to emphasize the basics and get them learned in four years. Second, in the good agricultural areas only about one-third of families will provide a small commercial farmer for the next generation as some of the youth will leave for the cities. All need to get a good grounding in the basic skills as half will be working in rural non-farm occupations for which basic literacy and numeracy are essential.

Using agricultural modernization examples is fine of course. In that context, some integration of the formal schools with extension education would help instill the value of extension people and provide examples for both reading and numeracy. With respect to girls' education, schools should use examples of women using reading and numeracy in the rural non-farm sector where they are disproportionately represented and in rural institutions such as cooperatives to increases awareness in boys and girls of the value of women taking leadership roles in those institutions.

PUBLIC HEALTH EXPENDITURE

Rural health expenditure varies immensely across countries. However, per capita expenditure in rural areas is almost universally less than in urban areas. That may be in part because dispersion leads to higher costs, but it probably also reflects a lack of political concern for rural compared to urban areas. A few countries (e.g., China) have made a point of reducing those rural disparities with a significant effect on rural health. Government expenditure on health in low- and middle-income countries has been slowly increasing as a share of both government expenditure and of gross domestic product (GDP) except in Sub-Saharan Africa where it has been declining (Lu et al. 2010).

Foreign Aid to Health

Foreign aid emphasizes health since it resonates well with home political constituencies. That accounts for a high proportion of health expenditure in low-income African countries that are large recipients of aid, such as Ethiopia, Rwanda, and Tanzania. For those countries, foreign aid provides 36–46 percent of public health expenditure (Table 10.3) Otherwise it is a small proportion of national expenditure. Carol Lancaster (2008) estimates close to 40 percent of US Development Assistance goes to various aspects of health and it has hovered around that figure in recent years.

Lu et al. (2010) in a careful quantitative analysis of the health sector in low- and middle-income countries makes estimates of the impact of foreign spending on a recipient's national expenditure. Extrapolation from the quantified analysis suggests that in Sub-Saharan Africa the withdrawal of national funds is roughly on a dollar for dollar basis with foreign aid. That may be sensible all around. The recipient country still has a high level of expenditure on health, perhaps even as much as it can manage efficiently, and funds are released for solving long-term problems through growth.

Table 10.3 Foreign aid as a proportion of government health expenditures

Country	External resources for health (% of total expenditure on health)[a]
Bangladesh	11.8
Pakistan	8.0
India	1.0
Indonesia	1.1
China	0.0
Ethiopia	41.7
Rwanda	46.2
Tanzania	35.9
Ghana	15.4
Nigeria	6.7
Bolivia	3.2
Guatemala	2.0
Mexico	0.4
Egypt	1.3

World Bank—see below
[a]From the World Bank: "External resources for health are funds or services in kind that are provided by entities not part of the country in question. The resources may come from international organizations, other countries through bilateral arrangements, or foreign nongovernmental organizations. These resources are part of total health expenditure"

Further, the technical assistance aspect of that foreign aid may be especially important for building essential institutional structures. In no case reported does the foreign aid component of public health expenditure rise as far as half. Thus the technical assistance part of foreign aid does have a multiplier effect on national public expenditure.

As a personal observation, the foreign aid effect on health sectors is positive both technically and practically, and is perhaps more efficient than placing those funds in the production areas, given the current practices in those areas. For example, the Clinton Foundation with its heavy emphasis on health has had a useful impact on the effectiveness of health expenditure by both donors and recipient governments.

Rural Health Status

Globally, 93 percent of households using untreated surface water live in rural areas and 70 percent of those are without access to improved sanitation. Ninety percent of open defecation is in rural areas. Fifty percent of the global population is rural but 38 percent of nurses and 25 percent of physicians are in rural areas. Rural areas have worse health problems and less treatment. The greatest spread in the rural to urban incidence of illness is among young children. That obviously affects learning, both formal and informal. It should be noted that rural areas in high-income countries also have a lower density of nurses and physicians than urban areas. But rural people in high-income countries have better access to urban specialists.

Rural areas do have a faster growth rate than urban areas in improved water and sanitation, but at a low 0.6 and 0.3 percent growth rate, respectively. Again the point must be emphasized that rural infrastructure is important to both the spread of health facilities and the presence of nurses and doctors.

The incidence of unavailability to work due to illness is much higher in low- and middle-income countries than in high-income countries. That is not surprising given the widespread malnutrition and poor health facilities and knowledge. Even though there is substantial underemployment, illness has a negative effect on production through its impact on family labor for which replacement is often not possible due to a cash constraint on hiring labor and the inefficiencies of hired labor. Onset of poor health is one of the most important risk factors with respect to income in rural areas of low- and middle-income countries. The social suffering from illness is immense in low-income families that are close to the margin of subsistence.

Investment in physical infrastructure will improve access to health facilities. The reduction in poverty from rapid agricultural growth will increase nutritional status, particularly in reducing lack of calories. All these elements interact with the health institutions to increase the returns to those institutions.

Modernization brings increased returns to the use of pesticides and with that a rapidly increasing use. Because pesticide use on farms is essentially unregulated in low- and middle-income countries the negative effect on health is substantial and that in turn has a negative effect on agricultural productivity (Antle and Pingali 1994). At the very least, research and extension must focus on this problem and increase the extension input.

POOR QUALITY OF RURAL EDUCATION AND HEALTH

The preceding paragraphs show the poor coverage of rural areas by health and education institutions. The problem is compounded by poorer quality that is not reflected in those statistics. The low quality has two components.

First, in general in low- and middle-income countries most educated people would rather live and work in urban areas with much better amenities, especially for children. That leads to, on average, the least qualified ending up in rural areas. This is less the case in high-income countries that have good rural schools and health facilities, excellent transport systems, and better access to urban areas.

Second, even those in rural areas must often live some distance from where they work in order to obtain minimum living facilities. Transport is often unreliable, which leads to a frequent decision not to go to work. The problem of worker absence is compounded in education by the increased absence of students who also have a commuting problem, worsened by uncertainty as to whether or not the teacher will be there. Both problems are mitigated by physical infrastructure investment and prospering market towns, fostered by rapid agricultural growth. Education and health and agricultural growth are mutually reinforcing.

Once rural physical infrastructure is upgraded and agricultural growth becomes rapid the core of the poor-quality problem is on the way to being solved. In that context, direct efforts to improve quality can be effective.

HEALTH AND CASH CROPS

There is some controversy that cash crops cause farm families to consume less of the more nutritional foods. First, this book is clear on the relation between increased farm production and increased income, not only for farmers but also for the large rural non-farm population. That income is converted efficiently into increased caloric intake, the first requisite of healthy diets. Second, the income elasticity of demand for high-value foods, livestock, and horticulture is high. Therefore, the higher incomes associated with cash cropping lead to better diets. However, that relation is less close than desired because of lack of information, a problem logically met with education.

An IFPRI (Kennedy et al. 1992) comparative study of six countries with respect to impact of cash crops on nutrition found a substantial cash income increase, much higher incomes, and no negative effects on health. A later study by Carletto et al. (2017) was broadly supportive of the earlier finding, counter to some of the arguments in the literature. However, there was no significant reduction in illnesses of preschool children. The one exception was Guatemala where the cash crop program had a social service/health component. The study emphasizes the desirability of programs for higher income having an associated extension action for improved nutrition and health.

PESTICIDES AND HEALTH

Modernization brings increased returns to the use of pesticides and with that, rapidly increasing use. Pesticide use on farms is essentially unregulated in low- and middle-income countries. Antle and Pingali (1994) report for the Philippines, consistent with most other low- and middle-income countries, that the negative effect of pesticide use on farmer health is substantial. That in turn has a pronounced negative effect on agricultural productivity. At the very least, research and extension must focus on this problem and increase the extension input. Research needs to emphasize non-chemical approaches to insect and disease control.

OBESITY

Obesity is a rapidly increasing problem in low- and middle-income countries as well as in high-income ones. However, the focus of this book is on the large numbers of people below the poverty line defined by adequate caloric intake, and those people do not, in general, have an obesity problem. Their problem is earning an income adequate to provide basic calories. In rural areas of low- and middle-income countries, the second priority is increasing the consumption of high-value commodities. In high-income countries, education appears to be the focus in dealing with obesity.

IMPORTANCE OF HOME ECONOMICS EXTENSION

Health practices and interrelated nutritional status do respond to income. As incomes rise expenditure on high nutritional value horticulture and livestock products increases more than proportionately. That is generally from a very low base. A home economics specialist can emphasize the benefits of the home garden and other measures to increase consumption of high nutritional value commodities, simple health practices including cleanliness, and low-cost components of a healthy diet. Such programs were effective in high-income countries, but such efforts are non-existent in contemporary low-income countries. They are not part of foreign aid programs even though they were important at one stage in the development of high-income countries.

REFERENCES

Antle, J. M., & Pingali, P. L. (1994). Pesticides, productivity, and farmer health: A Philippine case study. *American Journal of Agricultural Economics, 76*(3), 418–430.

Carletto, C., Corral, P., & Guelfi, A. (2017). Agricultural commercialization and nutrition revisited: Empirical evidence from three African countries. *Food Policy, 67,* 106–118.

Huisman, J., & Smits, J. (2009). Effects of household-and district-level factors on primary school enrollment in 30 developing countries. *World Development, 37*(1), 179–193.

Kennedy, E., Bouis, H., & Von Braun, J. (1992). Health and nutrition effects of cash crop production in developing countries: A comparative analysis. *Social Science & Medicine, 35*(5), 689–697.

Lancaster, C. (2008). *Foreign aid: Diplomacy, development, domestic politics.* Chicago: University of Chicago Press.

Lu, C., Schneider, M. T., Gubbins, P., Leach-Kemon, K., Jamison, D., & Murray, C. J. (2010). Public financing of health in developing countries: A cross-national systematic analysis. *The Lancet, 375*(9723), 1375–1387.

Martin, T. C. (1995). Women's education and fertility: Results from 26 demographic and health surveys. *Studies in Family Planning, 26*(4), 187–202.

Montenegro, C. E., & Patrinos, H. A. (2014). *Comparable estimates of returns to schooling around the world* (Policy Research Working Paper No. 7020). Washington, DC: World Bank Group.

CHAPTER 11

Prices and Price Policy

The thrust of this chapter is that government subsidies to cereals output and input prices have a prohibitively high opportunity cost in foregone investment in rural infrastructure, education, health, and the institutions of agricultural technological change. They are a bad idea. Relative agricultural output and input prices do provide important signals for adjusting to changing national and global circumstances. The rural poor may be driven into extreme poverty with long-term loss of productive capacity owing to rising cereal prices. In that case, intervention to assist the poor is a good idea, especially, as is often the case, if it is paid for with non-fungible funds by foreign assistance donors.

In agricultures dominated by small commercial farmers (SCF) and with widespread rural poverty a rapid increase in the production of cereals places little downward pressure on domestic cereal prices. Consumption of cereals increases roughly in line with production. That is radically different to the strong downward pressure on prices from rapid cereal production growth in high-income countries.

Governments can influence cereals' supply–demand balances through policies that affect demand as well as supply. In this and other contexts, agricultural prices serve an important signaling function. Government's agricultural growth-oriented policies, particularly infrastructure investment, reduce marketing margins, facilitate a concurrent increase in producer prices and a reduction in consumer prices.

Agricultural prices are always politically important. They affect the real income of all families and especially those of low-income families and farmers. In low- and middle-income countries those two groups collectively dominate rural areas and are important nationally. Families in poverty spend 70–80 percent of their income on food. Even for middle-income households, agricultural prices have a large impact on real incomes. Of course small commercial farmers derive their income almost entirely from agriculture. Farmers' incomes are also affected by weather and disease as well as technology, but prices seem more immediate

© The Author(s) 2017
J.W. Mellor, *Agricultural Development and Economic Transformation*,
Palgrave Studies in Agricultural Economics and Food Policy,
https://doi.org/10.1007/978-3-319-65259-7_11

and more subject to control by the political system. These forces push govern-ments towards interventionist cereal price policies that are detrimental to the growth that can raise the income of small commercial farmers and eventually eliminate poverty.

Agricultural price policy and analysis have a quite different context and requirements when associated with rapid agricultural growth as compared to slow-growth agricultures. Technology-based agricultural growth increases incomes of both farmers and the rural poor. In that context, it is equivalent to increased prices for farmers and decreased prices for the poor—a simultaneity that cannot be accomplished by price policy. These issues are treated in the predecessor to this book (Mellor 1966), at length in Mellor (1969), and Mellor and Ahmed (1988), with the emphasis on income distribution (Mellor 1978), and Timmer (1986, 2015) who refers to the food price dilemma—the differen-tial impact of cereal prices on farmers and on the poor.

Cereals receive special attention in price policy. As compared to perishable commodities they have low storage costs, allowing prices to be influenced through stocking policy. They are also the prime determinant of real income of the poor and commonly the most important crop to farmers. As countries rise into middle-income status the importance of livestock and horticulture increases to eventually exceed that of cereals. These perishables have special price policy problems. Agricultural export commodities also have special price issues. The last section in this chapter deals with an eventual widening income gap between small commercial farmers and the general population, and the implications of that on price policy.

COMMON GOVERNMENT AGRICULTURAL PRICE INTERVENTIONS

Most high-income countries provide subsidies to farmers. That is normally justified on the grounds that they are presumed to lose from technological change in agriculture that shifts most of the gain to consumers through a decline in prices and because of the substantial political weight of farmers, which is disproportionately large relative to their numbers. International prices have generally followed a downward trend driven by the accumulation of the above phenomena across a large number of high-income countries. In recent years, there has been a shift from subsidized price supports to highly subsidized insurance. The costs of all these subsidies are high. But they are income transfers from the very large, non-agricultural sector to the now—relatively small, agri-cultural sector—a small burden on the many for a large transfer to the few.

Within low-income countries the extent of price interference varies tremen-dously over time and among countries. Many low- and middle-income countries had a substantial period of trying to tax agriculture, often through overvalued exchange rates which depressed agricultural prices relative to other prices. Some governments have built large stocks of cereals at high cost (e.g., India), in order to support cereals prices. Subsidy of fertilizers is substantial in a few countries (e.g., India), and the World Bank has vacillated as to whether that is good or bad.

Inevitably these policies have had a high cost in reducing the availability of funds for investment in rural infrastructure and the technology generation systems. Many governments in low-income countries subsidize food to low-income consumers, as do several large foreign aid programs.

CEREAL PRICE STABILIZATION

In a low-income country, a high proportion of increased cereal production is consumed by the rural non-farm sector and with the modest increase in consumption by the small commercial farmer 90 percent of the increased production is consumed in the rural sector. That plus urban consumption and allowance for seed, feed, and waste roughly matches the increase in production and so there is little or no downward pressure on cereal prices. Understanding this relationship is essential to understanding how food security is provided, the price stabilizing forces at work in agricultures dominated by small commercial farmers and with a large share of the rural population in poverty, and the role of price policy in such economies.

Because of its importance and complexity this process is analyzed in detail. Ethiopia serves as a representative low-income country with a small urban sector, a high agricultural growth rate, and a large cereal sector. During the period of very rapid agricultural and cereal production increase (1995–2015) the trend in real prices of cereals remained flat (Fig. 11.1). The Ethiopian government bans private sector cereal exports and imports. The government imports modest

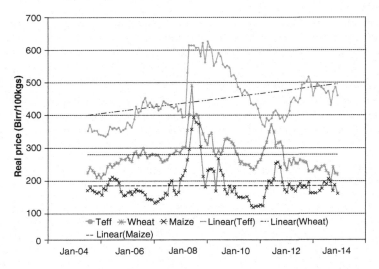

Fig. 11.1 Real price trends of major cereals (deflated by Consumer Price Index (CPI)) (Source: Price data obtained from Ethiopia Grain Trade Enterprise (EGTE) and (CPI) from Central Statistical Agency (CSA). Addis Ababa wholesale price considered as representative price and deflated by CPI (general consumer price index))

quantities of wheat on a regular basis but that has not affected the trend in prices. When international prices surged far above domestic prices, as in the international food crisis in 2008, the government was unable to prevent illegal cross-border cereal exports and the domestic price temporarily responded with a sharp upward spike. However, that was much less than the international price spike.

The following analysis quantifies the stabilizing effect on agricultural prices of the connection between cereal production to consumption by the rural poor, estimates the shares of increased cereal consumption by household class, and demonstrates the impact on food security of the poor.

The analysis is for the income inelastic cereals—maize, wheat and sorghum—that comprise the bulk of food consumption by the poor. Teff, an income elastic cereal is consumed hardly at all by the poor and largely by urban households and to some extent by higher-income rural households. The poor consume a small quantity of teff, usually mixed with lower-priced cereals. The real price of teff has trended up despite rapid growth in production. Most low-income countries have a superior cereal with an elastic demand (e.g., Basmati rice).

Assumptions for this analysis are presented in Table 11.1. There are two cereal-consuming rural household sectors (small commercial farm and rural non-farm) and one urban. In each household sector cereal demand is a function of population growth and income growth. Population growth is faster for the urban sector than for the rural non-farm sector due to migration from rural areas. Income in the urban sector is exogenous to agriculture. The income of small commercial farmers is entirely from agricultural production; the income of the rural non-farm (RNF) households is entirely from expenditures by small commercial farmers.

Income growth in the urban sector is assumed at a rapid 8.0 percent rate. That for small commercial farmers (SCF) is assumed at 6.6 percent, the actual rate for the past 12 years for Ethiopia. A subsequent analysis assumes a slow three percent rate to show the quite different impact of a traditional agricultural growth rate displayed by small commercial farmers.

Income is converted into demand for cereals by multiplying the income growth rate by the income elasticity of demand for cereals. The latter is derived from published numbers developed from large-scale consumer surveys in

Table 11.1   Base data for demand equations and Table 11.2

Sector	1 Base consumption of cereals excluding teff, tons	2 Population growth rate (%)	3 Income elasticity, demand	4 Base population, millions
SCF	6,654,000 (35%)	2.6	0.30	36.14
RNF	10,218,000 (54%)	2.6	0.74	36.14
Urban	2,088,000 (11%)	3.1	0.49	13.95
LCF[a]	–			
Total	18,960,000 (100%)	2.7	0.51	86.23

[a]Large commercial farmers

Table 11.2 Incremental production, incremental consumption aggregate for each household class, net surplus over human consumption, and cereals and income growth rate for the rural non-farm class (all numbers are aggregate tons except where specified as %)

Item	With a 3 percent growth rate	With a 6.6 percent growth rate	With a 6.6 percent growth rate, income elasticity is half
Increment to production	554,577	1,220,069	1,220,069
Increment consumption, SCF			
Population effect	173,004	173,004	173,004
Income effect	7984	79,848	39,924
Total	180,988	252,852	212,928
Increment consumption, RNF			
Population effect	265,668	265,668	265,668
Income effect	87,006	427,327	213,663
Total	352,674	692,995	479,331
Incremental consumption, urban			
Population effect	64,728	64,728	64,728
Income effect	50,133	50,132	24,555
Total	114,860	114,860	89,283
Total human consumption	648,524	1,060,707	781,542
Surplus (deficit) over human consumption	(93,947)	159,361	438,527
	(−17%)	+13%	36%
% human consumption, SCF	28	24	27
% human consumption, RNF	54	65	61
% human consumption, rural/small town	82	89	88
% human consumption, urban	18	11	12
% Growth rate/RNF/cereals per capita	0.9	4.2	2.1
% Growth rate/RNF income (per capita)	3.75 (1.15)	8.25 (5.65)	8.25 (5.65)

Ethiopia. Annex 1 provides the spreadsheet and a full statement of the equations. Mellor and Kumro (2017) provide a full explanation of the calculations.

Table 11.2 summarizes the results, with a column each for 6.6 percent growth (actually achieved by Ethiopia), three percent growth (normal without modernization), and again 6.6 percent growth but with income elasticities reduced by half. The rows present the production growth in tons, then the aggregate consumption growth for each household class divided into population effect, income effect, and total. The sum of consumption for all household classes is compared to the production, and net surplus or deficit for human consumption is calculated. Those numbers are used for various calculations in the succeeding rows.

Results from a 6.6 Percent Growth Rate in Cereal Production I (Table 11.2)

Increased Consumption by the Rural Non-Farm Population
Growth in cereal consumption is dominated by the rural non-farm households. Of the total increase in human consumption of cereals, 65 percent is by rural

non-farm households. All the income for purchasing those cereals is from the increased expenditure of the small commercial farmers out of their increased agricultural income. Dominance of the rural non-farm sector lies with that sector's initially high proportion of cereal consumption, and the relatively high income elasticity of demand for cereals. Those are all normal relationships for low-income countries.

Cereal consumption per capita of the rural non-farm population is shown to increase at a 4.2 percent rate. As this increase accumulates, it has a profound effect on calorie intake and food security of the low-income rural population, and on measured poverty reduction. This is consistent with an approximately 50 percent reduction in the proportion of Ethiopia's rural population under the poverty line between the early 1990s and the present (World Bank 2014).

Nearly two-thirds of the incremental consumption of the rural non-farm sector is due to the income effect. The population effect also requires an increased expenditure by the small commercial farmer to maintain the per capita income as the population grows.

Increased Consumption by the Small Commercial Farmer

Although approximately the same size population as the rural non-farm sector, the increment in consumption of cereals by the small commercial farmers is only 36 percent as large as for the rural non-farm population. That is largely because both the base of cereal consumption is far lower and the income elasticity of demand is only 40 percent as large as that for the rural non-farm population. Nevertheless, that still represents 24 percent of the increased consumption by all households.

Combined with the rural non-farm sector, increased rural consumption represents 89 percent of the increased production. The entirety of this consumption increase is driven by income generated from agricultural production growth of the small commercial farmer.

Increased Consumption by the Urban Population

The urban population in Ethiopia is growing slowly compared to urban growth rates of most other African countries. This difference is likely due to the agricultural sector growing rapidly, stimulating increased income and employment in the rural non-farm sector and migration to small market towns that are not classified in the CSA data as urban. This classification is useful since the small town population is supported largely by prospering rural areas.

Thus, the urban sector accounts for only 11 percent of incremental human consumption of cereals, which is lower than its 14 percent share of the population. However, 35 percent of teff, the income elastic cereal, is consumed in urban areas, suggesting an overall increment of 13 percent of all cereals, including teff. As for the small commercial farming sector, the income effect on consumption is modest despite a high growth rate in income.

The Balance in Production and Domestic Human Consumption

The total increase in human consumption falls short of the increased production by 13 percent, or by one percent of total production (Table 11.2). The standard figure for "feed, seed and waste" is 15 percent (FAOSTAT 2015). Crop cutting includes significant field losses as demonstrated by the universal gleaning of fields by low-income women. Seed is a significant part of output, and working animals are fed some cereal when they are working. Thus, we have slightly over-explained the increased supply by increased human consumption, 90 percent of which is driven by the income from increased production. Thus, real cereal prices have not had a noticeable downward trend.

Results from a Three Percent Growth Rate in Cereal Production

With a decline in the cereal growth rate to three percent the relative importance of the urban sector increases, but the bulk of cereal consumption increments remains in the rural sector. The relative importance of the rural non-farm sector declines from 68 percent of incremental consumption to 58 percent. The increase in rural consumption with these assumptions still accounts for 90 percent of the production increase. There is a deficit for human consumption over production, which will trigger demand for imports or increased prices, both of which are detrimental to growth of the urban sector.

Future Decline in Income Elasticity of Demand for Cereals

Rapid growth in income of the rural poor and the high growth rate in cereal consumption will eventually reduce the income elasticities of demand for cereals. The effect on demand will be substantial. The far right column in Table 11.2 shows the effect of reducing all the income elasticities by half. Human consumption takes 60 percent of the increment to production. The following analysis suggests that it will be some time, a decade or two, before those elasticities decline radically; in the meantime, demand for livestock products increases sufficiently to absorbed this surplus over human consumption.

Analysis by Shubh Kumar-Range of World Bank household surveys sheds considerable light on this question. There is no sign of a slowing of the increments to cereal consumption in rural areas. She notes that as people approach 80 percent of calorie requirements they slow their rate of growth of cereal consumption (i.e. reduce their income elasticity), and accelerate consumption growth in high-value foods. She finds only a small proportion of the rural population reaching this point. In this context, it will be a substantial number of years before the income elasticities decline sharply—at least a decade.

New Sources of Demand for Cereals

What potential is there for upward shifts in demand when demand elasticities for cereals commence their inevitable decline. Decreasing prices to export parity may not be viable. However, at current income growth rates, the demand for livestock products is growing in the order of eight percent per year. Based on concentrate feed requirements such a growth rate in intensive livestock production would absorb the surplus shown with low cereal demand elasticities, either directly or through shifting the cereal production area to high-quality forage crops. A shift of this magnitude would require a government focus on the livestock sector comparable to the Ethiopian government's current focus on cereals. In fast agricultural growth countries, both supply and demand are potentially dynamic and subject to policy.

PRICE ISSUES FOR SMALL COMMERCIAL FARMERS

The same argument as for subsidies holds for protecting the small commercial farmer from production and income fluctuations. The money is better spent on the requirements of modernization. The poor face more serious problems, and are treated separately in a following section.

Fluctuating Weather

Everyone suffers when production declines due to failure of rainfall or other weather-related events. There is less income generated, farmers spend less on the rural non-farm sector reducing the income of the poor, reinforced by the effect of food price increases. Farmers may also suffer from good weather if prices decline by as much as or more than the production increase. However, that is far more of a problem in high-income countries than in low-income countries because of the interaction of supply and demand, as described above, in low-income countries.

Rapid agricultural growth makes total production fluctuate up more (weather increase plus trend increase) and down less (weather reduction minus trend increase). As demonstrated above, in the context of small commercial farmers and large numbers in rural poverty, steady production increases from technological change tend not to be accompanied by a significant price decline. That describes the situation even, as is common, in food economies closed to trade. Thus, the small commercial farmer's income increases roughly in proportion to the increased production and similarly for the rural poor. Of course if prices decline the poor benefit from the price decline rather than the income increase, but the latter is preferable for overall growth. The price fluctuations are substantial even in economies open to trade because of transaction costs and market imperfections related to countries that are normally not in those markets.

Small commercial farmers in low- and middle-income countries tend to carry stock over from high-production years to low-production years. They have a very low opportunity cost of capital in the face of a bumper crop—their incomes are up, as a result their cost of capital for storing is low. They see storage costs as low. Widespread focus group say that home storage costs are low with low storage losses, and this is confirmed by Kaminsky and Christiaensen's (2014) World Bank findings of one to five percent storage losses. After all, small commercial farmers are rational, store with care, and monitor their storage closely. Thus they may put a few percentage points of production in storage in a good crop year. They then take that back in a poor crop year. That not only modestly stabilizes their incomes but also those in the rural non-farm sector as their expenditures vary less from good to bad crop years.

A major problem does occur in the case of two or more major bad crop years in a row. Farmers rarely store for two successive bad crop years. The cost is too high so the second bad crop year has no smoothing effect by farmers. The concern is that they will reduce production the next year due to shortage of credit and the debt overhang. The appropriate government action is to help the finance agencies, through special loans, to refinance loans and lend to farmers to meet current needs and to maintain production the next year. Such government assistance is common in high-income countries with well-established specialized agricultural finance systems. This is another reason why specialized finance institutions are needed to serve the small commercial farmer. Government forgiving loans is poor policy as it undermines the integrity of the farm finance system.

Speculation

When domestic prices rise sharply in low- and middle-income countries the government tends to respond to popular outcry, especially in urban areas, by claiming that traders are hoarding cereals on purpose to drive up prices and thus to profit from their hoarding. Of course if traders did not hold stocks the price would fall more at harvest and rise more at later periods. Government-forced divestment early in the season simply causes the later rise to be larger than otherwise.

In low- and middle-income countries, private traders rarely carry stocks over from one year to another. They are, however, the principal means of stocking for smoothing consumption over the year, between harvests. That activity requires prediction of what stocking famers are doing, as well as other traders and perhaps the government. There is considerable uncertainty about these estimates. Traders are, in effect, speculating on future prices with very limited information. They will in some years collectively err, by overstocking and facing less price rises than predicted or understocking and facing more rises than predicted. Their errors result in substantial year-to-year fluctuations in price seasonality.

The classic analysis, based on a solid year of intense interaction with Indian traders, in a country where markets work reasonably well, showed on average seasonal price increases consonant with storage costs (Lele 1971). That is what would be expected with well-operating markets. In apparent contrast Kaminski et al. (2016) found for Tanzania seasonal increases up to three times the "international reference market." However, regarding how well markets operate, the comparison should be with local storage costs, and probably Tanzanian markets are not fully competitive. In any case, their study was directed at the impact of seasonality on the poor. On that they found a ten percent seasonal adjustment in consumption by the poor, but they also state that the poor effectively smoothed consumption seasonally—i.e., seasonality was not a problem.

PRICE ISSUES FOR THE POOR

In poor crop production years cereal price increases fall harshly on the poor creating a difficult tradeoff between investing in the long-run modernization of agriculture and protecting the poor from those price increases. Starting from the high poverty levels in low- and many middle-income countries it will take 10–20 years of rapid agricultural growth to essentially lift all of them out of poverty. In the short run, special programs can reach large numbers of the poor but with a high opportunity cost in growth. The tradeoff can be avoided by foreign aid that may not be fungible into growth. Chapter 4 provides detail on these issues.

LARGE INCREASE IN INTERNATIONAL PRICES

International prices fluctuate more than domestic prices in fast agricultural growth, low- and middle-income countries. There were very large increases in international cereal prices in 1973, 1978, 1980, and 2009, an average of once every ten years, although there was no such predictability. The 2008–2011 price spike was extreme and received considerable international attention and a substantial subsequent literature (e.g. Headey 2011; Anderson et al. 2014).

The spike was greater than would be expected from production trends although there was an unusual concurrence of poor crops in major exporting countries. The effects were magnified by trade-related policies—exporters, notably India and Vietnam barring exports, and other countries trying to increase imports. There was an international consensus that poor people in low-income countries were hard hit and trade-related efforts were instituted to insulate domestic markets from the spike in prices. The insulation of course added to the spike in international prices, so that those not insulated were worse off. Anderson et al. (2014) estimates that the net effect of those policies increased poverty by eight million people in 2008. Not a very good record.

Ethiopia exemplifies the efforts at insulation by a very poor country that had rapid agricultural growth and still immense poverty. The domestic cereal price rose substantially towards the international price even though there was an export ban (Fig. 11.1). Apparently, substantial leakages of exports to neighboring countries occurred. However, domestic prices in Ethiopia rose in 2008 and later years by a small fraction as much as international prices. Ethiopia did protect its domestic consumers and international aid increased support for the safety nets. The rural poor received considerable protection but still suffered immensely.

Timmer (2015) provides a thoughtful extended discussion making the case for domestic markets and especially the poor in low- and middle-income countries to be protected from huge swings in prices completely unrelated to domestic conditions. This chapter is clear that given the prevailing elasticities in low- and middle-income countries, cereal domestic supply and demand tends to shift so as to significantly stabilize prices. That strengthens the case, as for Ethiopia, for insulating against uncorrelated swings in international prices. Unfortunately, the Ethiopian case shows how difficult it is to insulate against international markets.

Most low- and middle-income countries have a comparative advantage in producing cereals, and in a few countries root crops, sufficient to at least provide basic food security for their population. Thus they can insulate themselves from international markets, at least partially mitigating the problem of internationally driven price spikes. Insofar as there are leakages to exports, it is good policy to let prices rise to restrain consumption of high-income people and particularly of livestock production in conjunction with safety-net programs for the poor.

Some low-income countries, largely in Sub-Saharan Africa, have chosen not to develop their national capacities to provide basic food security domestically and hence they regularly import substantial quantities of food. They cannot insulate themselves against international prices. The price spikes show the immense human cost of such policies, so such countries need to get active in developing their agricultures.

The Special Problem of Export Commodities

International prices of export commodities fluctuate considerably with none of the self-correcting processes described for domestic cereals in low-income countries. National policy would like to see steady growth in production and exports of commodities, in which a country has a comparative advantage, and as domestic policy reduces the cost of production through the processes of modernization. Large downward fluctuations in prices may seem to interfere with that objective.

There are three reasons to stay with the fluctuating international prices. First, domestic policies should be continually and significantly reducing the cost of production. Second, export crop producers are almost all well above the poverty line. They can absorb temporary reductions in prices. Third, money spent on protecting domestic farmers from price changes will obtain better returns from lower cost of production oriented expenditure on physical infrastructure, education, and the institutions of technological change.

The Special Problem of Livestock and Horticulture

The most disturbing price relationship in low- and middle-income countries is the tendency for prices of livestock products and horticulture products to increase relative to other food and all other prices. That is a signal of demand increasing more rapidly than supply. Because both the income and price elasticities are quite elastic, even a small, perhaps somewhat hidden relative price increase, is a sign of demand increasing much more rapidly than supply. That is disturbing because increasing livestock and horticultural production is a major opportunity for small commercial farmers to increase their incomes and their employment multiplier to the poor. That is particularly important as the potential for high rates of catch-up growth in cereals declines.

THE SPECIAL PROBLEM OF A WIDENING INCOME GAP BETWEEN SMALL COMMERCIAL FARMERS AND THE GENERAL POPULATION

A serious political problem for all developing countries is a tendency for urban per capita incomes to surge ahead of those in rural areas. This book shows that condition is in fact a matter of choice. A six percent growth rate in agricultural production is a feasible proposition for the responsive agricultural areas of all low- and middle-income countries. The bulk of the farmers are in responsive areas—that applies just as much to countries with large drought prone areas, such as Mail and Chad, as it does to China and India. The bulk of agriculture can prosper with rates of income increases comparable to urban areas, and similarly for the rural non-farm population. That requires rapid growth in infrastructure and education and the full set of modernization institutions developed in the next four chapters. In that context, urban populations in market towns will grow and prosper. Continued migration to major urban centers will also be desirable and hence some income differential will continue at least for the lower-income families, but the gap need not be widening.

However, as countries move well into middle-income status the growth rate for agriculture tends to drop as the catch-up is largely achieved and domestic demand slows. However, that is well after a major shift into livestock and horticulture and tropical exports. As that happens agriculture as a share of total GDP becomes modest. The solution becomes increasingly like that of high-income countries in which a modest burden on the non-agricultural economy translates into a large transfer to the agricultural sector. Subsidies such as in high-income countries become feasible and political pressures may well support that.

ANNEX 1: CALCULATION OF THE EFFECT OF INCREASED CEREALS PRODUCTION ON THE DEMAND FOR CEREALS

The Equations

Table 11.3 defines the notation used in the equations below as well as the stated coefficients.

$$P = C,$$

and

Table 11.3   Definition of notation and coefficients in the equations

Notation	Coefficients
% I = percent increase in income	0.2 = The percentage addition to RNF cereal consumption to cover the rest of consumption to provide the total base consumption
P = production of cereals	0.7 = Growth rate of non-cereal production as a percentage of the cereals' growth rate
C = consumption of cereals	0.4 = Percentage of small commercial farmer income spent on the rural non-farm sector
% p = percent increase in population	−1.25 = The multiplier to cover expenditure by rural non-farm on its own sector; 20 percent of income iterated stabilizes at 25 percent
s = small commercial farmer	
r = rural non-farm	N = income elasticity of consumption
u = urban	I = income
l = large commercial farmer	T = total
o = consumption other than from the four human sectors	
p = population	

$$Ps + Pl = Cs + Cr + Cu + Co;$$

where $Cr = F(Ps)$

At present, we show that Co is small, covering a standard item of feed, seed and waste. We also show that it has the potential to become large as demand for livestock products catalyzes rapid growth.

Our concern is with the details of each of the elements in the equation. These components are presented below.

Increment in Cereal Production, Tons
From the small commercial farmer (SCF):

$$\Delta P_s = (\%P_s)*(P_s) \qquad (11.1)$$

From the large commercial farmer:

$$\Delta P_l = (\%Pl)*(P_l) \qquad (11.2)$$

Increment in total cereal production:

$$\Delta P_T = \Delta P_s + \Delta P_l \qquad (11.3)$$

These equations give us the annual increment of cereal production in tons, to be compared with the calculated increment in consumption. In the base case, the growth rate for cereal production is the trend rate of 6.6 percent for this set of cereals.

Percentage Increase in Income, Rural Non-Farm (RNF) Sector

$$\%I_r = \left((\Delta P_S) + ((\Delta P_S)*(0.7))*(0.4)\right)/(C_r*1.2)*(1.25) \qquad (11.4)$$

The overall result is sensitive to this calculation and is used in Eq. 11.9. The driving force behind this equation is the percentage increase in RNF income from the expenditure by the SCF from increased cereal and other agricultural production on the RNF sector. This is applied to calculating the increase in cereal consumption for the rural non-farm sector.

Growth in Human Consumption of Cereals
The following equations partition the growth in human consumption of cereals among three cereal consuming sectors. The sectors have very different income elasticities and base consumption of cereals. Those differences drive the results. For each sector, total consumption increase represents the sum of increased consumption from population growth and from income increase.
From the small commercial farmer sector:
From population growth

$$\Delta C_{sp} = (\%P_S)*(C_S) \qquad (11.5)$$

From income growth

$$\Delta C_{si} = ((\%I_S) - (\%P_S))*(C_S)*(n_s) \qquad (11.6)$$

Total

$$\Delta C_{sT} = \sum \Delta C_{sp} + \Delta C_{si} \qquad (11.7)$$

From the rural non-farm sector:
From population growth

$$\Delta C_{rp} = \%P_{rx}*C_r \qquad (11.8)$$

From income growth

$$\Delta C_{ri} = ((\%I_r - \%P_r))*(C_r)*(n_r) \qquad (11.9)$$

Total

$$\Delta C_{rT} = \sum \Delta C_{rp+} \Delta C_{ri} \qquad (11.10)$$

From the urban sector:

From population growth

$$\Delta C_{up} = (\%P_u)*(C_u) \tag{11.11}$$

From income growth

$$\Delta C_{ui} = (\%I_u - \%P_u)*(C_u)*(n_u) \tag{11.12}$$

Total

$$\Delta C_{uT} = \sum \Delta C_{up+} \Delta C_{ui} \tag{11.13}$$

Human consumption total

$$CT = \sum C_{sT}, C_{rT}, C_{uT} \tag{11.14}$$

Surplus over human consumption

$$O = P_T - C_T \tag{11.15}$$

References

Anderson, K., Ivanic, M., & Martin, W. J. (2014). Food price spikes, price insulation, and poverty. In J. P. Chavas, D. Hummels, & B. D. Wright (Eds.), *The economics of food price volatility* (pp. 311–339). Chicago: University of Chicago Press.

FAOSTAT. (2015). *Food and Agriculture Organization* (various years).

Headey, D. (2011). Rethinking the global food crisis: The role of trade shocks. *Food Policy, 36*(2), 136–146.

Kaminski, J., & Christiaensen, L. (2014). Post-harvest loss in sub-Saharan Africa: What do farmers say? *Global Food Security, 3*(3), 149–158.

Kaminski, J., Christiaensen, L., & Gilbert, C. L. (2016). Seasonality in local food markets and consumption: Evidence from Tanzania. *Oxford Economic Papers, 68*(3), 736–757.

Lele, U. (1971). *Food grain marketing in India. Private performance and public policy*. Ithaca/London: Cornell University Press.

Mellor, J. W. (1966). *The economics of agricultural development*. Ithaca: Cornell University Press.

Mellor, J. W. (1969). Agricultural price policy in the context of economic development. *American Journal of Agricultural Economics, 51*(5), 1413–1420.

Mellor, J. W. (1978). Food price policy and income distribution in low-income countries. *Economic Development and Cultural Change, 27*(1), 1–26.

Mellor, J. W., & Ahmed, R. (Eds.). (1988). *Agricultural price policy for developing countries*. Baltimore: Johns Hopkins University Press.

Mellor, J. W., & Kumro, T. (2017). *Rapid growth in cereals production generates much of its own demand in low income countries.* Under review by John Mellor Associates.

Timmer, C. P. (1986). *Getting prices right: The scope and limits of agricultural price policy.* Ithaca: Cornell University Press.

Timmer, C. P. (2015). *Food security and scarcity: Why ending hunger is so hard.* Philadelphia: University of Pennsylvania Press.

World Bank Group. (2014). *Ethiopia poverty assessment* (Report no. AUS6744). Washington, DC: World Bank Group.

CHAPTER 12

Research and Extension

The foundation for agriculture's role in the economic transformation is largely public modern science institutions producing a steady flow of improved technology. That technology must be locally based to ensure suitability to highly variable local conditions. Agriculture stands out relative to other sectors in the centrality of modern science to its progress. Research results must reach farmers and farmers' requirements must feed back to research. As a result, research and extension must be tightly integrated. The research system is also the repository of the best technical knowledge and all the other institutions feed off of it. It is central to rapid agricultural growth, which is usually underinvested, and often grossly so.

The Green Revolution: A Revealing History

In the mid-1960s the Rockefeller and Ford Foundation financed institutions in Mexico and the Philippines made breakthrough releases in wheat and rice. In 1964, outside my office at the Indian Agricultural Research Institute, I could see the first trials of Lerma Roho and Sonora 58. It was extraordinary. After an immense political battle India, to save time, short-circuited growing its own seed and imported from Mexico a modest tonnage of the new seed, and followed immediately with large orders. The green revolution was on.

Those events heralded radical change in plant breeding research throughout the low- and middle-income countries of Asia and Africa. The best way to understand the drama of that history and the substance of this and the next three chapters is best seen by a graph of radically different research station results for India and the United States from the pre-green revolution period.

Figure 12.1 shows the pre-green revolution years—the early 1960s. In West Bengal and Orissa the very low peak yields were reached with very low levels of fertilizer input. Indian researchers accepted the conventional wisdom that their farmers were too poor and uneducated to use commercial fertilizer except at very low levels. In Arkansas and Texas researchers had a very different philosophy—breed

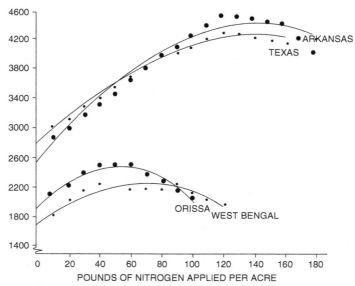

POUNDS OF NITROGEN APPLIED PER ACRE

Source: Herdt, Robert W., and John W. Mellor, "The Contrasting
Response of Rice to Nitrogen; India and the United States,"*Journal
of Farm Economics*, XLV (Feb. 1964), 150–160

Fig. 12.1   Before the green revolution, averaged experiment station data, contrasting
response of rice yields to nitrogen, India and the United States

varieties that would respond to high levels of fertilizer use and rise to very high
yields. At its simplest this was to create short, stiff-stemmed varieties that would
not lodge (fall down) with high levels of fertilization. The international research
centers took the US approach, and that of other high-income countries, one that
eventually spread throughout the national research systems. It turned out in
practice that small commercial farmers were quite ready to use large inputs of
fertilizer and pay for it if their yields went up dramatically. That was the green
revolution and Fig. 12.1 accurately predicted it.

Rates of Return on Research

Large public investment in agricultural research and the associated extension is
central to the modernization of agriculture that is, in turn, central to the
economic transformation and to rural poverty reduction.

There have been literally hundreds of studies of rates of return on research and
many for extension, a high proportion published in refereed journals. There is
tremendous dispersion in the results as should be expected. Research is risky,
with lots of failures, but lots of successes. Several studies survey this vast literature
and report the median returns (e.g. Alston et al. 2000; World Bank 2008; Pratt
and Fan 2010; Thirtle et al. 2003; Alston and Pardey 2001; Pardey et al. 2016).

The central tendency from all these studies is in the order of a 40 percent internal rate of return for Sub-Saharan Africa and 60 percent for the rest of the low- and middle-income countries. The international centers (CGIAR) come out at about 70 percent. The conclusion is clear: there is major underinvestment in research and extension in all regions.

There are, however, a small number of contrary papers, generally by the same authors as the findings being criticized. Alston et al. (2011), who also did much of the research cited above, calculates a low return for the United States in the order of ten percent. Hurley et al. (2014) reexamining a large number of studies across large areas of Asia and Africa and using a "novel method" come up with the same roughly ten percent rate of return. It is noted that the higher rates of return seem implausible. There may be a publication bias—journals preferring positive findings to negative findings—and the researchers themselves may have been prone to that bias. It is notable, however, that Pardey et al. (2016) who plow ahead with the same methodology as is criticized in Hurley et al. (2014) have three authors in common between the two papers arguing a lower rate of return, including the respective senior authors.

I have look at all the research carefully and have reached the same conclusion as above: research/extension has high rates of return and is grossly underinvested. I conclude on the logic that given the growth rate of agriculture in Ethiopia over the past 20 years, in the green revolution period in Asia, in Japan's agricultural growth rate from after the Meiji period (1868) onwards, and likewise for Taiwan, I see that in every case new crop varies and cropping patterns came straight from the agricultural research stations and dominated agriculture. We would be nowhere without institutionalized agricultural research/systems, no matter how much is invested elsewhere.

The variability in rates of return around the median tell us an important story. Returns to research vary greatly with circumstances. Some national research systems are so underfunded that they produce little or no useful research, some systems allocate resources to the more difficult situations, such as low rainfall areas, some have generally poor leadership and lack priorities, and often farmers lack the critical complements for effective application. We must understand the factors that determine agricultural research success. Results may also be biased by difficulties in attribution of production changes to various casual factors.

Most studies of returns to research show substantial spillover effects from the geographic area for which the research was financed. That could be seen as contrary to the view that every country needs its own research. However, work by Evenson has shown that countries that spend a lot on research receive the most benefits from other countries' research. That is of course logical. Your own researchers are the ones who notice and then adapt research from elsewhere. They are also the ones that researchers from the international system and from other countries want to interact with.

What can we conclude from these studies? Given the high returns, countries and the international community are underspending on research. Africa shows lower rates of return on research than other areas (see also Pardey et al. 2016).

That is partly because of much lower levels of spending on all the complements to research, from rural roads to rural education to agricultural extension—that is the story of Africa. It is also partly because, with less commitment to agriculture, there is less emphasis on ensuring productive research systems. Africa spends 66 cents per hectare on research compared to $3.13 in Asia (Thirtle et al. 2003). It is notable that the agricultural research system in Ethiopia is highly productive because the government ensures the money is spent well and the complements are there.

Rate of Return on Extension

Studies of the rate of return on extension are less in quantity and more limited in their findings than that for research. There is also more widespread criticism of extension than research. The correlation between extension, usually measured as farmer visits, and agricultural production was significant in only nine of the 15 studies (Birkhaeuser et al. 1991). However in the cross-section of studies reported above for research the median rate of return on extension was 30 percent in a set of ten studies, mostly by leaders in this field of analysis; only three were under 34 percent and they clustered around 15 percent. A 2010 study by the World Bank and IFPRI found an 80 percent rate of return on extension investment. The studies for the United States were all over 100 percent rate of return.

Extension effectiveness interacts with roads (Dercon et al. 2009). Returns on extension interaction with schooling tend to show more schooling equals a lower impact of extension. That is probably a reflection of the low quality of most extension in low- and middle-income countries and the need to upgrade the technical competence of extension workers as farmers become better educated. The returns on extension in the United States are the highest of all countries and the education level of farmers is very high.

The wide variability in returns on extension probably reflect poor to excellent complements, including research and poor to excellent integration of research and extension. The even greater variability when extension was measured for specific crops undoubtedly reflects the differences in potential. The bottom line on this is that extension has the potential for high rates of return that can be realized by effective complementary actions.

Numerous studies show that female farmers have poor access to extension. Farmers' wives, who are important in family discussions of farming, lose access to farming information as the focus shifts outside the village. These are serious problems that are discussed later in this chapter.

EXPENDITURE ON RESEARCH

Low- and middle-income countries underspend much more on research compared to high-income countries. The United States in recent decades was spending about three percent of agricultural gross domestic product (GDP) on public agricultural research. The private sector, rising from very little to prominence, was matching that level in the recent past to result in the very high level of six percent of agricultural GDP being spent on agricultural research. Low- and middle-income countries are well under one percent of agricultural GDP spent on research. Many are at half a percent or even less. They have immense potential for increasing that expenditure and receiving its high returns.

It is notable that high-income countries spend twice as much per researcher as do low- and middle-income countries. Analysis of expenditure patterns shows that result is largely due to very little operating budget for travel or assistants in low- and middle-income countries. This is doubly uneconomic because of the scarcity of top-level researchers. They should be given more support than in high-income countries not less.

The World Bank reports (2008) that the knowledge gap is widening between high-income and low- and middle-income countries—that is, expenditure is growing more rapidly in high-income countries. While investment in agricultural research tripled in both India and China during the few decades of rapid growth, at the same stage in Sub-Saharan Africa it grew by less than a fifth, while declining in nearly half the African countries (Pardey et al. 2016).

EXPENDITURE ON EXTENSION

Despite small increases in private sector extension in some high-income countries and large increases in New Zealand, 95 percent of the half million extension workers in the world are in the public sector.

The United States spends twice as much on research as extension. In contrast, in the early decades of their development low- and middle-income countries spent twice as much on extension as on research—probably in the incorrect expectation, held by donors as well as recipient countries, that technology could be easily transferred from high-income countries to low-income ones. As the realization spread that this was not the case low- and middle-income countries were soon spending as much on research as extension. However, it is rare for them to reach the ratio of high-income countries.

The World Bank concludes from its analysis of projects that the reasons for the low quality of many extension systems is poor support levels, weak linkages with research, and low motivation and accountability of extension staff.

Modern communications technology has the potential to increase the cost effectiveness of extension programs (see Aker 2011). The cell phone is already widely owned throughout the agriculture sector of low- and middle-income countries.

Attention is drawn in several places in this book to women's poor access to extension services. Women's severe time constraints, in part because of their many tasks, has been discussed in several contexts in this book. The social and human losses are immense and the specific reasons for this failure need to be addressed (e.g. see Saito and Weidemann 1990).

INTEGRATION OF RESEARCH AND EXTENSION

Research and extension are more efficient if tightly integrated. Particularly if many of the senior researchers are urban oriented, extension is essential for ensuring close relations with farmers not only for disseminating research results but for researchers to receive an inflow of information from farmers as to their problems: what is working and what is not, and why. Demonstrations are a critical part of extension. Researchers need to be involved in those demonstrations to ensure they are technically sound.

The US Model

The US model is to fully integrate research and extension with university level teaching and research—the land grant university approach. All three functions are located at the university. University researchers integrate with national government researchers and extension is fully integrated with research and also influences practical teaching. The University level extension workers in turn link with the local, county level, extension agents. In some cases the extension workers are integrated in the subject matter departments. In others they are separate. However, both methods work.

The Japanese Model

The Japanese model involves having research and extension people integrated at the regional research stations, with little link to universities. An American would argue that method reduces the link within university researchers who may then concentrate more on basic research and this loses a link for more practical teaching. From an agricultural production point of view the Japanese model is at least as effective as the American system.

The Low- and Middle-income Countries' Norm

The norm in low- and middle-income countries is to have extension and research separated in different administrative units. These countries often have good integration plans but little implementation. The result is poorer performance by both. That separation is surprising, given the strength of American foreign aid at the formative stage of many systems in Asia and Africa.

To make the best of a bad situation a complete system of regional research stations needs to be built as effective research institutions and the extension coordinated at that level. Alternatively, demonstrations can be jointly developed by research and extension personnel and integrate through that, but, in general, not even that happens. The result is a much lower level of performance by both research and extension, which then weakens the case for financial support for each one.

FARMER CONTROL OF EXTENSION

Extension is more effective when farmers play a major role in control. In the United States that happens at the local (county) government level. In most low-income countries, even in rural areas those local bodies, surprisingly, tend not be closely related to the agricultural sector and hence they serve as a poor coordinating body. The need is to broaden the political participation of small commercial farmers in local government, or possibly to use cooperatives as part of the coordination mechanism.

PRIVATE SECTOR EXTENSION

Private sector extension is significant in high-income countries. The fertilizer and seed distributors are large scale and can benefit from providing extensions services related to the products they sell. Farmers are still happy for the public extension service, keeping the private traders "honest." Private firms provide management services for a fee to farmers with the emphasis on futures trading in which farmers hedge against price changes. That is a long way from the practical problems faced by farmers in low- and middle-income countries.

Gomez and his colleagues at Cornell University, in an as yet unpublished research paper, analyzed a large data set on private sector extension services in Asian and African low- and middle-income countries. These include NGOs (non-governmental organizations) and private for-profit firms. Private firms tend to concentrate in sub-areas, such as advising on fertilizer use. NGOs, in addition, cover broader social areas. They are complements to public services not substitutes, particularly given their limited coverage.

That brings us to a key reason why extension services will, for a long time, remain in the public sector for low- and middle-income countries. In New Zealand 10,000 farmers produce over 80 percent of the agricultural output. In a typical medium-sized low- or middle-income country there would be several million small commercial farmers. That is a very large system to service with private sector extension.

The basic requirement is that there be full national coverage of integrated research extension systems. That will generally require a public system, usefully supplemented by whatever private systems develop. Finally, competition is always a good thing.

PRIVATE SECTOR RESEARCH

The private sector is increasingly important in agricultural research in high-income countries. The large-scale private sector (e.g. DuPont, Monsanto) is important in some sub-fields of agricultural research—principally hybrid crops and application of the most advanced basic science. Five or fewer firms now dominate the application of advanced science (for a discussion of the advantages and disadvantages of such research see Qaim (2001)). Their research results are patentable, can be controlled by the research institution, and can therefore be sold profitably (e.g., a high-yielding, patented hybrid maize or a weed-killing, spray tolerant variety). They use their research base to sell seed internationally, showing some potential for breeding crop varieties with a wide range of applications. Partly because of the limited areas in which they work they cannot be seen as substitutes for public sector research. There is of course scope for productive interaction.

Setting Public Sector Research Priorities

A common problem in low- and middle-income countries is maintaining an initially correct concentration on cereals well beyond the time when additional commodities need to be added. Part of the problem is inadequate spending, even for cereals, and hence very inadequate spending on a larger range of commodities. Expenditure needs to grow and the emphasis should be on adding new commodities.

The research systems' priorities should derive from the national vision and its priorities. In that context, the first step is to state the relative importance of each of the major agricultural commodities. Much applied research is commodity specific. The potential growth rate for each commodity is derived from the experience of researchers as to production potentials and for domestic demand growth and exports. From that, the relative importance of each commodity set is calculated, which provides guidance for personnel and budget allocations. With that base the size and composition of research that cuts across commodities, including basic research, is developed.

Table 12.1 provides an example, for middle-income Pakistan, of such a matrix. Note that dairy, livestock, and horticulture comprise 74 percent of incremental agricultural GDP. That is a product of their large initial weight and the high growth rate assumed. The latter is possible because of little land

Table 12.1 What is the likely commodity composition of a 5.3 percent agricultural growth rate, Pakistan—a base for setting research priorities

Commodity	Base % agr. GDP	Growth rate	Incremental growth (%)
Dairy (milk & meat)	39	7	51
Other livestock	16	4	12
Horticulture	7	8	11
Wheat	11	4	8
Cotton, rice, SC	16	4	12
Other crops	8	3	5
Forestry/fisheries	3	2	1
Total	100	5.3	100

Source: Base percentage agricultural GDP from Pakistan Bureau of Statistics, 2014; commodity growth rates estimated by author from historical growth rates and calculated demand growth rate in a high-income growth rate context
Note: Author's calculation

constraint for these sectors and rapid growth in domestic demand. Most middle-income countries err in allocating very little to these areas. In a low-income country these sectors will be much smaller, while the potential growth rate in the basic field crops will be higher.

Initially, unimportant crops or new introductions will receive little or no weight in the allocation of research resources. That is because even with very rapid growth it will take many years to build a base large enough to have an aggregate impact. If the private sector fosters growth in these sectors they may reach a size where public resources should be devoted to them.

In low- and middle-income countries there is a common trend of developing an export horticultural commodity, having a rapid growth rate, and then suddenly a disease or insect hits and production plummets. That trend is then repeated with another crop. Guatemala is a good example. In the United States with its highly developed research system, particularly for horticulture in California, that rarely if ever happens. That is because the research system spots the problem early and in the several years it takes for a disease to have an aggregate impact a solution is found.

Normally when a high-value crop develops an export potential it results in a high density of production in a limited area greatly increasing susceptibility to serious disease problems. The research system needs to prioritize diagnosing that potential early and catering for it.

Basic Research

It is argued that low- and middle-income countries should put all their research into applied research. On the contrary, basic knowledge helps attract some of the best minds, including overseas nationals, to the research institution. An important case is that of genetically modified organisms (GMOs).

Until a few decades ago, the core theory driving plant breeding was Mendelian genetics based on a research breakthrough some 150 years ago. In recent decades, massive breakthroughs have occurred in our understanding of plant biology with the potential to greatly accelerate changes in plant productivity. Those breakthroughs are in the popular mind aggregated into GMOs. As with all radical change an argument ensues about banning such products.

For high-income countries the cost of banning such research in agriculture has little cost of living impact because food is such a small part of consumer expenditure. Much more serious would be a ban on such research in the medical fields which are more important to high-income consumers. That of course does not occur. In low-income countries the problem is reversed. Breakthroughs that provide basic caloric intake increase and eventually higher-quality diets are the changes having the largest health impact. The more high-income countries steer clear of these research breakthroughs in agriculture the more low- and middle-income countries need to develop capacity.

One needs trained people in these sciences in order to deal with problems that may arise not only from domestic research but that done in other countries, and to provide the insights for the essential regulation needed if the problems are to be avoided.

No-one knows what potential will rise from future basic research. The point here is not specifics but the fact that basic science breakthroughs greatly speed the pace of new practical applications. All the more reason for low- and middle-income countries to increase their research expenditure so their contributions can benefit from these breakthroughs, diagnosing and preventing problems, and for constant vigilance as to what assistance the small commercial farmer will need in order to participate.

Tropical Export Commodities

Foreign assistance, especially as exemplified by the CGIAR system, has a strong bias towards basic food crops, particularly cereals, and that attracts national resources in that direction. This penalizes the tropical export commodities in particular. The national system should resist that bias but usually does not.

As an exception, when Malaysia, against World Bank advice, decided to build a large oil palm sector it sent researchers to the then Belgian Congo (Zaire)—at that time the location of the world's premier oil palm research system—and immediately set up its own system modeled on the Congo's. Right from the start, Malaysia built a strong oil palm research and extension system. In sharp contrast, the several African countries for which comparative advantage is strongly towards tropical export commodities, allowed existing research systems to deteriorate. An African exception to this is Ghana: it achieved rapid growth in its cocoa sector by building its research extension system for cocoa and ensured a rapid decline in rural poverty in the large coffee-producing area.

Climate Change

Most studies (e.g. Nelson et al. 2009; Wiebe et al. 2015) of climate change show substantial reduction of yields, increased prices, and hence a heavy burden on the poor. There is clearly a lot of little-understood regional variability in the causes and effects of climate change that call for adaptive responses.

Because foreign aid programs tend to emphasize climate change it is important that recipient countries have clear priorities. First, and most important, the national research systems need to be much larger and more expensive than without climate change. That is in the context in which spending is well below the optimal level. Second, for most countries extra research attention needs to be given to heat resistance, both through new cropping patterns and breeding for heat tolerance. Third, research on water use efficiency must be increased. If supplies dwindle, urban areas will use their economic power to pull water from agriculture. Fourth, in monsoonal areas research is needed on ground water development as monsoonal rain increases and the dry season becomes drier.

Improving the predictability of climate change at the national level would also be helpful.

Most important, the basic thrust to accelerate the agricultural growth rate in the most productive and efficient manner should not be subverted by specialized climate-oriented research. For a low-income country, the most important adaptation to climate change is increasing the resource base and getting its population well above the poverty level.

WIDESPREAD REGIONAL RESEARCH SUB-STATIONS

Political pressures encourage the proliferation of research stations, which is in general desirable. Research results have to be tailored to micro differences in the environment that affect not only the combination of enterprises but the productivity of specific varieties. Multiple sub-stations have two other important advantages. Of course fully adequate financing must be provided, as discussed throughout this chapter.

First, they locate the researchers close to farmers and provide, in the collectivity of sub-stations, a wide range of experience. Second, senior government officials may use the station as a central point for addressing and interacting with rural populations, particularly the politically influential small commercial farmers.

I remember sitting with the Director for Agriculture in Paktikia Province, Afghanistan, and asking him what he thought of foreign aid to help redevelop the old agricultural research station in his Province. Without hesitation he said "that would do so much for my reputation." To the farmers in the area he is the government. In a situation of nation building, encouraging the support of influential, small commercial farmers is essential.

HIGHER EDUCATION

Because agriculture is so science oriented for its growth, and requires a large number of complex public and private sector institutions staffed by highly knowledgeable and educated staff there must be a rapid expansion of the agriculture-related higher education system. In the mid-twentieth century, the United States foreign aid system provided long-term assistance to develop agricultural universities in essentially every Asian country and in a few African countries. That assistance ended prematurely but it provided a core which in many countries has continued to grow and to occupy a major role in thinking about and staffing the agricultural growth institutions. It is striking how higher education related to agriculture has continued to grow in countries like the United States where agricultural production has dropped to a very small portion of the economy. However, input supply and highly complex marketing have caused the total integrated sector to grow. Education and research have responded by greatly broadening their work. In general, such expansion and broadening has not happened in low- and middle-income countries.

The great tragedy of US foreign assistance is the premature abdication of the United States from that enormously useful effort in which it had an immense comparative advantage. All low- and middle-income countries are the losers but the greatest loss has been in Sub-Saharan Africa. I was Chief Economist of USAID at that time, saw it coming, understood the bureaucratic forces at work, but proved helpless in stopping it: a horrible experience.

The Consultative Group on International Agricultural Research (CGIAR)

Let us close on a positive note. In the 1940s the prescient Rockefeller Foundation, based on a seminal report commissioned from Professor Richard Bradfield, an agronomist at Cornell University, started an international research center in Mexico for maize and wheat breeding (CYMMT), with some ancillary areas of research. It proved to be a highly productive investment. Twenty years later the Rockefeller Foundation was joined by the Ford Foundation under the leadership of ex Cornell Professor F. F. Hill to set up a similar center for rice in the Philippines. Robert Chandler the founding Director of IRRI had a very simple objective: to double rice yields.

The somewhat earlier efforts of the American foreign aid program had created land grant universities similar to national institutions throughout Asia, while concurrently the Rockefeller Foundation was strengthening national agricultural research institutions. Several governments had built the beginnings of a fertilizer distribution system. That provided a favorable environment for the release of extraordinarily productive fertilizer responsive rice and wheat varieties from CYMMT and IRRI. They had a truly revolutionary effect on cereal production throughout Asia.

That extraordinary impact resulted in the World Bank and many other donors, including strong USAID leadership, jumping on the band wagon to finance the present 15 CGIAR Research Centers, a now over one billion dollars a year system. As the system grew it placed an increasing emphasis on increasing the national impact by helping to build and work through increasingly effective national systems. Consistently, the measurement of the rate of return on the investment in CGIAR has been very high.

It should be noted that there are effective, international, agricultural research centers that not part of the CGIAR system (e.g., the international fertilizer center and the international vegetable crops center) but they too are valuable institutions.

Four key points about CGIAR are as follows:

First, it is valuable, needs to be maintained and even to grow gradually, with increasing control and financing from the research systems of Asia, Africa, and Latin America.

Second, low- and middle-income countries benefited from the international centers in direct proportion to the strengths of their national systems. This relation was reinforced by the CGIAR researchers' finding that they were most effective when working with strong national systems. The result was a boost to building national systems and a multiplier on the work of the army of CGIAR researchers.

Third, as the system grew, the governing body, dominated by the high-income donor countries, gradually moved to lower-level foreign aid and foreign ministry administrators from the very top level that had initiated the system and governed it in the early years. The result has been an increasingly bureaucratic system responding to a very wide range of donor specific concerns and hence a reduction in the efficiency with which growth (particularly crop yield) objectives were pursued to the detriment of the larger objective of poverty reduction. The individual CGIAR boards all have very strong, professional, developing country members, and likewise research staff. As the central bureaucracy grew the control by the individual CGIAR boards inevitably diminished and concurrently so did the CGIAR Directors General and their staff. Research systems need to have a clear focus, not be spread thinly over many, sometimes conflicting, objectives. With bureaucratic control the system has also become less flexible. Research Center Directors General, their Boards and their research staff have been able to manage the system so as to preserve some of the basis for much work that still has an immense impact. But CGIAR's efficiency has declined. Eventually the system needs to be more substantially financed by, and as a result becomes more strongly influenced by, the research systems of countries in Africa, Asia, and Latin America.

Fourth, the system followed a donor obsession with basic food crops and hence the export crops so important to the income growth of many low- and middle-income countries were neglected. The same is true of the high-value commodities such as horticulture and intensive livestock production that represent a major share of future high growth rates and improved nutrition. This latter point is not a main criticism of the CGIAR system, which indeed benefited from the narrow focus on food crops to draw attention to remaining problems and the consequent development imbalance.

REFERENCES

Aker, J. C. (2011). Dial "A" for agriculture: A review of information and communication technologies for agricultural extension in developing countries. *Agricultural Economics, 42*(6), 631–647.

Alston, J. M., & Pardey, P. G. (2001). Attribution and other problems in assessing the returns to agricultural R&D. *Agricultural Economics, 25*(2–3), 141–152.

Alston, J. M., Marra, M. C., Pardey, P. G., & Wyatt, T. J. (2000). Research returns redux: A meta-analysis of the returns to agricultural R&D. *Australian Journal of Agricultural and Resource Economics, 44*(2), 185–215.

Alston, J. M., Andersen, M. A., James, J. S., & Pardey, P. G. (2011). The economic returns to US public agricultural research. *American Journal of Agricultural Economics, 93*(5), 1257–1277.

Birkhaeuser, D., Evenson, R. E., & Feder, G. (1991). The economic impact of agricultural extension: A review. *Economic Development and Cultural Change, 39*(3), 607–650.

Dercon, S., Gilligan, D. O., Hoddinott, J., & Woldehanna, T. (2009). The impact of agricultural extension and roads on poverty and consumption growth in fifteen Ethiopian villages. *American Journal of Agricultural Economics, 91*(4), 1007–1021.

Hurley, T. M., Rao, X., & Pardey, G. (2014). Re-examining the reported rates of return to food and agricultural research and development. *American Journal of Agricultural Economics, 96*(5), 1492–1504.

Nelson, G. C., Rosegrant, M. W., Koo, J., Robertson, R., Sulser, T., Zhu, T., et al. (2009). *Climate change: Impact on agriculture and costs of adaptation* (Vol. 21). Washington, DC: International Food Policy Research Institute.

Pardey, P. G., Andrade, R. S., Hurley, T. M., Rao, X., & Liebenberg, F. G. (2016). Returns to food and agricultural R&D investments in sub-Saharan Africa, 1975–2014. *Food Policy, 65,* 1–8.

Pratt, A. N., & Fan, S. (2010). *R & D investment in national and international agricultural research: An ex-ante analysis of productivity and poverty impact.* Washington, DC: International Food Policy Research Institute (IFPRI).

Qaim, M. (2001). Transgenic crops and developing countries. *Economic and Political Weekly, 36*(32), 3064–3070.

Saito, K. A., & Weidemann, C. J. (1990). *Agricultural extension for women farmers in Africa* (World Bank Discussion Paper No. 103). Washington, DC: World Bank Group.

Thirtle, C., Lin, L., & Piesse, J. (2003). The impact of research-led agricultural productivity growth on poverty reduction in Africa, Asia and Latin America. *World Development, 31*(12), 1959–1975.

Wiebe, K., Lotze-Campen, H., Sands, R., Tabeau, A., van der Mensbrugghe, D., Biewald, A., et al. (2015). Climate change impacts on agriculture in 2050 under a range of plausible socioeconomic and emissions scenarios. *Environmental Research Letters, 10*(8), 085010.

World Bank Group. (2008). *World development report 2008: Agriculture for development.* Washington, DC: World Bank Group.

CHAPTER 13

Purchased Inputs

The core of agricultural modernization is yield and income-increasing technology based in modern science. Associated with new technology is a shift from inputs produced on the farm to those that are purchased and dramatic increase in the quantity of those purchased inputs. That in turn requires new types of servicing businesses and institutions.

The large increase in the biological mass removed from the land means that a large quantity of soil nutrients must be replaced by purchased nutrients. Organics produced in situ are complementary to the purchased inputs and increase their productivity, and vice versa. There is a contrary view, specific to Sub-Saharan Africa, that emphasizes low-input agriculture. Giller et al. (2009) provide a strong counter to that argument with many references to low-input literature.

Research provides a constant requirement to increase fertilizer use and purchase new varieties of seed and those in turn have to be repurchased annually in the case of hybrids and every few years in the case of open-pollinated varieties. There are many other purchased inputs made highly profitable by new technology, including pesticides and machinery. Although more a capital investment than an operating expense, the profitability of irrigation also increases with modernization and a large increase in irrigated area often occurs. Similarly, the large increase in labor use creates labor bottlenecks, even in the context of considerable underemployment of labor, and consequent mechanization.

There is scope for increased efficiency in the use of purchased inputs and there are environmental problems that must be addressed. However, they are essential in large quantities to modernization and all its benefits. Five types of purchased inputs are discussed in this chapter: fertilizer, irrigation, seed, pesticides, and machinery.

© The Author(s) 2017
J.W. Mellor, *Agricultural Development and Economic Transformation*,
Palgrave Studies in Agricultural Economics and Food Policy,
https://doi.org/10.1007/978-3-319-65259-7_13

FERTILIZER

Fertilizer is the dominant purchased input at early stages of modernization. Since it is so large in quantity and so essential, governments must give special attention to ensuring that a high growth rate is achieved.

Variability in the Intensity of Fertilizer Use

Regional differences hide a great deal of variability among countries within a region. However, it is useful to start the analysis with a broad picture. Nitrogen use gives a better picture of impact on growth rates because it is normally used first and in the greatest quantity.

All the growth rates are surprisingly slow as compared to sub-periods of very rapid growth (Table 13.1). Europe shows a negative growth rate reflecting initial very high levels of application and concern about the environmental effects at those high levels. North America is also very slow-growing, reflecting a high degree of maturity in agricultural production and similar pressures to increase fertilizer efficiency.

South and East Asia have reached a moderately mature stage of cereal production and have failed to grasp the potentials for large-scale growth in fertilizer-intensive horticultural crops and so fertilizer use is stagnating at levels of high use, largely on cereals.

Sub-Saharan Africa, as is to be expected, is at an early stage in fertilizer use. However, at the current levels of use a rapid agricultural growth program would require a ten percent or higher growth rate for fertilizer. The huge Sub-Saharan African area uses only five percent of the world's fertilizer. South Asia uses five times that amount. India during its period of rapid, green revolution fueled, agriculture growth increased nutrient use by ten percent per year for the period 1967/68–1976/77. Other Asian countries had similar growth rates at that stage of development. Those high growth rates were off a substantial base and continued for a decade or so beyond 1976–1977. Ethiopia has maintained a ten percent growth rate in fertilizer use for 20 years and should maintain that as cropping patterns change for at least another decade or two.

Table 13.1   Growth rate in nitrogen use and share of total use, selected regions, 2014/2018

Region	Growth rate, percent	Share of total use, percent
World	1.4	100
Sub Saharan Africa	4.6	5
South Asia	1.7	25
East Asia	1.0	29
North America	0.5	26
Western Europe	−0.3	15

Source: FAO Stat 2011

Table 13.2   Variability in nitrogen use, selected countries, 2013

Country	Total tons N	Kg per hectare of arable land	Per capita GDP (US $)
Bangladesh	452,040	208.7	1211.7
Pakistan	2,564,311	135.3	1429.0
India	12,332,509	157.5	1581.6
Indonesia	3,634,210	204.6	3346.5
China	29,225,324	364.4	7924.7
Ethiopia	–	19.2	619.1
Rwanda	–	9.3	697.3
Tanzania	–	4.7	864.9
Ghana	–	35.8	1381.4
Nigeria	170,200	17.8	2640.3
Egypt	2,362,360	636.4	3614.7
United States	8,891,335	131.9	55,836.8
Japan	596,072	256.7	32,477.2

Source: FAOSTAT

Consistent with the data in Table 13.1, individual Asian countries use far more fertilizer than African countries (Table 13.2). Within Asia, Bangladesh is high reflecting a national effort to accelerate agricultural growth in a context of a high proportion of the land with good water control and double cropping. Pakistan is somewhat lower than India despite a much higher proportion of irrigated area and double cropping, reflecting poor agricultural growth efforts. Indonesia reflects the higher income level and excellent irrigation achievement.

The United States has low use per arable acre because a high proportion of the arable land is in dry areas on which moisture restricts crop yields to low levels, and the offtake of nutrients is low. In Japan most of the land is in lowland areas with ample rainfall and irrigation and soil structures that favor very high yields. Ghana has a large proportion of area planted to high value export crops (e.g., cocoa) that respond well to high levels of fertilizer use and provide high rates of return. Egypt is essentially all irrigated land with excellent soil structure and a long history of intensive cultivation. That results in amongst the highest levels of fertilizer use. The three East African countries reflect an early stage or no emphasis on modernizing agriculture. Even Ethiopia, which has pushed fertilizer use, is less than ten percent the intensity of use of the high-using countries.

Types of Fertilizer

As intensive crop production continues nutrients become depleted and must be replaced. Nitrogen is heavily used in plant growth and normally becomes the first nutrient depleted by high-yielding crops. Nitrogen is naturally fixed from the air, but in very small quantities relative to the high-yield crop offtake. The response to commercial nitrogen is high and uptake comes early in the modernization process. Eventually phosphate becomes lacking and concentrated forms such as super phosphate come into use. Finally, potassium becomes limiting and use grows, often in the form of mixed fertilizer containing all three of these major nutrients. Further, in cropping intensity various trace elements and minerals will be found lacking. Of course the order and the levels required vary according to several features of the underlying soil composition and structure.

Ideally, a system of soil testing delineating small areas with differing requirements is needed. However, that is a sophisticated system requiring large numbers of trained people and management. Experience is that a low-income country can quickly build a base of use and maintain a high growth rate (e.g., ten percent per year) for a decade or two without such a complex system. Of course, the sooner the basis can be built for such a system the better, but not at the expense of a broad-based research system fully integrated with a massive extension system. Such sequencing of requirements will be a constant refrain in these chapters.

The case is often made for mixed fertilizers. That is a risky choice prior to detailed, widespread, soil testing because a given mix is likely to be inefficient for many farmers. The result is they are paying for nutrients that are not yet limiting and often in the wrong combination. The rate of return to fertilizer may thereby be reduced to an unprofitable level.

Environmental Concerns

Fertilizer use practices that result in fertilizer entering the ground water and run-off, particularly into water bodies, is a major concern in areas of high levels of application. It is important to start with the understanding that farmers do not want to pay for nutrients that end up in the water table or in surface bodies of water. They will respond to efforts to increase the efficiency of use. Also, the impact of run-off may be exaggerated. A detailed study in the United States in an area of heavy fertilizer use found little impact on ground water (Sharpley et al. 1987).

An underlying problem is that fertilizer is so profitable that it is better to err on the side of too much rather than too little. The research and extension program needs to emphasize optimal use. There are examples of success such as pelletizing fertilizer and optimal placement. Increasing efficiency increases the rate of return on fertilizer and induces some offsetting increase in use. Nevertheless, these measures conserve by increasing the output per unit of fertilizer.

Health Concerns

Inorganic fertilizer is taken up by the plant in the same manner as naturally occurring nutrients. Thus, from a health point of view there is no difference between nutrients naturally in the soil, added through weather events, or as purchased nutrients. That is, of course, very different to the position with respect to pesticides and hormones and antibiotics for animals. The health issues covered in those other areas do not apply to fertilizer and should not be used to confuse fertilizer policy.

WHAT DETERMINES THE GROWTH RATE IN FERTILIZER USE?

In much, but not all, of Asia fertilizer use has been highly profitable for several decades and use on cereals is now at levels suggesting only modest further growth. Rapidly growing demand for horticulture for some export crops and high-quality roughage for livestock has not been met and to do so will greatly increase fertilizer use on these highly fertilizer-responsive crops.

Africa has initially a very low use of purchased fertilizer—less than one tenth the levels of Asia. Cereals receive very little fertilizer. On the surface, that offers the opportunity for fertilizer-dominated growth for a decade or two. Therefore, it is important to understand specifically for fertilizer what drives rapid growth so as to direct effective investment and policy. In specific terms, why did fertilizer use grow at more than ten percent per year in Ethiopia while it only grew at four percent per year in Tanzania and probably almost all of the latter was on large-scale farms. In both Ethiopia and Tanzania, fertilizer use was at least initially of a similar profitability.

Fertilizer Profitability and Efficiency

Sub-Saharan Africa stands out from all other regions in having a substantial literature that suggests low responsiveness to inorganic fertilizers. For reviews of such studies as well as contrary views see, for example, Vanlauwe et al. (2014), Giller et al. (2009), Marenya and Barrett (2009), Morris (2007), and Kumwenda et al. (1996).

It is argued that in Africa soils have been cropped so intensively for so long that they are degraded and organic matter is very low. In that context, response to fertilizer is said to be low. The problem is compounded by high temperatures. But that surely also applied prior to the green revolution to much of Asia (e.g., the Indo-Gangetic Plain).

Producing organic matter by composting is labor intensive and carrying manure and compost to the fields is even more labor intensive. Farmers even on depleted soils tend not to use organic matter except on fields close to the homestead. Time-pressed women use organic matter less than men. New, high-yielding crop varieties and low-cost purchased fertilizers change that. The complementarity with inorganic fertilizers needs to be emphasized by extension through demonstrations.

Most surveys of fertilizer response in Africa do not classify the data by size of farm and region. The study that classifies by region shows 21 percent of the area with no response to inorganic fertilizer. Most likely that accounts for only 15 percent of production. Much of that area has no long-term future in agriculture. For a portion of that area, research should be able to generate profitable recommendations.

The comprehensive 2007 World Bank report on fertilizer use in Sub-Saharan Africa (Morris 2007) is clear that there is "little doubt that fertilizer use must increase in Africa." The geographic area oriented surveys show a large output response to nitrogen for over half of the cropped area. It would be reasonable to assume this higher-yielding land provides well over three-quarters of output. That would support a simple fertilizer seed strategy that can give large sustained increases in production. The Ethiopian experience with such a thrust shows the aggregate impact is very large, leading to a long period of rapid agricultural growth.

Numerous studies of fertilizer use in early stages of adoption (e.g. for Ethiopia), show farmers using less than optimal mixes of nutrients, applying one dominant application instead of the split dosages over the season as is usually recommended, and using less than optimal amounts of fertilizer. Those practices have been adopted by enough farmers to show that they are profitable. The research/extension/demonstration system needs to actively push for greater homogeneity in adoption.

Farmer Motivation

Farmers are like the rest of us, with complex objectives that vary from one another and over time. They may take pleasure in a reputation for good husbandry, high yields, and a clean looking farm. They may want to contribute to a sense of community. A government policy that has a national vison and an explicit fundamental role for farmers is likely to appeal to many of them, as in Ethiopia. Motivation is greatly accelerated if the farmer's wife has full access to knowledge about fertilizer, by participating in demonstrations that fit her busy work schedule, maintaining the traditional family interaction on important issues.

Risk

Much is often made of small commercial farmers' aversion to risk. That is misleading in the context of production-increasing innovation. Incomes of most small commercial farmers are sufficient to absorb the bulk of risks associated with production innovations. That is particularly so after a few of the more prosperous farmers have demonstrated success. The literature on high-risk aversion seems to be based on that "average" farmer who is poor. Of course farmers want reassurance on profitability—and they often get wrong information. An effective research and extension system should meet that need.

Supply Side Push

In a seminal research report on fertilizer use, IFPRI researcher G.M. Desai (1982) showed the importance of a supply-side push to accelerate growth in fertilizer use—a national fertilizer production system with enough pressure to disseminate its product, or in the case of Ethiopia importing to target and disseminating the fertilizer to cooperative unions and then on to the primary cooperatives, putting pressure on the system to further disseminate the fertilizer to the farmer. Fertilizer needs to be moved into use to avoid storage losses. The policy is to ensure that supply is considerably greater than demand at each stage of distribution, with consequent pressure to disseminate the supply. The objective is not to push for uneconomic use of fertilizer but to overcome inertia in taking up profitable use.

In theory if fertilizer is profitable to farmers, private sector traders will meet that demand. Grain traders, already trading with a bulk commodity, can easily take up fertilizer distribution. It is fully complementary with grain trading in the use of capital, storage, and management. Private importers should be ready to respond to trader demand and indeed predict it and import to start the process, but in practice this seems not to happen. The private trader, perhaps not surprisingly, responds more to actual farmer demand than predicted demand. There is a chicken and egg problem: farmers are not using fertilizer, so it is not profitable to make it available; or only a few big farmers use it and they can arrange their supplies in a major city. Because the traders are not demanding fertilizer, importers do not supply it.

More likely governments will have to start the process. That starts with not predicting the demand but having a demand target, based on the more responsive areas. First come the imports. A logical target would be for one-quarter of the responsive area (adequate rainfall and all-weather roads) to be fertilized with one-quarter of the recommended rate. After that a ten percent growth rate would fit the norms for rapid fertilizer growth situations. Import that quantity, have programs to disseminate the fertilizer and be prepared for some carryover stock. The objection to targets is that they may end up being met by fakery rather than recognizing shortfall and analyzing why it occurred, and how to ameliorate the constraints.

Cooperatives are the normal target for governments to disseminate the supply of fertilizer. Alternatively, they may facilitate private traders to stock fertilizer on short-term credit terms—payment in a month or two giving time for the fertilizer to be sold. Governments usually want to regulate margins in a case like this but competition should make that unnecessary. However, setting margins on the basis of actual costs and a reasonable margin should not serve as a disincentive. The objective is not the lowest possible price to the farmer but rapid growth in availability.

Supply push has a cost. Ethiopia, in effect, used this strategy and a research effort by Rashid et al. (2013) calculated the cost at about 15 percent of the wholesale price. That is a high estimate since three-quarters of the cost was for carryover stock, some of which was essential to normal operations. This could be considered as a subsidy, but is not considered in the next section because it is short term and easily removed as use approaches the optimum level.

Foreign aid agencies often push, in the name of privatization, "one stop" supplies of inputs. Aside from the unlikelihood of government bureaucrats coming up with the private sector solution to a problem, this suffers from the quite different nature of fertilizer, a very bulky commodity, from other input and output services. Best to let the market operate, with prodding from the government and the cooperative sector.

Subsidies

This book consistently argues against subsidies on the grounds that the opportunity cost of subsidies is high in foregone investment in research, extension, infrastructure, and education. Governments have difficulty in meeting the CAADP target for ten percent of government expenditure on agriculture. The argument is particularly relevant for fertilizer in which the rate of return to the farmer from purchasing fertilizer is high in the context of effective research and extension systems. That argument is greatly reinforced by the extreme difficulty of removing subsidies once instituted. Fertilizer subsidies are very cheap when hardly any fertilizer is used and rapidly become very expensive as the country moves to optimal levels of fertilizer use. India is the prime example of fertilizer subsidies that have gone horribly wrong.

The World Bank vacillates on the issue of fertilizer subsidy. Several decades ago, it conditioned a loan to India on the government's agreement to subsidize fertilizer use and then spent the entire time since then unsuccessfully trying to get the government to eliminate that subsidy. It of course stopped recommending fertilizer subsidies. Then, in recent decades, it returned to recommending fertilizer subsidies in Africa, presumably partly to compensate for high transport costs. After a generally poor record on subsidies in Africa it again stopped recommending them.

There has been considerable research on fertilizer subsidies in Africa. In a comprehensive review article Jayne and his colleagues (2013), for the period of "smart subsidies" supposedly more efficient than in earlier periods, concluded that in no scenario in the three countries studied (Malawi, Kenya, Zambia) "do the financial program benefits outweigh the program costs." That is substantially because of practical problems in implementation, including that 33 percent of subsidy program fertilizer is diverted before being received by the intended farmers; already substantial use was converted to subsidized fertilizer; traders who were not included in the program in many cases exited distribution; and female-headed households received less benefit than male-headed households.

They note further that the government distribution favored the larger holdings (which we argue in this book is fine if the objective is to increase agricultural production) but was considered unfortunate in the program. Targeting farmers who produce very little is hardly the right approach to accelerating the growth rate. The program was concentrated in areas of weak credit and infrastructure—raising the question of why not spend the money on those requirements. They conclude that studies that show positive benefits from subsidies neglect to account for diversion and crowding-out effects. The upshot of that is that subsidies are inefficient where the institutional resources for agricultural growth are weak. Those same institutions are required to make the subsidies work.

In widely quoted experimental research Duflo et al. (2011) took an unusual approach—look for a small, tightly targeted subsidy that would induce substantial uptake of fertilizer at a low cost. They note that farmers in the study areas failed to take up profitable fertilizer investments (as argued more generally in this chapter) and that simply providing free delivery of fertilizer at harvest time resulted in a 47–70 percent increase in fertilizer use. Farmers normally buy fertilizer at the time of use, not at harvest time, so the experiment changed the timing of fertilizer purchase in what appears to be an uneconomic direction. The experiment did not include a high-quality research/extension program with demonstrations and credit as a control.

The conclusion in the context of this book is that it is possible to design subsidies that are less costly than the usual ones. But, it still evades the issue that the Ethiopian approach of strong institutional structures provided a higher incidence of fertilizer use than even the targeted subsidy. The extension education/ demonstration approach has the growth advantage of improving practices and hence the productivity of the fertilizer. In passing, the farm price of fertilizer is lower in Ethiopia, without subsidy, than in Kenya with subsidy (Rashid et al. 2013).

IRRIGATION

Irrigation differs from fertilizer in that in Asia there was a long colonial history of investment in very large-scale irrigation. It has in common a powerful interaction with modern high-yielding varieties.

The green revolution brought to much of Asia rapid growth of small-scale irrigation, particularly from ground water. In many areas, the ground water reserves were large and deep wells to serve many farmers and shallow wells to serve only one or a few were rapidly developed with a major impact on production. As a result of those investments Asia has developed the bulk of its irrigation potential. There remain considerable opportunities, however, to increase irrigation water productivity.

Small-Scale Irrigation Projects

Small-scale projects are at the scale of the individual farmer or a small group of farmers. Farmers or small groups of farmers make the investments directly. They do so when the rate of return is substantial, most likely because of modernization. It is then important that credit institutions be available and prepared to make loans on terms appropriate for such intermediate-term investment.

There is a latent problem of drawing from the water table beyond its capacity to replenish withdrawn water. It is the usual "problem of the commons"— private benefits pursued to the point of reducing overall benefits. Where that potential is present government must be prepared to legislate, based on an analysis of ground water potential. It is difficult (impossible?) to solve the problem when as is usually the case existing wells are already drawing down the water table. Wells are continually deepened until many farmers quit.

Small watersheds may also provide opportunity for dams to collect water for irrigation on a small scale. Again credit will be needed and often a system for groups to agree on watersheds that cut across several households.

Large-Scale Irrigation Projects

Large-scale schemes are normally developed by governments, often at high cost with a subsidy. They have been massive in scale in many countries. Large-scale irrigation projects seem generally to have major operational problems. These are of two types. Problems due to poor design including salinity and waterlogging;

and, problems due to management, largely less than optimal allocation of water among users.

Large-scale projects were commonly badly designed. Most attention has been focused on the huge colonial period projects in the Indus basin. Faulty design is particularly a problem of inadequate provision for drainage. As a result, water backs up causing waterlogging from excess quantity and salinity from constant replenishment of water as it evaporates bringing larger and larger concentrations of saline materiel. Eventually the land becomes unproductive. The solution is drainage that continually draws a substantial quantity of water. That may be expensive since it must connect all the irrigated areas with a principal water course, such as a major river. This was a problem in the United States, and is still a problem in Pakistan.

Pakistan epitomizes the problem of poor management. Water release starts at a main canal and passes though many farms on its way to the last user. The upstream users draw off excessive amounts of water, leaving inadequate quantities for those downstream. The solution is democratically organized water users' associations. That is difficult, and apparently impossible to achieve when households of the same district have greatly different wealth and political influence. Perhaps the realistic approach is to accept the misallocations, as is often done in the United States, and work for optimal use of the actual amounts of water available at each farm. Rosegrant and Binswanger (1994) provide a comprehensive analysis of the potential for increasing water use efficiency through various approaches to pricing.

Taiwan is an excellent example of successful development and operation of water users' associations (Barker and Levine 2012; Levine et al. 2000; Wai 1996). The period to examine is prior to 1980. In more recent years, the increasing wealth of Taiwan has made it possible to remove all the water charges from the farmers' associations. The Taiwan water users' associations ensured that users would control the water including negotiations with the water authority and user responsibility for payment of all water charges including operation and maintenance. They also paid for many improvements to the system (Barker and Levine 2012; Lee 1971). Water use efficiency has been very high with a high level of agricultural output.

Potential in Africa

Only six percent of Sub-Saharan Africa's cultivated area is irrigated. However, that suggests a not inconsequential 12 percent of output is from irrigated land. You et al. (2011) estimates that area could be nearly doubled, which suggests 25 percent of crop output from irrigated land.

As an example, Malaysia with an area physically comparable to the humid tropic forest of West Africa, grows irrigated rice in the river valleys and upland high-value tree crops, rubber, and oil palm on the area between the river basins. The analogous area of West Africa has a large potential for irrigated rice, which is already at the early stages of development.

Ethiopia has begun to realize the potential for irrigation in its upland agriculture, much like the rest of East Africa, by exploring, with the help of German aid, ground water and small river basins to obtain a second crop in the dry season and increased output during the rainy season by eliminating dry spells through irrigation.

There is also scope for large-scale schemes on the great rivers of West Africa. The high cost of past development, perhaps tracing from high levels of corruption, discourages future development, but perhaps that can change.

SEED

Improved seed starts at the research station that creates and tests the new varieties and makes decisions about releasing them. The research station normally produces seed for sale to the seed companies that then multiply it for broader use. The seed may be sold by those companies, both public and private, directly to farmers or to retail establishments and cooperatives that then sell to farmers. A common problem is governments imposing restrictions on the private sector seed producers, often largely to protect the government system, which interferes with generating productive interactions between seed producers and farmers. In conclusion, it is best to let markets operate.

Hybrid and Open-Pollinated Plants

Plant breeding makes very large advances through producing improved hybrids—varieties that are bred within the type for several generations to eliminate bad features and increase good ones, and then crossing two strains to get what is called hybrid vigor. The seed from hybrids does not breed true and hence has to be replaced every year. Hybrid seed production requires scientifically more complex and large-scale production systems and gravitates to large-scale firms. As that expense rises the importance of specialized finance institutions for small commercial farmers increases.

Open-pollinated seed is much less complex to produce, can be saved and replanted, and dominates most crops. In a relatively few years, the seed quality tends to deteriorate and so high-yielding open-pollinated varieties need a seed system that allows replacement after a small number of years. However, those seed systems are not complex and the larger of the small commercial farms can shift to producing seed of a reasonable quality. Certification would be helpful in assuring quality.

Role of Government and the Private Sector

The seed production industry is so large that efficiency generating competition requires a large, normally dominant, private sector. As in other areas the long-term role of government is to estimate the feasible growth rate, take steps to encourage the private sector, provide the essential regulatory environment including certifying private providers and, in the short run, to step into gaps. That is a substantial role requiring numerous well-trained people. Foreign technical assistance can be very helpful.

As pointed out previously, the existing private sector tends to be trade not production oriented. That shortcoming, especially for hybrids, is likely to be filled by technical people short on business skills. In that context, government will expand into full-blown seed production from the research system base. As the demand grows rapidly into large aggregates the government inevitably falls behind the rapid growth in demand, and scarcity arises. The government has a vested interest in seed production both for jobs and income and rationalizes measures that block private sector competition. The government must have a strategy for gradually moving out of seed production as the private sector expands. There are too many cases of farmers denied access to seed because of inadequate to the task government monopolies.

There is of course a vital role for government in regulating the private sector seed industry. Farmers need to be assured of quality seed by certification programs usually initiated by government. This is an important function requiring substantial human and institutional resources and is a bottleneck to effective private sector growth. It is a natural area for foreign technical assistance.

Production of open-pollinated seed may gravitate to many relatively small producers, certified and supervised by the government.

THE ROLE OF CREDIT

Seed and fertilizer are classic examples of inputs that are divisible into small units. In theory, farmers short of capital can start using small amounts and then take the profits to expand. With a normal 20 percent rate of return it takes only a few years to move to the optimal level of use. Why the process does not normally work in that way is not clear.

It is most likely that farmers look more at the total impact on income rather than the percentage return and if they cannot operate at the optimal level or some major fraction of that they will not take up the innovation. The perfect divisibility turns out to be irrelevant. Nevertheless, farmers do take up fertilizer and move to substantial levels without credit programs. That has been particularly true in Africa where credit is rarely available to the small commercial farmer. Focus group studies tend to show farmers underusing fertilizer by about 30 percent in the absence of credit.

PESTICIDES

Pesticides cover a wide range of targets from insects to diseases to weeds. Pesticides are like seed and fertilizer in one respect. They offer a potential high rate of return on controlling crop losses and in that sense are complementary to seed and fertilizer.

There is however a serious health problem. In low- and middle-income countries they are largely unregulated. Poor extension by the selling firms and by national extension systems, and low educational levels, result in often universal incidence of famer illness from pesticide use. Examples of the large literature on this subject are in an early study reported by Pingali et al. (1994) for the Philippines and Maumbe and Swinton for Zimbabwe (2003).

Pesticides differ from seed and fertilizer in four respects.

First, they are produced by large-scale firms but can be marketed through a diversity of small-scale retail channels including health shops and in rural areas. They tend to be readily available. Second, they have a significant negative impact on the environment, particularly including poisoning farmer users. Third, there are biological controls that can substitute for chemical pesticides. Fourth, pesticides come largely from a small number of large-scale firms.

Thus, the environmental negative aspects can be dealt with by breeding crops that are immune to attack by insects and diseases. Concern for environmental factors requires more expenditure on such research and extension.

Biology with respect to weeds works differently. It is possible to breed crops resistant to weed killers, greatly increasing the effectiveness of weed killers. Since the benefits come from the sale of weed killer it pays large-scale chemical companies to engage in plant breeding for that purpose. That is why most private sector research in agriculture is carried out by what were once dominantly bulk chemical companies—for example, Monsanto and DuPont. They grew rapidly in plant breeding by buying large, existing, free-standing plant research firms. Low- and middle-income countries will be price takers and must carefully analyse the relative costs and returns.

MACHINERY

While labor productivity rises markedly with yield-increasing technology, total labor requirements also increase. That creates labor bottlenecks at particular seasons which in turn calls for mechanization. Concurrently, higher yields increase the returns to irrigation increasing the incentive to purchase engines and pumps for ground water development. The increased demand for machinery sales and repairs rapidly expands an industry that can adapt to providing other machinery-related output for distant markets, hastening and broadening the economic transformation and strengthening growing market towns as growing centers of economic activity.

Machinery differs from most of the previously discussed inputs in its indivisibility and hence requirement for substantial lump-sum investment placing a new pressure on lending agencies. However, rental markets in various forms have risen. China has been out front in developing a variety of institutional structures for facilitating farm machinery rental including government initiated machinery stations.

Although less so than for fertilizer, governments do consider subsidies to agricultural machinery. The literature, as for most agricultural subsidies, tends to show poor rates of return to these investments. There is discussion about government discouraging farm mechanization because of the presence of under-employed labor. As stated, mechanization may actually increase employment. It is best to let the market operate. Do not provide artificial discouragement or encouragement, but recognize that mechanization is often employment creating by breaking seasonal bottlenecks and smoothing labor demand over the year.

REFERENCES

Barker, R., & Levine, G. (2012). *Water productivity in context: The experiences of Taiwan and the Philippines over the past half-century.* Colombo: International Water Management Institute.

Desai, G. M. (1982). *Sustaining rapid growth in india's fertilizer consumption: A perspective based on composition of use* (International food policy research institute (IFPRI) research report 031). Washington, DC.

Duflo, E., Kremer, M., & Robinson, J. (2011). Nudging farmers to use fertilizer: Theory and experimental evidence from Kenya. *The American Economic Review, 101*(6), 2350–2390.

Food and Agriculture Organization. (2011). *The state of food and agriculture: Women in agriculture, closing the gender gap for development.* Rome: Food and Agriculture Organization.

Giller, K. E., Witter, E., Corbeels, M., & Tittonell, P. (2009). Conservation agriculture and small holder farming in Africa: The heretics' view. *Field Crops Research, 114*(1), 23–34.

Jayne, T. S., Mather, D., Mason, N., & Ricker-Gilbert, J. (2013). How do fertilizer subsidy programs affect total fertilizer use in sub-Saharan Africa? Crowding out, diversion and benefit/cost assessments. *Agricultural Economics, 44*(6), 687–703.

Kumwenda, J. D. T., Waddington, S. R., Snapp, S. S., Jones, R. B., & Blackie, M. J. (1996). *Soil fertility management research for the maize cropping systems of smallholders in southern Africa: A review* (NRG paper 96–02). Mexico: CIMMYT.

Lee, T. H. (1971). *Inter-sectoral capital flows in the economic development of Taiwan, 1895–1960.* Ithaca: Cornell University Press.

Levine, G., Sheng, K. H., & Barker, R. (2000). The evolution of Taiwanese irrigation: Implications for the future. *International Journal of Water Resources Development, 16* (4), 497–510.

Marenya, P. P., & Barrett, C. B. (2009). State-conditional fertilizer yield response on western Kenyan farms. *American Journal of Agricultural Economics, 91*(4), 991–1006.

Maumbe, B. M., & Swinton, S. M. (2003). Hidden health costs of pesticide use in Zimbabwe's smallholder cotton growers. *Social Science & Medicine, 57*(9), 1559–1571.

Morris, M. L. (2007). *Fertilizer use in African agriculture: Lessons learned and good practice guidelines.* Washington, DC: World Bank Publications.

Pingali, P. L., Marquez, C. B., & Palis, F. G. (1994). Pesticides and Philippine rice farmer health: A medical and economic analysis. *American Journal of Agricultural Economics, 76*(3), 587–592.

Rashid, S., Tefera, N., Minot, N., & Ayele, G. (2013). Can modern input use be promoted without subsidies? An analysis of fertilizer in Ethiopia. *Agricultural Economics, 44*(6), 595–611.

Rosegrant, M. W., & Binswanger, H. P. (1994). Markets in tradable water rights: Potential for efficiency gains in developing country water resource allocation. *World Development, 22*(11), 1613–1625.

Sharpley, A. N., Smith, S. J., & Naney, J. W. (1987). Environmental impact of agricultural nitrogen and phosphorus use. *Journal of Agricultural and Food Chemistry, 35*(5), 812–817.

Vanlauwe, B., Wendt, J., Giller, K. E., Corbeels, M., Gerard, B., & Nolte, C. (2014). A fourth principle is required to define conservation agriculture in sub-Saharan Africa: The appropriate use of fertilizer to enhance crop productivity. *Field Crops Research, 155*, 10–13.

World Bank Group. (2007). *Poverty and the environment: Understanding linkages at the household level.* Washington, DC: World Bank Group.

You, L., Ringler, C., Wood-Sichra, U., Robertson, R., Wood, S., Zhu, T., et al. (2011). What is the irrigation potential for Africa? A combined biophysical and socioeconomic approach. *Food Policy, 36*(6), 770–782.

CHAPTER 14

Finance for the Small Commercial Farmer

In the context of modernizing agriculture, loans to small commercial farmers increase their investment and significantly accelerate the agricultural growth rate. Increased lending to those farmers requires a specialized lending agency such as that in all high-income countries and the bulk of Asian countries. Competition in lending is desirable so a plethora of other lending institutions is desirable but the core is the specialized agency.

All high-income countries developed specialized agencies for meeting the financial needs of small commercial farmers early in their development. Those institutions were universally effective with high repayment rates. Most Asian countries developed similar institutions prior to the 1990s with substantial foreign assistance. However, they tended to have large overdue rates for loans, often misinterpreted as bad debts. That experience caused a negative attitude towards such agencies. Foreign assistance and then much of the academic literature turned to favoring other modes of providing credit. The effect was that few Sub-Saharan African countries developed on a nationwide basis the specialized agencies so effective in the high-income countries and in Asia in meeting the credit needs of small commercial farmers. A small number of late developing Asian countries (e.g., Nepal) also failed to develop such institutions.

Thus a major thrust of this chapter is how to develop finance institutions in the self-supporting manner of the high-income countries. In a review paper, Nagarajan and Meyer (2005) note that the rural finance lending of the World Bank in recent years, "following the new rural finance paradigm, has....promoted institutions providing small loans and savings services instead of financing lending operations for large rural and agricultural enterprises." The implicit definition of large includes what we define as the small commercial farmer.

This chapter starts with background information and then provides brief points on the wide range of rural lending institutions. That is followed by analysis of the required specialized agricultural lending institution suitable to the small

© The Author(s) 2017   181
J.W. Mellor, *Agricultural Development and Economic Transformation*,
Palgrave Studies in Agricultural Economics and Food Policy,
https://doi.org/10.1007/978-3-319-65259-7_14

commercial farmer. The chapter closes with a discussion of recent literature that presents saving, insurance, and borrowing as interchangeable.

SOME EXAMPLES OF CREDIT AVAILABILITY

From 2006 to 2010, in rural Uganda, households with access to credit increased from 27 percent to 42 percent (Khandker and Koolwal 2014). All of the increase came from modern institutions, as traditional sources declined. Households with a belief that lack of collateral would bar them from borrowing dropped from 23 to 14 percent. While the percentage who did not borrow because they did not know of a lender or otherwise lacked access dropped from 30 percent to five percent. Presence of infrastructure (roads and electricity) made households more likely to borrow from modern institutional sources.

In Rwanda (Ali et al. 2014), 32 percent of households were unable to obtain modern forms of credit with one-third of that due to lack of collateral. Loans for consumption are relatively more important from traditional lenders and loans for investment are a higher proportion of borrowing from modern institutions. The Rwanda study shows that access to modern forms of credit is greater with more schooling, larger farms, and being a member of a cooperative.

An Ethiopia study (Abate et al. 2016) shows cooperative credit (aimed at the small commercial farmer) had a much larger impact on technology adoption than that from micro-credit. The cooperative impact was on both adoption rates and intensity of adoption. Both the cooperatives and micro-finance devoted over two-thirds of their lending to smallholder agriculture: with micro-finance at the lower end and cooperatives at the upper end of the size of farm scale.

RETURNS TO CREDIT

In the Ethiopia study 99 percent of rural households with access to modern forms of credit used fertilizer while 74 percent without access used fertilizer. However, the striking difference occurs in the intensity of use. Those without access to modern credit applied fertilizer at only half the recommended rate. Taken across a set of improved practices, those with access to modern credit had a 32 percent higher adoption rate and used 51 kg more fertilizer than those without access. These results are corroborated, reporting a 30 percent increase in fertilizer use if credit was available, by focus groups under the USAID AMDe project in Ethiopia.

In the Rwanda study, being credit constrained reduced the likelihood of non-farm self-employment by 6.3 percent. This shows that credit is also a constraint in realizing the full benefits of the increased demand for the rural non-farm sector. Lack of access to credit also reduced fertilizer use by half and lowered yields.

TYPES OF RURAL FINANCIAL INITIATIONS

Rural areas have a wide range of financial institutions. Competition is desirable: lack of it results in decreased efficiency and productivity. A range of institutions is a plus whenever it results in multiple sources of financing for the small commercial farmer even, as we argue, for the dominance of a specialized agency.

Family and Friends

The dominant source of borrowing in traditional agriculture is the extended family. It is often without interest payments and used primarily in times of stress. This source, in effect, reduces the risks in farming by spreading them over many related families. Typically, half of rural households borrow from friends and family, a proportion that holds steady or declines over time, particularly when institutional credit becomes available. It is rarely a major source of funds for investing in income-increasing working and fixed capital.

This source is described in current literature as informal insurance— protecting against unfortunate events. It is much more available and effective for small commercial farmers than the poor in the rural non-farm population. Poor people tend to have poor relatives.

Village Money Lenders

It is common in traditional agriculture for a few well to do families in a village to lend to low-income families primarily for consumption in times of stress. Both repayment and interest rates are high. The combination of lending in times of stress and ensuring repayment by frequent contact has spawned a large literature of exploitation by money lenders.

Village money lender rates come down when alternative sources become available, suggesting that without competition village money lenders overcharge compared to a competitive situation. Even so, the money lender rates are too high relative to the returns from modernization investment. This form of lending tends to decline rapidly when institutional credit is available. In the Uganda study cited earlier, this class of lenders covered only two percent of households.

When the donor community fled from specialized credit agencies for small commercial farmers a literature developed extolling the benefits of the village money lender. However, these lenders are poorly adapted to meet the needs of modernizing agriculture. Most important, they lack integration with national and international credit markets so they cannot use their own funds profitably when local demand declines seasonally or draw on those sources when demand dramatically increases, both seasonally and over a long period of time. They are an inefficient source of funds for agricultural growth.

Traders

As small commercial farmers increase buying and selling, traders become an increasingly important source of credit. Competition from institutional forms of credit is important to keeping their lending rates and conditions competitive. Off lending by larger commercial banks to traders for lending to small commercial farmers is a potentially important source of credit and desirable as long as there is competition. However, their importance declines when a specialized agricultural lending agency is provided.

Contract Farming

Contract farming is lending provided by large-scale businesses under contract to market output and provides input and technical guidance. The system may be large and dominant in small specialized situations. It is not a substitute for national coverage from a specialized institution. Contract farming has become common in specialized areas, such as poultry, in high-income countries, but is much less widespread in low- and middle-income countries.

Micro-Finance

Micro-credit became common when publicized by Nobel Peace Prize recipient, Muhammad Yunus, founder of the Grameen Bank in Bangladesh. It is a system of small groups, often of women, generally poor, formed to promote savings followed by a very small-scale lending program. Borrowing is very risky for the poor because their incomes have no scope for interest payments: they are already at the margin of existence. That is why the emphasis is on savings, building a reserve in good times.

With the growth in popularity of micro-credit there has been a spate of commercial efforts to enter the field. That has in general brought a bad name to micro-credit since the focus is on making loans that all too often cannot be repaid. The exposition here is of the traditional type of micro-credit which continues to grow.

Research consistently shows that micro-credit in rural areas increases agricultural production. The studies and focus groups also show that among farmers it is only those at the lowest end of the small commercial farm size that receive micro-credit: it does not reach those who produce the bulk of agricultural output (Khandker and Koolwal 2014). The proportion of rural households accessing micro-finance grows rapidly up to about one-third and then stabilizes. That is equal to a major share of the rural non-farm population that includes subsistence farmers.

Micro-credit first developed in the United States, but received enormous popularity through the successful efforts of the Grameen Bank in Bangladesh. That model is one of large numbers of small groups, first emphasizing savings, then loans backed by the group, and the constant emphasis on small group solidarity. The small groups form a pyramid that develops into a national organization. The result is very high repayment rates and low administrative costs.

In the context of the growth processes in this book, micro-credit has a useful role in facilitating and enlarging participation in the growing rural non-farm sector. The basic constraint on that sector is not capital but lack of demand for its output, a problem solved by small commercial farmers' rising incomes. However, in that context some poor households, and women in particular, may have trouble raising the required small amounts of working capital. Micro-credit is helpful in that circumstance. It may also be available to the smallest of the small commercial farmers—those just above the poverty line.

Micro-credit is not appropriate for the bulk of small commercial farmers on two counts. First, there is a vast difference between the $50–$200 loans typical of micro-credit and the several thousand dollar loans required by the small commercial farmer. The nature of the loans and what it takes to be profitable differ greatly from the usual requirements of the micro-credit institutions' normal clients. Second, the repayment system, depending on group solidarity and guaranteeing each other's loans works well in a savings context and very small loans. It works less well for farmers having to guarantee loans of many thousands of dollars. I recall discussing this with an Indonesian farmer who said, "I would not even guarantee a ($1000) loan to my brother let alone to someone completely outside the family." Of course in cases of highly cohesive communities, group guarantees could work for small commercial farmers, but systems should not be set up assuming that as the norm.

There is an argument that the strong emphasis on repayment represents a desirable culture for lending to small commercial farmers and so the micro-credit institutions could convert to lending to these wealthier families. The most important argument against that is one put forward by leaders in micro-credit systems: "Don't destroy what we have. We have a wonderful institution for lending to the poor and lifting them up." The system is keyed to that group so when it is recalibrated to the small commercial farmer the poor will be lost. When the Grameen Bank in Bangladesh was asked to lend to small commercial farmers it set up a parallel structure for that purpose and kept its micro-credit focused on the poor.

Micro-credit can bring competition in lending to small commercial farmers by providing some competition at that end of the size scale. That would complement the commercial banks, as stated next, in competing at the larger end of the size scale.

Commercial Banks

Commercial banks will eventually be an important component in the agricultural finance systems of currently low- and middle-income countries. That will not happen quickly despite efforts by foreign aid agencies.

Commercial banks in high-income countries are important lenders to agriculture, including to family farms, which are similar to what we define as small commercial farms in size of labor force. In the United States, over half of lending to agriculture is by commercial banks. For a long period of time, branch banking was not allowed. That meant that what are now termed community banks, often in rural areas, had special access to making farm loans and became important lenders. They had a technically trained agriculture loan officer as a prominent staff member. That person worked with farmers to develop farm budgets and loan programs and followed up to ensure repayment. The default rate was close to zero except for that caused by bad weather. The rural banks had a risk problem from a high proportion of loans in weather susceptible agriculture.

In low- and middle-income countries the commercial banks are located in major urban centers and are reluctant to expand into rural areas. That is because they see difficulties in scale for local branches and consider lending to agriculture risky because of their lack of in-house agricultural expertise. Typically, less than five percent of rural households apply for commercial bank credit. In India, ten percent of commercial bank loans are to agriculture, but that is because the law requires this and then it is to the largest most urbanized farmers.

In the long-run commercial banks will gradually expand to cover smaller and smaller urban centers and will eventually become a useful source of competition in lending to small commercial farmers. They are attracted by the large potential to increase deposits from rural areas.

To be effective in agricultural lending, commercial banks must fulfill two conditions. First, they must operate large numbers of rural branches, essentially in all of the larger market towns. Second, they must staff at each branch a technically qualified agricultural loan officer. Hopefully, a few banks will start with a few branches that fulfill those conditions, more will follow and the commercial banks will become an important part of a competitive agricultural credit system. That would include lending to agri-businesses and large-scale deposit mobilization.

A SPECIALIZED FINANCIAL INSTITUTION FOR THE SMALL COMMERCIAL FARMER

A specialized financial system is required to serve the small commercial farmer, filling the otherwise wide gap between micro-credit and commercial banks. Such a system has a large number of loan offices staffed specifically to reach the small commercial farmer. This system is normally either comprised of cooperatives or takes a cooperative form. Systems that are run out of the normal government bureaucracy are rarely successful.

Agriculture has special technically-based requirements which are very different to those facing urban-based lenders. It requires dedicated, specialized loan officers. This is particularly true in low- and middle-income countries. Risk is greatly reduced by a knowledgeable loan officer.

Crop agriculture has a seasonality that dictates the precise timing of loans and repayment periods. That timing differs from region to region and even from farm to farm within regions depending on the specific crops grown and physical conditions. The loan officer must become knowledgeable about technical agriculture and the local conditions.

The clientele of agricultural cooperatives is largely small commercial farmers, the natural clientele for a production agriculture oriented credit system. Indeed, cooperatives are often criticized for focusing on farmers above, or more commonly well above, the poverty line. Subsistence or near subsistence farmers are less concerned with purchased inputs and marketing than the small commercial farmer and thus the economic services of the cooperatives are of less interest to them.

Key Features of a Specialized Agricultural Credit System

Four features are key to providing finance to small commercial farmers on a national scale: many branches; an agriculturally trained loan officer in each branch; a local branch level board; and an apex level oversight body.

Many Conveniently Located Branches Surveys repeatedly show that convenience of location (i.e., nearby) is the most important single factor stated by farmers with respect to a financial system (Desai and Mellor 1993). They know that to use the system requires many visits and having to go to a distant major city is out of the question. Local branches are also important to ensuring that the loan officer knows the borrowers.

There is a tension between many branches close to the borrowers and achieving adequate scale to spread the overheads of loan officers and accounting across sufficient business to contain administrative costs to reasonable levels. The first effort to obtain adequate scale is for the loan officer to expand lending by working with farmers to find additional profitable investment opportunities. The objective of the system is to accelerate the aggregate agricultural growth rate and incidentally to have a scale sufficient to cover overheads.

The second way to increase scale is to mobilize deposits. That adds a second fee and in effect doubles the scale. In a mature agricultural finance system, the volume of savings by farmers is always larger than the volume of loans. Farmers have a high marginal propensity to save, driven partly by conservatism with respect to maintaining their consumption through a bad year as well as the desire to build larger reserves. Thus the financial system actually funnels resources out of agriculture, hopefully to expanding rural non-farm businesses as well as to the urban centers. This is one reason why a well-functioning rural finance system is not inflationary.

In most countries, adding deposits will require meeting banking regulations. That in itself is desirable although it will take time—the lending operations might come first followed after a few years of growth by the deposit function. If it is desirable to add deposit mobilization sooner then an arrangement can be struck with a commercial bank to mobilize deposits and pass them on to the commercial bank, the branch in effect serving as a local agent for the bank. All banks are eager to increase deposits.

The third means is lending to the rural non-farm sector as farm incomes drive rapid expansion of that sector. Credit is not initially the constraint in that sector but as it grows, and particularly as opportunity arises to serve a large market for the more sophisticated small enterprises, credit for the system from small commercial farmers could logically expand into that area.

The Loan Officer The second essential is a specialized, technically competent, loan officer at the branch level to ensure a large and growing volume of profitable loans that are repaid in full and on time. This is a key position in the system. It is here that sound loans are made, that repayment is ensured, and that loan growth is rapid. That officer must be trained at a high level in technical agriculture as well as being experienced in agriculture. A period of service in the extension service is a logical recruiting ground and loan officers need training in accounting, farm budgeting, and lending rules. The loan officer works closely with the local Board and is well paid relative to extension workers.

A survey for the Reserve Bank of India's analysis of overdue loans (which I was involved with) showed that farmers see those overdues as debts that must be paid—a moral responsibility—but they "somehow never get around to it!" The evidence is also clear that even in situations where such overdues are substantial, farmers who have substantially profited from a loan are most likely to repay on time. The loan officer ensures that there is a profitable farm plan for use of the loan proceeds and then follows up regularly to ensure on-time repayment.

The question often arises of lending for consumption, especially including maintaining consumption in a difficult time. The studies generally show consumption loans make up about half of all rural lending. The loan officer's task is to ensure that the loan generates income to allow its full repayment. That the proceeds are in fact fungible—they can be diverted to other purposes—is irrelevant if a plan is implemented that is profitable enough for repayment.

The problem with repayment is most likely to arise in unexpected circumstances: two bad crop years in a row, illness or a death in the family, a completely unexpected degree of price decline. In those circumstances the loan needs to be rescheduled and stretched out over a longer period. That is an important function of a loan officer.

What if there are three bad crop years in a row? Fortunately, that is uncommon. It is destabilizing to the system that is specialized in agriculture for good reason and hence is not diversified across other sectors. That is when governments inevitably step in, as they do in general banking failures. That has been the tradition in the United States and is in effect a form of government subsidized insurance. The loan officer attempts to minimize the extent of this government assistance and it should occur infrequently. Governments are tempted to gain political support by forgiving loans. That is, of course, destructive to the essential discipline of a viable system. Loan refinancing is the correct route.

The huge number of trained loan officers required poses an important problem that is met by rapid expansion of the agricultural universities. During the period of rapid expansion of the national rural financial system in India, that system was easily the single most important job destination for graduates of those institutions. The social objective of more people participating in higher education is assisted by the large demand for trained agriculturalists for a growing agricultural finance system. In the short run, since the financial system likely follows by some years the extension system, the best of the extension agents can be given special training in finance and become loan officers.

A Community Level Board The third essential feature is a local board of knowledgeable farmers, farmers' wives, and female-headed households to ensure sound loans and full repayment, not by personal guarantees but by proper selection and oversight. It is not usual for small commercial farmers to guarantee each other's loans as is the practice in micro-credit. The loans are too large relative to incomes reinforced by a business attitude of focusing on one's own business and not that of others. It is for the loan officer to do that. However, a group of respected farmers and farmers' wives on an elected board can ensure that repayable loans are made and apply social pressure to ensure that the branch is solvent so that lending can continue. The board brings local knowledge of farms and farmers that can supplement the intensive work of the loan officer and bring stability to the branch.

There are two reasons why it is essential to have substantial women's representation on such a board. First, women, in survey after survey, prove to be more committed to repaying loans than men. That attitude is important to a board. Second, women bring somewhat different specialized knowledge about both farming and the farmers applying for loans. Third, it is important not to have a bias against female-headed households, particularly since they tend to be on average lower income than male-headed households, and they face greater difficulties.

The pool of female-headed households tends to be low so farmers' wives are also logical board members. Women tend to be underrepresented on such boards partly because of nascent prejudice but more because they tend not to be included in the dissemination of knowledge about the new, technically-based agriculture. Experience on such a board is a logical stepping stone to other positions of influence.

An Apex Body The fourth essential is an apex body to raise funds for the branches to lend, manage sophisticated accounting and analysis, spot problems at a branch and rectify them, and set policy for the system. Large countries will probably have two levels: an appropriate number of unions to manage the branches and an overall apex at the national level, with an appropriate division of labor between them.

It is most efficient to manage the accounting at the apex level. The advent of the cell phone facilitates this—leaving the loan officer at the branch to primarily make farm plans and supervise lending and repayment—with the accounting data sent directly to the apex.

What Is the Timing for a National Institutional Finance System?

As modernization of agriculture begins, the core element is seed for improved varieties and the associated commercial fertilizer. These are both divisible inputs that lend themselves to self-financing. If that is the case, instituting the required finance program can be delayed for several years. The experience seems to be that without credit divisible input use rises on average to about 70 percent of the full profitability level. Credit is needed to go beyond that: and some farmers never start without credit.

There are of course resource shortages with the finance system not being the first priority. Perhaps the best position is to start early and build the system carefully and effectively to ensure full repayment of loans.

SPECIAL ISSUES

There are three especially important issues that cut across all agricultural finance systems: collateral; risk; and interest rate policy. Inflation is also a factor.

Collateral

Much of the literature on credit to farmers in low- and middle-income countries emphasizes the importance of lack of collateral as a barrier to lending. In that context, they note poor land records and lack of legal titling of land. Titling in the long run is a good idea, but providing collateral for agricultural loans should not be a primary reason.

It is a general rule in agricultural lending in high-income countries that operating capital loans (e.g., for fertilizer and seed) must be made on the basis of the profit and loss statement not on collateral such as land. That is the rule in high-income countries and it is essential in low-income ones because of difficulties in land titling and the reluctance of farmers to mortgage the land which is their source of livelihood. Intermediate-term loans, such as to buy a tractor or an irrigation system, can be backed by the instrument that is the purpose of the loan.

In high-income countries, much of agricultural lending is to purchase land either for farm enlargement or to finance generational changes. For that purpose, using land as collateral is usual and appropriate. However, that is essentially never important in low- and middle-income countries. Thus the issue of collateral should not be an important issue in such countries if a national system is in place with sound loans based on analysis of the profit to be made from the loan. The loan officer is central to success in that context.

Risk

Agricultural loans are often said to be high risk, that implies large risk premiums on the interest rate, which in turn makes the loans non-viable. Risk must be held at a very low level by detailed knowledge of the borrowers, including a farm plan, to ensure a high rate of return on investment of borrowed funds. That is the job of the specialized loan officer backed by a community-based board. Such systems have negligible default rates.

That in turn introduces a new risk—concentration of the loans geographically and in terms of weather. A large institution is needed to span a wide range of weather conditions. Even so, an occasional series of years with major price or weather event causes a large-scale inability to pay. As discussed earlier, most small commercial farmers can manage one bad year by using carry over crops and savings. With two bad years in a row, rescheduling of loans is the usual practice. In case of a larger event, governments step in to assist. The loan officer is key to that eventuality.

Interest Rate Policy

This book's consistent opposition to subsidies continues with respect to interest rates. They should not be subsidized. That makes it important to ensure low costs of lending to contain interest rates.

The data (e.g. Desai and Mellor 1993) are clear that, in contrast to high-income countries, in low- and middle-income countries farmer demand for credit is elastic with respect to the interest rate while savings are inelastic. The logic of that is that small commercial farmers have a high marginal propensity to save. They do so with little impact from the interest rate, presumably being driven by conservatism in the face of substantial fluctuations in weather and other attacks on production and income, and a desire to protect their assets in times of stress. They want to increase production, have opportunities to do so, and will borrow more as interest rates decline, increasing their ability to repay. Thus, from a growth point of view, keeping agricultural interest rates low is desirable. Without subsidies that means that costs must be kept low.

Three sets of costs must be covered: the pure interest rate for agency borrowing, for example from the central bank; the losses from bad loans; and the administrative costs of operating the system.

The pure interest rate should be as low as the central bank feels comfortable with in terms of its larger requirements. Off-lending at a low rate will increase borrowing, production, and incomes. Bonds with a government guarantee can be floated at low interest rates.

The loan losses should be kept to an absolute minimum, probably driven by an occasional personal disaster such as a death in the family and illness. The loan officer is to ensure that sound, profitable loans are made, ensuring full repayment. Successful systems have very low loan losses.

First and most important the loan officer must ensure that the loan is for a profitable purpose. Of course loan proceeds are fungible: they may be acquired on the basis of a profitable plan for increased income, but actually be spent on a wedding. That is not a problem as long as the loan was made in the context of a monitorable expansion of the business that ensures the increased income to pay the loan. The loan, after approval by the loan officer, should be approved by a loan committee of local farmers, and finally the loan needs to be approved by the union.

Once the loan is made the loan officer must track it regularly to ensure that the plan is being followed or modified appropriately to changing circumstances. That follow-up coincides with follow-ups to ensure repayment on time.

Administrative costs include the loan officer, modest other expenses at the branch, and a share of the costs of the union. Those costs must be contained.

In sum the costs might look like: three percent real interest, two percent for loan losses, and four percent for administrative costs, for a nine percent interest rate (abstracted from inflation coverage). Farmers I talk to see that as taking half the profit from investment—perhaps a sensible way to look at it.

Inflation

Central banks are concerned that the overall development effort is forcing inflation-creating deficit spending. Commencing large-scale lending to the small commercial farmer is seen as increasing that problem.

At least in the early stages of agricultural growth finance is used largely for short-term investments: the return from improved seed and fertilizer comes within a crop year, which is considerably less than a calendar year. Technically that has no inflationary effect. That assumes complete repayment and failure to repay is of course inflationary.

Interchangeable Savings, Credit, and Insurance

There is a literature (e.g. Karlan et al. 2012; Dercon and Christiaensen 2011; Barrett 2007; Besley 1995) that states that savings, credit, and insurance are substantially interchangeable and then makes the point that failure in these markets results in decisions that are rational for the individual but result in inefficiency as compared to well-operating markets. Besley (1995) is explicit about the lack of institutions for trading in risk in low- and middle-income countries. There is an implication that providing competitive markets in these areas would change decisions in a manner that would raise household incomes. They make special mention of failure in insurance markets, and of the role of informal markets. In reflecting that literature it is important to differentiate the poor from the small commercial farmer. These issues are discussed at various points in this book and summarized here.

The basic problem for the poor is that their incomes are so low that they cannot pay interest costs on debt or premiums on insurance even when they are available. That is compounded by the likelihood that their relatives are poor also and hence not a source of informal insurance. That is why the emphasis in micro-credit is first on savings, very small and presumably in the more favorable periods, then borrowing from the group's pool of savings. This book advocates micro-credit programs for the poor and public safety nets—and of course more employment to get out of poverty. In describing the behavior of the poor in adversity it is noted that they liquidate assets to preserve consumption and otherwise reduce consumption, with unfortunate effects.

The small commercial farmer is able to self-insure by storing cereals across years, is unwilling to pay the commercial cost of crop insurance, and more broadly insures on the informal market, borrowing from relatives. This book advocates specialized agricultural finance systems (lending and saving) and is clear that for all subsidies that subsidize crop insurance, even when at low cost from indexing, should not be instituted on the grounds of the high opportunity cost in income growth.

REFERENCES

Abate, G. T., Rashid, S., Borzaga, C., & Getnet, K. (2016). *Rural finance and agricultural technology adoption in Ethiopia: Does the institutional design of lending organizations matter?* (IFPRI discussion paper no. 1422). Washington, DC: International Food Policy Research Institute.

Ali, D. A., Deininger, K., & Duponchel, M. (2014). *Credit constraints and agricultural productivity and rural nonfarm participation: Evidence from rural Rwanda* (Policy Research Working Paper No. 6769). Washington, DC: World Bank Group.

Barrett, C. B. (2007). Displaced distortions: Financial market failures and seemingly inefficient resource allocation in low-income rural communities. In E. Bulte & R. Ruben (Eds.), *Development economics between markets and institutions: Incentives for growth, food security and sustainable use of the environment* (pp. 73–86). Wageningen: Wageningen Academic Publishers.

Besley, T. (1995). Savings, credit and insurance. In J. Behrman & T. N. Srinivasan (Eds.), *Handbook of development economics* (Vol. 3A, pp. 2123–2207). Amsterdam: Elsevier.

Dercon, S., & Christiaensen, L. (2011). Consumption risk, technology adoption and poverty traps: Evidence from Ethiopia. *Journal of Development Economics, 96*(2), 159–173.

Desai, B. M., & Mellor, J. W. (1993). *Institutional finance for agricultural development. An analytical survey of critical issues and food policy review* (1st ed.). Washington, DC: International Food Policy Research Institute.

Karlan, D., Osei-Akoto, R., & Udry, C. (2012). *Agricultural decision after relaxing credit and risk constraints* (NBER working paper series no. 18463). Cambridge, MA: National Bureau of Economic Research.

Khandker, S. R., & Koolwal, G. B. (2014). *Does institutional finance matter for agriculture? Evidence using panel data from Uganda* (Policy Research Working Paper No. 6942). Washington, DC: World Bank Group.

Nagarajan, G., & Meyer, R. L. (2005). *Rural finance: Recent advances and emerging lessons, debates and opportunities* (Reformatted version of Working Paper No. AEDE-WP-0041-05). Columbus: Department of Agricultural, Environmental, and Development Economics, The Ohio State University.

CHAPTER 15

Cities, Consumption, and Marketing Dynamics

The economic transformation, associated rapid growth of cities and small towns, rising incomes, and expanded export markets bring large changes in the level, location, and composition of agriculture consumption. These in turn bring major opportunity for change in the size and composition of agricultural production and a large increase in the proportion of consumer expenditure on post-farm marketing.

These are immense new opportunities for the small commercial farmer and consequently for further poverty reduction and economic transformation. They require major adjustments, particularly from government and all the institutions supporting agricultural growth (see for example Pinstrup-Andersen and Watson 2011). Those adjustments have often been lacking with consequent loss of opportunity for agricultural growth and poverty reduction.

The growth of cities immediately increases marketing expenditure. Marketing expenditure from the farmer to the major city consumer in a low-income country is in the order of 30 percent for cereals and 80 percent for fresh vegetables. More dramatic is the consumption shift, started by rising incomes and reinforced by urbanization, to livestock products and horticulture. These are high-value perishable commodities, increasing in middle-income countries to well over half of the value of farm-level agricultural output. The complementary rise of urban supermarkets has a further major impact.

These transformative changes have dominated the scene in many low- and middle-income countries far earlier in development than their original entrance in contemporary high-income countries. It tells much about how rapidly the importance of the marketing function has increased by noting that in the third edition of the premier book of articles on agricultural development (Eicher and Staatz 1998), the only article on marketing gave details of a technological change in rice processing! None of the above was mentioned. Now there is a multitude of research reports in this area (see for example the range of publications listed in the references by Reardon).

© The Author(s) 2017
J.W. Mellor, *Agricultural Development and Economic Transformation*,
Palgrave Studies in Agricultural Economics and Food Policy,
https://doi.org/10.1007/978-3-319-65259-7_15

There is also a shift in trade towards income-elastic tropical export commodities partly driven by rising incomes in low- and middle-income countries. Off-season horticulture is an example. That shift also occurs with traditional export commodities. For example, coffee and cocoa demand is shifting towards higher quality with a more elastic demand. The source of demand is shifting towards low- and middle-income countries with higher demand elasticities. Unfortunately, all these commodities have elastic prices for domestic consumption: failure to meet demand results in modest price increases that divert that demand to other goods and services. Thus the opportunity for small commercial farms is unnecessarily lost.

Foreign aid, with its direct action poverty focus, tends to concentrate within agriculture on the basic sources of low-cost calories, cereals, and root crops. This has helped divert attention from the large new opportunities for agriculture and poverty reduction as the economic transformation progresses.

In the context of these major changes, small commercial farmers maintain a cost of production comparative advantage but face problems in meeting the new requirements with respect to what they produce and in marketing. Those problems can be met but require further progress in the basic institutions and investments that drive agricultural production as well as new or improved institutional structures. Unfortunately, these opportunities have been poorly grasped in the bulk of middle-income countries. Specifically, the research and extension systems need to make large additions to all aspects of marketing.

The private sector maintains its dominance in marketing but must make major adaptations. Cooperatives have the opportunity for a greatly increased role, and government must define its rapidly changing requirements in these processes.

THE RAPID RISE OF CITIES

Urbanization has been growing rapidly in less-developed countries relative to more-developed countries as a proportion of total population (Table 15.1) (see also Cohen 2006; Duranton 2015). By the year 2030, 79 percent of urban populations will be in less-developed countries, compared to 44 percent in 1950. Urban growth typically occurs 60 percent from a natural increase (births in the urban area), 25 percent from migration from rural areas, an important factor, and 15 percent from reclassification of areas outside the city to inside the city.

Table 15.1 Distribution of urban population by development level

Region	1950	1975	2000	2030
More developed	58	46	31	21
Less developed	44	54	69	79
World	100	100	100	100

Source, World Bank. The more-developed regions comprise Europe, North America, Australia/New Zealand, and Japan. The less-developed regions comprise all regions of Africa, Asia (except Japan), Latin America and the Caribbean, plus Melanesia, Micronesia, and Polynesia

However, in low- and middle-income countries half the urban population is in cities of less than 500,000. In some countries, a substantial proportion of the rural non-farm population working in non-agricultural occupations is classified as rural including many in market towns with their economies still driven by expenditure from agricultural income. Despite these proportions, government urban development expenditures are generally concentrated in the dominant capital city to the neglect of smaller cities and towns. The literature is clear: this is unfortunate for national growth and of course even more so for rural development. Rapid agricultural growth drives growth of the market towns and governments need to facilitate that to favor a dispersed urbanization pattern. For a broad discussion of these issues see Vandercasteelen et al. (2016).

Cities have a two-way impact on agriculture. On the one hand, they provide a market. That is relatively unimportant for the income-inelastic cereals. As shown in Chap. 4, in a fast agricultural growth, low-income country only 11 percent of incremental income-inelastic cereal consumption was in urban areas. Urban areas are a major source of demand for high-value, income-elastic commodities such as livestock products and horticulture. Governments have an important function in expanding the research and extension systems for these commodities to facilitate rapid growth with constant prices. There is also a complex task of ensuring distribution and marketing services—not only in the form of good roads but also electrification for cold storage and other functions, and technical assistance.

The second function is providing jobs for the rural sector's surplus labor. As shown in Chap. 2 the rapid agricultural growth areas will assure employment for the local labor force, including in the market towns. But the less-favored agricultural areas need the support of growing urban areas. The Lewis view of a need to increase agricultural productivity so as to release labor from agriculture may once have been true but continued rapid population growth has turned that argument around.

Urban poverty is growing even as a proportion of total urban populations and represents in the order of 50 percent of the urban population in most African countries. It is closer to 30 percent in other low- and middle-income countries. That discrepancy is mainly because agriculture has, in most African countries, been neglected. In Africa, urban areas are growing substantially because of a push out of increasingly poor rural populations rather than the combined pull and push in other parts of the world. A recent World Bank Development Report observed that "cities in Africa are not serving as engines of growth and structural transformation. Instead, they are part of the cause and a major symptom of the economic and social crises that have enveloped the continent" (World Bank 2009).

The result is swelling ranks of people looking for, but generally not finding, urban employment. They make do in part-time employment in very low-paying jobs. Urban amenities are lacking in the slums that house the bulk of urban poor. However, improving them simply makes the urban areas relatively more attractive compared to stagnating rural areas and the numbers and proportions of urban poor increase.

PRIVATE SECTOR ROLE IN THE INCREASING SHARE OF MARKETING COSTS

In a traditional agriculture only a small proportion of production by small commercial farmers is marketed outside of the local community and that is almost entirely cereals. The marketing is handled largely by private traders. Their margins are, on average, high as evidenced by the decline in margins when competition increases by cooperatives entering the trade. When infrastructure is poor, that is with a high cost of local transport, there is often only one or a few traders who can demand high costs and thus earn high margins.

As marketing expands, markets can be made more productive by the provision of central marketing facilities. That is an important public investment function in low-income countries. Traders tend to locate near each other in an urban context, but government provision of market yards, with facilities for example for storage, and checking weights and measures, facilitates entry into trading, increases competiveness among traders, and has a direct influence on efficiency. The specifics of such investments must be developed in consultation with the trading community that will use the facilities. Numerous horror stories exist of expensive facilities located inconveniently so they are not being used by traders.

Traditionally, the private sector operates as a trader. Traders, by definition, are not experienced in producing added services as the need arises. That can become a modest problem in cereal marketing when new types of cereals arise or demand calls for some change in the form of the cereals. The big problem arises, however, as demand grows for perishables—livestock, livestock products, and horticulture. These require entirely different approaches to marketing. The private sector must rise to the occasion, but government could have an important role to play in understanding the constraints to private sector operation and taking appropriate facilitative action.

Prominent is the need for improved roads, but electrification soon becomes essential as the importance of perishables increases. Governments can help with training programs for the newly rising, more-complex marketing functions and sometimes by helping cooperatives with technical assistance to set new standards. Foreign aid can also provide important technical assistance from countries more advanced in these functions.

Cell phone use has increased explosively (Tadesse and Bahiigwa 2015; Goyal 2010) and is particularly helpful in marketing perishables.

THE CRITICAL ROLE OF HIGH-VALUE PERISHABLES

The demand for livestock and horticulture grows rapidly with economic transformation. The demand is elastic with respect to income. Similarly, the demand for agricultural exports expands. The huge change that needs to occur is from the dominance of cereals in growth to the dominance of livestock, horticulture, and exports. Note, however, the position stated long ago by Adam Smith: development increases diversification nationally but increases specialization within the firm (the farm).

Typically, in low- and middle-income countries the elasticity of demand for cereals ranges from 0.6 to 0.3 and lower. Consumption increases at a slower rate than income. In contrast, the income elasticity of demand for livestock and horticulture ranges from 1.0 to 1.5 for a high proportion of the population. Expenditure on these items increases faster than income. That means, in a country experiencing rapid agricultural and urban industrial growth demand grows at eight or nine percent per year. With that level of growth, after only a few years that set of commodities represents one-half of agricultural gross domestic product (GDP), providing two-thirds of a six percent growth rate. Most countries fail to realize the potential and almost all middle-income countries have agricultural growth rates in the three to four percent range.

Unfortunately, demand is also elastic with respect to price. That is to be expected in a low- or even middle-income country. People turn away from these "luxury" agricultural goods as the price rises. Thus, if production and marketing facilities present barriers to increased supply, the loss is not highly noticeable since modest price increases will bring supply and demand into balance at low levels of production and consumption. It is widely noted in low- and middle-income countries that, over time, relative prices of high-value agricultural produces do rise and balance supply and demand at a low level.

Those commodities are labor intensive, provide increased job opportunities in agricultural production, and reinforce the comparative advantage of the small commercial farmer in farm-level production. They provide a large income per unit area of land greatly increasing the incomes of small commercial farmers. That in turn increases the incomes of the rural non-farm population and drastically reduces poverty.

As the economic transformation proceeds the nutrition problem changes from one of inadequate calories to a complex one of inadequate minerals, vitamins, and other constituents of livestock and horticulture products. Rather than driving consumption away with rising prices, governments need to provide education as to the nutritional advantages of livestock and horticulture products and meet the growth in demand with efficient domestic production and marketing.

In high-income countries massive scale and extraordinary density of livestock production has become common and it has seeped into some low- and middle-income countries (e.g., China). In contrast, it is production by small commercial farmers that is most effective for poverty reduction. There are ample examples of efficient, competitive livestock production in tropical and sub-tropical low- and middle-income countries. The most noted example is India with a large-scale smallholder livestock sector.

Massive-scale livestock production is, in a sense, a global problem of the commons. Quite aside from the humane consideration pressed by animal rights' organizations, is the dominance of intensive livestock in the use of antibiotics to prevent disease. That has the consequence of a rapid building up of resistance to antibiotics with a cost in human lives. Small commercial farmers have less-dense livestock farming systems and can compete on a level playing field. Governments need to be aware of that and provide extensive research, extension, and finance assistance.

In contrast, there is now considerable publicity as to the effect of livestock on CO_2 levels, hence on global warming and encouraging a strong anti-livestock movement. It is of the utmost importance to recognize the extremely low levels of animal product intake in low- and middle-income countries. They should not be deprived owing to the greater animal product consumption in high-income countries. The anti-livestock position is grossly misplaced in the context of low- and middle-income countries.

Middle-income countries typically import a substantial share of their horti-culture and livestock products. Rarely will a comparative advantage in the context of efficient government programs favor that. This is the result of insuf-ficient attention by governments to their usual functions of research extension and infrastructure investment, and expanding them to focus on the high-value, income-elastic commodities.

However, the marketing and, to some extent, production problems are substantial. The highest priority is improving the road system. Poor roads penalize high-value perishables more than the basic cereal staples. Intensive horticultural production is limited to very short distances from all-weather paved roads. Data for Guatemala show that the bulk of horticulture production is within seven kilometers of urban areas and on an all-weather road. There are scale economies in marketing high-value perishables so one tends to get con-centrations of production on good roads and relatively near urban centers. Because they are generally perishable, cold storage and chilling facilities are essential and they must be low cost to be competitive. That requires rural electrification, which in any case increases consumer incentives for increased production by small commercial farmers.

The more complex production problems require major additions to research and extension capabilities in addition to a wide range of Ministry of Agriculture marketing services ranging from statistics needed for planning (both by the private sector and government), quality control, weights and measures, and technical assistance to marketing firms. Here again we see sense in the rule of thumb of ten percent of government expenditure on agriculture in order to cover the many items that do not make the high-level priority lists but are nevertheless essential.

EXPORT COMMODITIES

There has been a view that the demand for tropical export commodities is inelastic and that therefore increased production results in lower total value of output. That view was strongly held in important parts of the foreign intellectual and donor aid community, and combined with the previously noted preference for emphasizing low-cost calorie sources to focus on direct action to reduce poverty, deflected attention from tropical export commodities.

In the modern world, demand for important tropical exports, such as horti-culture, but also traditional exports such as coffee and cocoa, is growing partic-ularly in low- and middle-income countries (e.g., Trostle and Seeley 2013), but also to some extent in high-income countries. Concurrently, the demand for high-quality products is increasing relatively more rapidly. It is notable in the case of coffee that the quality shift is also towards geographic areas in which small commercial farmers have an advantage over the large-scale plantations that grew up in the colonial era. It is the higher elevations, tending towards a rugged topography, that produce the highest-quality coffee, but which create management problems for large-scale plantations, Reinforcing these arguments for the emphasis on tropical export commodities is the potential to greatly increase productivity for these commodities. That increased productivity in a dynamic demand environment leads to increased incomes and poverty reduction. Increased cash-crop production by small commercial farmers is poverty reducing.

For low- and middle-income countries, to take advantage of growing export potential requires three major actions: (1) an extra emphasis on infrastructure and education investment; (2) An extra emphasis on research and extension; and (3) an emphasis on institutions to adjust quickly to the dynamics of production and consumption. These high levels of activity are required in part because of the highly competitive international environment compared to producing purely for the domestic market.

First, as is continually emphasized, the rural infrastructure, especially roads and electrification, must be constantly upgraded with large annual investment, and similarly for rural education. These requirements are particularly important to the export sectors which tend to be complex and dynamic. While broad consumption and production needs should be met for incentive and productivity reasons, there may need to be a special orientation of infrastructure to the special needs of coffee, horticulture, or whatever the major export potential happens to be.

Second, research and extension expenditure must be even higher than the high level required for other parts of agriculture. That is partly because they are competing in international markets where others will be pushing the technical fields. The scope to reduce the cost of production is great and research and extension need to be relatively larger for these export commodities to ensure that shifting demand is met and that competitive cost reductions are realized. That is reinforced by the lack of investment by international bodies. For example, the highly productive CGIAR (Consultative Group on International Agricultural Research) does not work in the tropical export commodity areas. National spending must compensate for underspending in the international system. It would of course be helpful to have an international system that provided the same kinds of services to tropical export commodities as are provided to cereals and root crops by CGIAR. It is notable that there is a highly productive international center for vegetable production, located in Taiwan.

There is a tendency for export commodities to have major scale economies in marketing and, to some extent, in production services that reinforces the physical environment pressure to concentrate production in specialized geographic areas. However, concentrated areas of production create an insect and disease hazard. This is rarely a problem in high-income countries with highly developed agricultural research systems with the capacity to diagnose a problem early and find a varietal or other solution before the problem has spread. For low- and middle-income countries with poor research and extension systems it is common, as in Guatemala, for production (particularly of horticultural commodities) to expand rapidly for several years, then to suddenly be hit by a disease problem and for production to rapidly decline, often to be replaced by another commodity a few years later. That is an inefficient process that mitigates against a sustained, high-growth rate.

Third, export areas are probably more dynamic than production for the domestic market. Specifically, demand tends to be dynamic, including shifts in tastes, requiring a flexible private trade in which competition results in meeting shifting demand. It is common for countries with a major agricultural export commodity to develop an oversight agency to ensure that the needs of the sector are met. An excellent example is Anacaffe, in Guatemala, that is allocated a share of export revenues and serves to provide services to the coffee sector, including research and extension and advertising in consumer markets.

The bias against tropical export commodities has hit Sub-Saharan Africa especially hard because several of those countries have a strong comparative advantage over much of their geographic area in those commodities. This bias against commodities on which they have a comparative advantage is part of the explanation of Sub-Saharan Africa's poor agricultural and poverty reduction record. Those commodities require special attention in such countries because of their importance and the historical bias against them; they have a more central role in those countries to reduce poverty and increase food security. An exception to the bias against tropical export commodities was the large assistance by the World Bank to the smallholder tea sector in Kenya, and there should be more such exceptions.

SUPERMARKETS

Supermarkets came slowly to contemporary high-income countries allowing time for adjustment, but came rapidly to contemporary low- and middle-income countries. They demand a high uniform quality and buy in large quantities. Supermarkets, in effect, impose high standards for quality, health, and traceability, and are often more demanding than governments.

Much of the requirements for quality are in fact labor intensive, which plays to the advantage of the small commercial farmer, but such farmers require help in achieving collective action to ensure these standard. Numerous studies (e.g., von Braun and Webb 1989) and many of Reardon's publications (e.g., Reardon 2015; Reardon et al. 2003) document the potential for the small commercial farmer to be fully competitive. However, all those studies are clear: substantial government intervention is required to succeed and this is frequently not available.

The natural reaction of supermarkets to these problems is to turn to large-scale farmers and if they cannot supply or are not present, to import. In practice, where there are both large-scale farmers and small commercial farmers the bulk of the purchasing gravitates to the large-scale farmers. That means loss of a highly desirable form of income to the small commercial farmer and, most importantly, the loss of a major means of reducing rural poverty. There are five main actions required to ensure that small commercial farmers participate fully in the highly desirable new opportunities.

First, as is continually emphasized in this book in so many contexts, physical infrastructure, not just roads but also rural electrification, is needed at a redoubled effort; and the roads must be paved. Initial emphasis could be given to the areas with the greatest potential for exports and supermarket supply. However, such areas are difficult to predict, so it is better to move rapidly with all the high-potential production areas.

Second, the specialized agricultural finance system needs to be checked to be sure it can finance the wide range of non-land requirements for supermarket servicing. Well-controlled irrigation must be expanded wherever it is economic: let markets operate but provide the finance and other institutional structures so they operate efficiently. Mechanization may become more profitable and require financing. Similarly, for on-farm cooling investment—and on and on. Lending must not be restricted to bureaucratically determined inputs: again let the market operate, but with full knowledge and ample financing.

Third, the research extension system needs to greatly expand, not only for a broader commodity coverage but also with a critical mass in the marketing and distribution sectors. In high-income countries, distribution is a major part of the research extension system, which extends beyond farmers to the businesses supporting farmers. Middle-income countries, in particular, are missing a major element in growth and poverty reduction.

Fourth, cooperatives are the obvious solution to the problem of marketing to supermarkets or for export. These must be real cooperatives, with farmer control, not fake government-run ones. They need to lead the way in consolidating farmer output, ensuring that traceability requirements and on-farm requirements for small commercial farmers are met. There are important scale economies in marketing in the supermarket or export context. Small commercial farmers can meet those requirements with proper organization.

The problem is, of course, how to start. Starting a cooperative for marketing perishables to supermarkets is difficult if the market is not there and starting after the supermarkets have found an import potential may also be difficult. Government can play a role but with the standard danger that the cooperative will become a government bureaucracy with little or no farmer control or input, with a consequent likely failure.

However, if cooperatives already exist for grain marketing and fertilizer distribution that base may be used either by adding the perishable marketing function or spinning off a related institution. The need is for technically competent marketing functions, including interacting with the producing farmers on marketing-related production issues as well as helping reduce the cost of production. Strong links to research should be expanded, and of course close links with the supermarkets and exporters developed. Cooperatives need to provide the conglomeration that reaches supermarket buying levels and ensure quality. That requires close outreach to the participating farmers.

In limited situations, contract farming may solve the problem of aggregating small commercial farmers. In that case the processor, or possibly a retail chain, organizes farmers, provides credit and technical services, and most importantly provides the services for ensuring quality and on-time delivery. They contract with farmers to purchase their output subject to the farmer following the defined system. Potential is limited in low- and middle-income countries owing to a lack of private sector operatives ready to develop a well-staffed institutional structure. There is also the danger of lack of competition in those contexts and therefore exploitation of the small commercial farmer. Part of the support for contract farming has come from foreign aid agencies that have the view that government bodies cannot provide efficient services. That may be true in some cases, but then—as has constantly been shown here—those countries cannot develop the agricultural sector.

Supermarkets themselves may fill this function. They are not likely to do so if there is the alternative of buying from large commercial farmers. The supermarkets also have the option of importing, as has become common in Indonesia. As for contract farming, governments should not rely on the supermarkets filling this function to achieve aggregate impact—the government needs to secure national coverage.

Thus, cooperative are not the only means of providing scale economies and oversight. Best to let the market operate, but to push the cooperatives to compete with the other alternatives, and vice versa.

Fifth, a whole host of individually minor government efforts are required and must be swung towards perishable commodities. This include statistical services, research on these commodities, research on the marketing issues, extension on all that—and on and on. One of the major reasons for a poor response to the new opportunities is the continued focus of government institutions, often pushed in that direction by foreign aid, on basic cereal crops. As livestock and horticulture grow to be more than half of the value of agricultural output it is imperative that more than half of the agricultural research, extension, and other services be allocated to these commodities. They are always grossly underfinanced by low- and middle-income countries and need proportionately larger investments than cereals because of the variability within them compared to the relatively homogenous cereal sector. Since cereals are usually underfinanced the resources for perishables must be additive.

The critical issue is for government to recognize the importance of the small commercial farmer being mobilized to take advantage of the profitable potential in these commodities and be organized to deal with their disadvantage on the marketing side. The advantage is with the small farmers, given the labor intensity of production of these commodities, as long as they have full research and extension support and government diagnosis of the constraints on the marketing side, and government is mobilized to assist the private sector to provide the essential services.

A final note. The preceding chapters detailed the various public institutions required for modernizing agriculture. All the functions detailed in this chapter are implemented through expansion and via those institutions. The big task is creating those institutions. They must then grow and evolve to meet the changing circumstances of dynamic modernization and growth.

REFERENCES

Cohen, B. (2006). Urbanization in developing countries: Current trends, future projections and key challenges for sustainability. *Technology in Society, 28*(1), 63–80.

Duranton, G. (2015). Growing through cities in developing countries. *The World Bank Research Observer, 30*(1), 39–73.

Eicher, C. K., & Staatz, J. M. (1998). *International agricultural development* (3rd ed.). Baltimore: Johns Hopkins University Press.

Goyal, A. (2010). Information, direct access to farmers and rural market performance in central India. *American Economic Journal: Applied Economics, 2*(3), 22–45.

Pinstrup-Andersen, P., & Watson, D. D., II. (2011). *Food policy for developing countries: The role of government in global, national, and local food systems.* Ithaca: Cornell University Press.

Reardon, T. (2015). The hidden middle: The quiet revolution in the midstream of agrifood value chains in developing countries. *Oxford Review of Economic Policy, 31*(1), 45–63.

Reardon, T., Timmer, C. P., Barrett, C. B., & Berdegue, J. (2003). The rise of supermarkets in Africa, Asia and Latin America. *American Journal of Agricultural Economics, 85*(5), 1140–1146.

Tadesse, G., & Bahiigwa, G. (2015). Mobile phones and farmers' marketing decisions in Ethiopia. *World Development, 68*, 296–307.

Trostle, R., & Seeley, R. (2013). *Developing countries dominate world demand for agricultural products. Amber waves, economic research service.* Washington, DC: United States Department of Agriculture.

Vandercasteelen, J., Tamru, S., Minten, B., & Swinnen, J. (2016). *Cities and agricultural transformation in Africa: Evidence from Ethiopia* (ESSP working paper no. 91). Washington, DC: International Food Policy Research Institute.

von Braun, J., & Webb, P. J. R. (1989). The impact of new crop technology on the agricultural division of labor in a West African setting. *Economic Development and Cultural Change, 50*, 313–338.

World Bank Group. (2009). *World development report 2009: Reshaping economic geography.* Washington, DC: World Bank Group.

CHAPTER 16

The Role of Foreign Aid

Foreign aid to agriculture needs to return to basics. That is just as true for middle-income as for low-income countries. First, there is a large need for foreign assistance, both financial and technical, to the agricultural research/extension systems including higher education. Large-scale training, with the emphasis on advanced degrees, is central. Second, is assistance to credit institutions, micro-credit for the rural non-farm sector, and a specialized lending agency for the small commercial farmer, with the emphasis on making them fully self-supporting. Third, if large-scale funds are available then the accelerated expansion of rural roads, electrification, and schools with the emphasis on subsidized girls' participation is essential.

Unlike in the health sector, aid to agriculture must be in the context of a clear national plan for rapid growth with a national level of support which is substantial and growing relative to the total to provide a high level of long-term development. Without that, foreign aid should not be provided. It is likely that, at least initially, the bulk of African countries will prove to have governments that will not make that commitment. It happens that this is the most effective way for foreign aid to reduce poverty in the recipient countries.

Rapid agricultural growth in low- and middle-income countries is possible because of the potential for a rapid catch-up with the present high-income countries. Thus, technical assistance from those countries should be especially valuable.

Poverty reduction is central as an objective of foreign aid and we have shown that that requires the rapid development of agriculture, led by the small commercial farmer. The small commercial farmer is not alien to foreign aid staff—the family farms of Europe and North America are, in terms of labor force, small commercial farmers—but foreign aid officials, now as compared to the early years of foreign aid, normally have little knowledge of their own countries' agriculture and its supporting institutions.

Numerous, international, foreign aid meetings reiterate the importance of agriculture. Thus, it is surprising that foreign aid has had a mixed record in

© The Author(s) 2017
J.W. Mellor, *Agricultural Development and Economic Transformation*,
Palgrave Studies in Agricultural Economics and Food Policy,
https://doi.org/10.1007/978-3-319-65259-7_16

increasing growth and productivity of agriculture, and hence of poverty reduction. While much of the following exposition describes and explains the ineffectiveness of foreign aid to agriculture it is in the context of a historical period of great success and of at least a few current successes.

THE GOLDEN AGE OF FOREIGN AID TO AGRICULTURAL GROWTH

In the 1960s and 1970s, an important formative period for many of the then low-income countries, the United States provided continuous large-scale technical assistance to the development of agricultural higher education, research, and extension systems in the Asian and a few African countries. That assistance took the form of relationships between highly committed US universities and counterpart agricultural universities being developed in the respective assisted countries. The large role of the US land grant universities also led them, at that time, to be strong supporters of foreign aid in Congress. The international agencies also provided support in this area as did several bilateral agencies.

Under foreign aid pressure, receiving countries gave more attention to agricultural growth than they had intended. The national agricultural universities then provided a long-term steady stream of well-trained professionals to the agricultural sector as well as solidifying institutional structures to undertake agricultural research. Large numbers of professionals were sent to the United States for graduate level training. The results are still there several decades after the grossly premature ending of those programs. Even in my work in recent decades, and IFPRI's work, it is high-level personnel with foreign training from those days who provide the core of national support. Asia, and even more so, Africa would benefit immensely from the reintroduction of those extraordinarily effective programs. Of course the capacity to implement such programs has declined but could quickly be reestablished from a remaining core effort.

Foreign aid donors, almost without exception, joined in creating and providing continuous financing of the Consultative Group on International Agricultural Research (CGIAR), notable as one of the great success stories in accelerating agricultural growth in low- and middle-income countries. The United States has been a major supporter from the beginning and continues to be, at a declining level, including providing substantial technical assistance and many deeply committed and distinguished Center Board members and members of various CGIAR commissions.

The other foreign aid success is in the safety net and food aid programs that lifted very large numbers of rural families out of poverty, particularly in periods of extreme stress. The human benefits of those programs are immense and they have continued throughout the history of foreign aid. They of course reach only a small fraction of those under the poverty line and are short-term palliatives not long-term solutions to the underlying problems. They are less valuable in the long run than the research and trained personnel efforts cited above. The palliatives continue, while much of the long-term solutions terminated.

FOREIGN AID TO AGRICULTURE

Foreign aid in total increased at an average rate of 2.3 percent per year from 1960 to 2010. That roughly equals the population growth rate in Africa. Foreign aid growth accelerated somewhat in the several years following 2010. There was a sharp drop in the late 1990s made up for by a subsequent sharp increase in the early 2000s to get back directly on the trend growth rate. For a broad review of foreign aid see Lancaster (2008).

Foreign aid to agriculture averaged 12 percent of total aid in the 1980s, comparable to education and twice that of health, including population. It then steadily declined to reach a low point of 3.3 percent in 2003–2005 and then stabilized around five percent subsequently. Given the central role of research to agricultural modernization it is striking that from 1984/86 to 1990/93 US aid to agricultural research declined by 73 percent! From 1990 to 1993 total foreign aid to agriculture decline by one-quarter for the United States and by one-third for the multilateral agencies. So much for continuity and reliability. It is only for the early 20-year period that foreign aid allocations showed any sense of priority to agriculture.

FOREIGN AID TO AFRICA

Foreign aid now gives special attention to Africa where the agriculture sector-specific allocations increased by 2.3 times from 2002 to 2010 (Table 16.1). However, the proportion allocated to agriculture held steady at between 6.5 and 7.8 percent of the total. That is twice the proportion for agricultural aid to all regions, but hardly shows a high priority to agriculture or, implicitly, to poverty reduction. The rest of the money was scattered over a large number of areas, presumably insufficient to have any significant impact.

Among African countries, Ethiopia has been the largest recipient of agricultural aid (see the sample of countries in Table 16.2). That is consistent with its unique focus on agriculture as central to its overall development strategy. However, Tanzania, which has not had such a focus, is essentially at the same level. It is also notable that Ethiopia is so high largely because of a large allocation from the multilateral donors who provided even more aid to Tanzania's agriculture.

As is common in Africa, several small donor projects have had success, but they do not add up to an aggregate impact. Rwanda, which has recently shown a commitment to agriculture comparable to Ethiopia's, is way down the list regarding assistance to its agriculture, although it is of course a very small country. Ghana, which for a substantial period showed rapid growth in agriculture, was one of five countries with over $100 million per year in aid to agriculture but in that case two-thirds came from bilateral donors. The agricultural growth success was largely in the coffee sector. Côte D'Ivoire, with a very important agricultural export sector and at least an early emphasis on agriculture, received 80 percent of its agricultural aid from the multilateral donors.

Table 16.1   Trend in foreign aid (average) disbursed to agriculture in Sub-Saharan Africa (constant 2010 USD millions)

Year	Total sector allocable	Agriculture allocation	Agricultural aid (%)
2002	268.08	18.22	6.8
2003	291.04	21.23	7.29
2004	333.28	22.76	6.83
2005	353.52	23.45	6.63
2006	392.45	25.83	6.58
2007	457.51	30.85	6.74
2008	510.79	32.93	6.45
2009	564.88	44.08	7.8
2010	611.74	46.62	7.62

Source: Alabi (2014); IFPRI

Table 16.2   Average of bilateral and multilateral aid to agriculture, selected countries, 2002–2010, millions of US$

Country	Total agriculture aid	Bilateral agriculture aid	Multilateral agricultural aid
Ethiopia	126	53	73
Tanzania	123	34	89
Kenya	75	42	33
Rwanda	36	19	17
Mali	104	56	48
Ghana	101	64	37
Senegal	66	48	18
Côte D'Ivoire	42	7	35

Source: OECD

It is striking that the allocation to sub-sectors within agriculture shows much less sense of priority in Africa as compared to the Far East (Table 16.3) (Mellor et al. 1987). In the Far East the three top categories accounted for two-thirds of the aid to agriculture. Agricultural policy is of course important, but in Africa 22 percent of resources went to that, compared to nine percent in the Far East. Perhaps that is a reflection of a worse policy environment in Africa, but as pointed out later in this section that should be a reason not to allocate to the sector. The other large allocation is to "agricultural development", which is a varied collection of field-based direct development efforts that have little or no aggregate impact, even though they may be beneficial to the small proportion of the population covered. They are not even set up to serve as pilot projects for later nationwide expansion. Most striking, the proportion of agricultural aid to research was only 8.5 percent, not much more than the Far East.

Table 16.3 Aid allocations to agricultural sub-sectors, Sub-Saharan Africa and the Far East

| Utilization | Sub-Saharan Africa | | | Far East | | |
	Mean	%	Standard deviation	Mean	%	Standard deviation
Agrarian reform	5.18	0.35	2.58	8.50	1.65	5.13
Cooperative	21.56	1.46	7.39	1.39	0.27	0.84
Agricultural development	366.08	24.78	148.68	111.85	21.66	33.69
Agricultural extension	65.69	4.45	15.12	9.53	1.85	2.13
Agricultural finance	19.85	1.34	17.04	15.30	2.96	16.41
Agricultural input	78.02	5.28	89.78	15.52	3.00	11.09
Agricultural policy and administration	318.69	21.57	145.83	45.08	8.73	20.01
Agricultural research	125.94	8.52	86.75	30.45	5.90	29.78
Agricultural service	59.86	4.05	20.24	3.76	0.73	1.96
Training	23.95	1.62	16.31	4.71	0.91	1.29
Alternative development	7.53	0.51	12.72	1.89	0.37	1.73
Export crop production	36.17	2.45	42.03	7.60	1.47	7.16
Food crop production	111.11	7.52	29.95	16.86	3.26	7.03
Land development	55.27	3.74	13.17	68.63	13.29	31.99
Livestock	55.99	3.72	9.36	12.28	2.38	2.97
Postharvest and processing	11.18	0.96	7.11	3.09	0.60	1.40
Veterinary	7.63	0.52	3.47	9.71	1.88	6.45
Agricultural water resources	108.92	7.57	33.18	150.24	29.09	77.48
Total agricultural aid	1477.60	100.00	503.23	516.43	100.00	101.51

Source: Computed by the author

THE IMPACT OF AID

Particularly in Africa, growth seems to have slowed in periods of increasing aid and accelerated in periods of declining aid. Doucouliagos and Paldam (2014) find, in a correlogram, no sign that aid can explain growth. Growth does seem to explain aid. That is, faster growth attracts more aid. In a further analysis of 141 papers with 1177 estimates of the effect of aid on growth they find a statistically significant positive effect but one so small as to be of no economic significance. They make a major point of "publication bias" (the preference for articles that have positive rather than negative findings) and correct for that. That needs to be kept in mind in the following analyses. See also Alabi (2014).

Juselius et al. (2014) find that in "27 of 36 Sub-Saharan African countries aid had a significantly positive effect on either investment or GDP or both. In seven countries the effect is positive but not significant. In two countries there is a significant negative effect." In an influential *American Economic Review* paper Burnside and Dollar (2000) found "that the impact of aid is greater in a good policy environment than in a poor policy environment." Also, "policy seems to be more important for aid effectiveness in lower income countries." However, they found that the positive policy effect was entirely from multilateral aid (for a broader discussion of multi-lateral versus bilateral aid see Mellor and Masters (1991)). They found "no significant tendency for total aid or bilateral aid to favor good policy." Policy was a set of macro policies. They also found "a marked trend towards better policies among low-income countries which means that the climate for effective aid is improving."

Charron (2011) shows "multilateral aid [is] strongly and robustly associated with lower corruption levels and that bilateral aid is insignificant in this regard."

An IFPRI study (Islam 2011) of Sub-Saharan Africa shows from an econometric analysis that foreign agricultural aid has a significant (at the 10 percent level) positive impact on agricultural gross domestic product (GDP) and agricultural productivity, and that disaster and conflict have a positive effect on the level of aid. However, a different approach testing for causality shows that foreign aid to agriculture does not influence growth in agricultural GDP.

Most convincing, from her deeply researched, definitive, book length analysis of foreign aid to agriculture in Africa, Uma Lele (1991; Lele and Nabi 1991) concludes, in cautious World Bank speak, that it is "difficult to find much connection between where donor assistance went (to agriculture) and where growth occurs." See also Riddell (2008) and Sachs (2005).

Perhaps the overall conclusion is that foreign aid may be effective in the exceptional cases in Africa where the government is committed and effective in implementing policies that ensure rapid growth in agriculture.

THE NEGATIVE IMPACT OF RAPIDLY CHANGING FASHION

Agriculture has suffered most from the rapidly changing fashion in foreign aid. This is partly because the greater relative emphasis on technical assistance provides a greater visibility and partly because agriculture is such a politicized sector in most high-income countries. However, the sector suffers more because the core of growth is public sector institutional development. That takes time and continuity. In the 1970s and 1980s, foreign aid maintained a steady large focus on agriculture and the resource flows were reliable. The subsequent radical decline in foreign aid to agriculture, then a wildly fluctuating horizontal path, made institution building far less efficient and indeed took the focus off much of that effort.

Foreign aid to agriculture seems to follow agricultural prices. When prices are down in the donor country, with bumper crops, interest and funding of agriculture drops. When a few bad crop years occur then interest jumps, flashy donor meetings on the agricultural crisis occur, rhetoric escalates immensely, and funding bumps up somewhat, only to decline again as crops improve.

In recent decades, fashions have popped up which not only detract from the growth/poverty focus, but lead to inefficiency in achieving the objectives of the fashion as well. The general problem is a specific focus that abstracts from and detracts from the priority thrusts for modernization of agriculture and poverty reduction. Three fashions are of note.

First, several chapters in this book focus on the vital role of women in rural modernization, their unnecessary decline in influence, and inadequate assistance to women in filling new or modified roles, particularly in local and national development institutions, the rural non-farm sector, and in livestock production. These have rarely been the focus of gender programs. A special emphasis on rural women, yes, but not a focus on ensuring they are leaders in the mainstream processes and, most important, have full access to rural modernization information. There is a focus on how much women labor in the fields, but power and influence come not from laboring in the hot sun but from modern information. As household income rises women tend to withdraw from laboring in the fields.

Climate change in low- and middle-income countries needs to be dealt with in the context of raising the poor substantially above the poverty line in the context of achieving rapid agricultural growth. Focus on climate change does not change the basics of agricultural growth. It does call for more production research and investment in water resource generation and conservation. The same as for gender, for climate change-oriented foreign aid to be effective requires mainstreaming in the growth and poverty reduction processes.

The private sector dominates agricultural growth, but focusing directly on privatization misses the crucial complementarities. Foreign aid must focus first on the public sector institutions essential to rapid agricultural growth. That greatly increases scope for the private sector. As the new enlarged functions for the private sector arise, foreign aid can provide vital technical assistance to ensure the adaptation of traditional management to new situations.

Recognizing the importance of each of the topics but implementing them in the context of the larger objectives will improve the speed of reaching the larger objectives and succeed more fully in forwarding these newly found objectives.

WHY WAS AID TO AGRICULTURE SO EFFECTIVE IN THE 1970S AND 1980S?

From 1976 to 1990 agriculture received on average 12 percent of sectorial allocated aid. Those were years of rapid growth in Asian agriculture. Not only was the percentage high, but the absolute amount was high also. Thus, part of the answer to the question is much greater funding. But an earlier section indicated that funding tends to follow growth not the reverse. So we must look deeper.

The background was a much greater and near universal emphasis on agriculture. I remember when Nicki Kaldor, a star Cambridge University macroeconomist, lectured in India, he would first say that agriculture was so critical to the country's future and that he assumed the country had experts for that, and then he would go on to his macro-economics. Can you imagine a contemporary macro-economist stating that in a public speech? Rather, "maybe agriculture is important, if so the market will take care of it."

It was a time when the United States Department of Agriculture was in a down-sizing period and so suddenly a large number of highly competent agriculturists of all disciplines was available for foreign aid. Concurrently, colonial institutions were winding down and again large numbers of experienced agriculturalists became available to foreign aid agencies, particularly the multilateral ones.

The highest-level agriculturalist in the World Bank reported directly to the President. The second rank from the top, in the American aid program, would include agriculturalists. The Chief Economist for the Agency could be an agricultural economist with a large, highly trained staff and reporting directly to the Administrator (head). Now the highest-level agriculturalist is many layers down the structure. The heads of agricultural divisions in all of foreign aid, multilateral and bilateral, were headed by technically trained and experienced agriculturalists. Now those divisions are often called rural development rather than agriculture and their heads, often as not, are not technically knowledgeable agriculturists. The bottom line is that in foreign aid technical competence was then far greater and reached far higher levels of influence.

The United States was particularly important in foreign aid in those days, and was heavily staffed with agriculturalists, supplemented by the large numbers of agricultural staff stationed in developing countries by American contract universities. That aid took the position that higher education in agriculture was lacking in Asian countries and was the most important institutional structure. Because of the nature of the institutions in the United States that meant a major emphasis on training people at the tertiary level to staff agricultural institutions, in research and in extension. The three most important institutions—agricultural universities, research, and extension—all received large, steady support.

The heads of the land grant institutions in turn influenced aid policy and Congress: they were a powerful lobby. Concurrently, the top of the aid institution was committed to agriculture and pushed hard at the highest levels of recipient governments for a matching concern, often with considerable success, against the heavy inclination to want to become modern immediately by investing in heavy industry according to the most fashionable economic theories of the time. The large numbers of highly competent technical assistance people added to the reach of emphasis on agriculture.

That massive foreign aid-driven institution building throughout Asia and in a few early independent countries in Africa (e.g. Ethiopia), built institutions that in general lasted and formed the basis for continuous progress. Even in the early stages they were critical to the rapid spread of the new cereal varieties coming out of the international research institutions.

It took the United States 50 years from the beginning of development of the land grant system, to having a noticeable impact on agricultural growth beginning in the late 1920s. So, ending that assistance in Asia and Africa after 20 years was grossly premature. And, it is true that in India institutions have since deteriorated under the pressure of communalism and corruption (Tamboli and Nene 2011). Everywhere the growth has been slower as a result of drawing back from those efforts. However, what potential we see now is partly due to those early, institution-building efforts.

What is the solution? The low- and middle-income countries are going to have to use their capacity to understand the role of agriculture and its requirements, put that into a clear strategy as in CAADP (Comprehensive Africa Agriculture Development Programme) for Africa, and use that to channel foreign aid, as does Ethiopia. They will have to recognize the key role in the catch-up of technical assistance and insist on its provision. That in turn will require returning the aid donor's country missions to a broad latitude for decision making, and hence ability to respond to and mesh with national priorities, and of course more willingness to reduce aid in inhospitable contexts.

Two countries have done very well in agricultural growth and its associated rapid decline in poverty without continuation of the high level and quality of foreign assistance discussed above for the 1970s and 1980s. They are Ethiopia and China. Both illustrate that public institutions are critical to rapid agricultural growth, that learning from other countries may involve very long lags between learning and fully impacting growth, and that the methods of learning may be quite convoluted. These points also illustrate the "better late than never" aspect. Foreign aid should be far more efficient, and faster, than the convoluted processes described below.

Ethiopia's success has been eveident for the past 20 years and is continuing. There were three elements in that success that had a basis in foreign aid.

First of all, Ethiopia was one of the few African countries to benefit from the golden age of US foreign assistance to agriculture. An excellent agricultural university was built which pumped out substantial numbers of well-trained agriculturalists, year after year, and trained sufficient numbers that several other agricultural universities have developed. Even with the heavy losses of trained people during the period of disruption prior to the present government, the numbers were large, especially compared to other African countries.

Second, partly because of the preceding, the African Union's very large, donor-supported effort to develop an Africa-wide strategy (African Union 2010) provided a blueprint that could be adapted by Ethiopia's own trained people. It was not only an excellent blueprint, but it was easily epitomized as being an African, and hence an Ethiopian, framework. The government was repeatedly explicit that this was the plan to be modified to fit Ethiopia.

Third, Prime Minister Meles, a strong leader, laid out his strategy of Agricultural Development Led Industrialization (ADLI). He repeatedly said that, during the period when he was leading troops that eventually took over the government, one of the books he read (he had a horseback load of books wherever he went) was entitled Agriculture on the Road to Industrialization. He converted it to a much better title but, more importantly, he saw in it a means of getting rural political support for his vision of a transformed economy. He then sold that strategy to the nation's people: it became their strategy.

The Chinese success in rapid agricultural growth is more complex. First came the radical land reform but, as in the case of Ethiopia, a land reform that did not lead directly to rapid growth. Second, and decades later, decision making at the farm level was turned over to the small commercial farmer. Third came the policies unleashing the peasantry and rapid growth. In both Ethiopia and China there was a long time period from radical land reform to rapid growth.

But, in China too, there was a foreign aid institutional catching-up effort, although in China's case its impact was nascent for a long period. Way back in the 1920s and 1930s two Cornell University connected individuals had a major impact on China. Professor Love, a plant scientist, played a major role in developing agricultural science in Nanking University. A large generation of Chinese scholars were trained in that tradition and multiplied. Concurrently, J. Losing Buck (the husband of a Nobel prize-winning author and also Cornell University associated) conducted massive farm surveys in China, bringing a series of Cornell Agricultural Economics Professors to China to work on that survey and to interact with Chinese scholars. From that massive, nationwide survey came a widespread understanding of the true nature of Chinese small commercial farmers and what was needed for them to succeed, and a core of academic excellence for such work. That work is still quoted by China scholars, but more important it started a tradition and trained a lineage of people who could act when finally the circumstances were right.

In no case is rapid agricultural growth achieved largely with the efforts of foreigners, but learning from them is important—it is catch-up growth. In these two cases, the process was drawn out and indirect but no less important.

THE CONTENT OF FOREIGN AID AND AFRICA

Barring a few countries in Asia, the prime problem of getting agriculture started now lies in Africa. Only Ethiopia has been a continuous major success story. What can foreign aid do? The context is much more favorable than at a comparable stage in Asia. First, the knowledge base, although little used by foreign aid agencies, is far superior to that when Asian countries were making their start. There is not only a great wealth of experience, good and bad, but an explosion of academic research. Second, there are prime examples of contemporary success: Ethiopia and several Asian countries. Third, the trade environment is much larger and more open, facilitating large-scale exports of high-value commodities.

Foreign aid to agriculture has tended to be cereal and basic food crop oriented. That has been disadvantageous to Africa since many countries have a comparative advantage in tropical export commodities which receives little emphasis. A striking exception is the substantial foreign aid received by Kenya for its smallholder tea sector—with a major impact not only on that sector but on the overall agricultural growth rate. The exception probably arose from the timely availability of expatriates with a lot of East African experience to the staff of the World Bank and UK agencies. That success underlines the missed opportunity more generally in Africa.

The urgency of course is huge. Most importantly, population has been growing rapidly for a whole generation with little done to provide the growth for absorbing it. The size of the underemployed, desperately poor, rural non-farm sector is far greater than a generation ago. Each passing decade makes the job of poverty reduction far greater.

The principal lessons are clear. First, technical assistance to help develop, nation by nation, a strategy and vision based on CAADP and the Ethiopian vision and strategy—a major role for agriculture in the economic transformation. In that context, the emphasis was placed on agricultural growth carried out largely by the small commercial farmer. Second, assisting to shift finances so the CAADP target of ten percent of government expenditure devoted to agriculture is met. Third, capital assistance and technical assistance to ensure massive investment in rural infrastructure and education. Fourth, large-scale (a few orders of magnitude larger than present), technical assistance and budget support for agricultural research and extension, and rapid expansion in the private sector of improved variety seed production and fertilizer use, growing at ten percent per year. Fifth, building the Ministry of Agriculture to fill the multiple functions needed to support broad-based, rapid agricultural growth. The analytical task is to find the bottlenecks with no ideology about where and when. With those priorities ensured at a high level, effort can go into innumerable areas that require technical assistance to build the base for later expansion once the seed fertilizer revolution has provided a sustained and rapid growth.

FOOD AID

Food aid is covered in Chap. 4 in the context of poverty and food security. In brief, it is seen: as a positive safety net for the poor, being additional to the total of such assistance; as generally well run by the major food aid donors; and as not reducing incentives for agricultural growth (Mellor and Pandya-Lorch 1992). Those are similar to the conclusions reached by Uma Lele (1991) in her exhaustive analysis for the World Bank of aid to African countries (see also Lele and Nabi 1991; Barrett and Maxwell 2007; Mellor 1989; Mellor and Pandya-Lorch 1992). For a broad review of food assistance with the emphasis on the range of instruments for its provision, see Lentz et al. (2013).

CGIAR: CLOSING ON SUCCESS

CGIAR has been a great success story for foreign aid to agriculture. The underlying problem for the system is the increasing micro-control by the high-income donor countries and the transfer of power from the high-level administrators who started the system to lower-middle-level foreign aid and foreign policy administrators and a concurrent increase in non-scientists (physical or biological for the crop and livestock centers) on Center Boards and even occasionally as Directors General of Centers, contrary to the norms for science research centers in high-income countries.

The instrument for the change is increasing bureaucratic donor control of Center budgets through special projects. Initially, each Center's budget was entirely in block grant's, not tied to specific donor-funded projects. Each Center's Board, management, and staff, working together and interacting with their host countries, determined the research program. By 1990, one-third of the funds were tied to special projects—projects initiated and supervised by donor country staff. By 2004 over half and by 2012 over 80 percent, were tied.

What is wrong with special projects? First they are developed by staff from high-income countries who are less knowledgeable than the researchers in low- and middle-income countries or the CGIAR staff. In that context, there is more attention to direct action according to the shifting fashions in national foreign aid objectives than to the realities of what biological science research can do. The effect is to reduce the emphasis on technology that increases yields, which is what the system succeeded at originally and is central to achieving any of the broader objectives.

What is to be done? The Centers are so vital to low- and middle-income countries that they need to contribute significantly to the budget, and with that gain (disproportionately) a power position in negotiations as to how the system is run. That is not easy to achieve since most low- and middle-income countries are massively underspending on their own national systems, in effect because they do not attach a high value to rapidly growing their agricultural sector—they are more urban oriented.

EFFECT OF FOREIGN AID TO AGRICULTURE ON THE AGRICULTURE OF EXPORTING COUNTRIES

Foreign aid agencies are responsive to their national political context as well as the values of their supporters. The latter leads to an emphasis on poverty reduction. That of course leads to an emphasis on rural areas and is consistent with the thrust of this book. However, the indirect processes described in this book may be too complex for constituency support. That requires simplifying the message.

A more complex problem arises with rural agricultural areas of high-income countries and their powerful lobbying institutions. At the level of broad foreign aid, the processes described in this book lead generally, in middle-income countries, to increased agricultural imports and hence agricultural exports of the aid-providing nations, particularly the United States. Development assistance accelerates economic growth and that causes a rapid increase in demand for livestock products. That demand grows sufficiently rapidly that supply tends to fall behind increased demand, which leads to imports. Note the big increase in China's livestock imports. More importantly, as their domestic production of livestock grows they cannot keep up with the demand for feed grains and protein sources and import large quantities. China again is a good example. Note the dominance of China in soybean imports. Overall low- and middle-income countries have a high population density which means that even at best they have trouble keeping up with growth in domestic demand for livestock and livestock feed when overall growth is rapid.

Aid to agriculture accelerates agricultural growth and its powerful multipliers to the non-agricultural sector and leads to imports as above. Those multipliers are the big story in this book. An additional point is that US farmers are, in general, traditional churchgoers and therefore want to help poor people. It is agricultural growth that ultimately lifts the poor.

References

African Union. (2010). *Comprehensive African Agricultural Development Plan (CAADP)*. Addis Ababa: The New Partnership for Africa's Development.

Alabi, R. A. (2014). *Impact of agricultural foreign aid on agricultural growth in sub-Saharan Africa: A dynamic specification* (AGRODEP Working Paper No. 6). Washington, DC: International Food Policy Research Institute.

Barrett, C. B., & Maxwell, D. (2007). *Food aid after fifty years: Recasting its role*. Abingdon: Routledge.

Burnside, C., & Dollar, D. (2000). Aid, policies and growth. *The American Economic Review, 90*(4), 847–868.

Charron, N. (2011). Exploring the impact of foreign aid on corruption: Has the "anti-corruption movement" been effective? *The Developing Economies, 49*(1), 66–88.

Doucouliagos, H., & Paldam, M. (2014). *Finally a breakthrough? The recent rise in the size of the estimates of aid effectiveness* (Economics Working Papers No. 7). Washington, DC: World Bank Group.

Islam, N. (2011). *Foreign aid to agriculture review of facts and analysis* (IFPRI Discussion Paper No. 1053). Washington, DC: International Food Policy Research Institute.

Juselius, K., Møller, N. F., & Tarp, F. (2014). The long-run impact of foreign aid in 36 African countries: Insights from multivariate time series analysis. *Oxford Bulletin of Economics and Statistics, 76*(2), 153–184.

Lancaster, C. (2008). *Foreign aid: Diplomacy, development, domestic politics*. Chicago: University of Chicago Press.

Lele, U. J. (1991). *Aid to African agriculture. Lessons from two decades of donors' experience*. Baltimore: Johns Hopkins University Press. pp. xix + 627pp.

Lele, U., & Nabi, I. (1991). Concessionary and commercial flows in development. In I. Nabi (Ed.), *Transitions in development: The role of aid and commercial flows*. San Francisco: ICS Press.

Lentz, E. C., Barrett, C. B., Gómez, M. I., & Maxwell, D. G. (2013). On the choice and impacts of innovative international food assistance instruments. *World Development, 49*, 1–8.

Mellor, J. W., & Masters, W. A. (1991). The changing roles of multilateral and bilateral foreign assistance. In U. Lele & I. Nabi (Eds.), *Transitions in development: The role of aid and commercial flows* (pp. 331–372). San Francisco: ICS Press.

Mellor, J. W., & Pandya-Lorch, R. (1992). Food aid and the development in the MADIA countries. In U. Lele (Ed.), *Aid to African agriculture: Lessons from two decades of donor experience*. Baltimore: The Johns Hopkins University Press.

Mellor, J. W. (1989). Agricultural development in the third world: The food, poverty, aid, trade nexus. *Choices, 4*(1), 4–8.

Mellor, J. W., Delgado, C. L., & Blackie, M. J. (Eds.). (1987). *Accelerating food production growth in sub-Saharan Africa*. Baltimore: The Johns Hopkins University Press.

Riddell, R. C. (2008). *Does foreign aid really work?* Oxford: Oxford University Press.

Sachs, J. D. (2005). *Investing in development: A practical plan to achieve the millennium development goals*. London: Earthscan.

Tamboli, P. M., & Nene, Y. L. (2011). *Revitalizing higher agricultural education in India: Journey towards excellence*. Secunderabad: Asian Agri-History Foundation.

CHAPTER 17

Conclusion

In keeping with Ernest Hemingway – tell the story in six words:[1]

Sustained rapid agricultural growth. Poverty gone.

Part 1 of this book explains how that happens. Part 2 states the initial conditions. Part 3 tells us how to do it. This chapter concludes in two contexts: first, national planning for implementation; and second, departures from current conventional wisdom.

Achieving rapid agricultural growth and rural poverty reduction in low- and middle-income countries is very different to current practice in high-income countries. The feasible rate of change is far higher because of the potential for catch-up growth. All the essential institutional structures and investments are in full operation in high-income countries with built-in mechanisms for adjustment to changing conditions. They are roughly on auto-pilot.

The task in low- and middle-income countries is building and adapting to changing circumstances the critical set of institutions and making large investments for agricultural growth. That is to be done largely in the public or quasi-public sector and in the context of acute scarcity of financial and trained personnel resources. That requires explicit national vision, strategy, and planning and priorities or sequencing of efforts.

The private sector implements the changes to achieve growth and poverty reduction targets. A government's task is to incentivize them, facilitate them, spur them on, and fill the gaps. As in high-income countries, the small commercial farmer requires a substantial set of public institutions.

© The Author(s) 2017
J.W. Mellor, *Agricultural Development and Economic Transformation*,
Palgrave Studies in Agricultural Economics and Food Policy,
https://doi.org/10.1007/978-3-319-65259-7_17

NATIONAL PLANNING FOR IMPLEMENTATION

There are three components to national planning for implementation: vision and strategy from the Chief of State; detailed planning from the Ministry of Agriculture; and planning and coordination with other ministries.

Chief of State

Success in sustained rapid agricultural growth requires mobilizing broad national support and intense rural support. The Chief of State must articulate the vison and strategy. It is the politician, not the academic, who successfully phrases and expresses the vision and strategy.

Prime Minister Meles, for very low-income Ethiopia, stated the vison as becoming a middle-income country in 25 years: given the starting point that was an expansive vison. The strategy was "Agricultural Development Led Industrialization." Prime Minister Meles ensured that the vision and strategy reached not only the government bureaucracy but the people throughout the nation. A large extension service assured that broad sustained acceptance in rural areas was achieved.

Part 1 provides many components of a vision that can assist a Chief of State in defining a vision and a strategy for widely participatory sustained rapid growth in agriculture that will largely end poverty. Everyone will have adequate food, and feel food secure. Along the way, rural people will have all-weather roads and electrification, and will be educated for good jobs. Small towns will grow rapidly and receive the full complex of urban amenities. Urban unemployment will largely disappear, and jobs for educated young people will grow rapidly. It will be a different country. A caveat: if political power lies entirely in the major urban centers this vision cannot be made appealing even though urbanites will be important indirect beneficiaries.

The Ministry of Agriculture

The initial task of the Ministry of Agriculture is to spell out the objectives of the plan, delineate the elements to be implemented in the Ministry and those to be implemented in other ministries. The objectives derive from the Chief of State's vision and strategy. They are the subject of Part 1 of this book. Chapters 4, 11, 12, 13, 14, and 15 spell out the tasks that the Ministry of Agriculture must perform; Chaps. 5, 9, and 10 tasks for other ministries.

A Policy Unit in the Ministry of Agriculture should coordinate the planning effort. It will ensure an appropriate plan from each Department of the Ministry of Agriculture, and from the other ministries, ensure systems for coordination, and generate a detailed budget. Alternatively, those functions may be performed by a special body reporting to the Prime Minister, or a unit in a Ministry of Planning. However, it is better to build that capacity in the Ministry of Agriculture as that will be the primary implementing body.

A representative with foreign experience would be useful. It is striking how there is widespread and deep interest in what other countries are doing in low- and middle-income countries—and what can be learned from that.

The Policy Unit in the Ministry of Agriculture has a broad set of plan-related functions, in addition to the administrative role stated above. It must, in broad consultation, provide the overarching commodity and geographic growth rate targets and the budgets for the respective components. It must then provide oversight and spot studies of how the effort is proceeding, diagnose the bottlenecks to achieving the goal, and delineate modifications to deal with errors and oversight in the planning process. The plan must have scope for adjustments to shortfalls and errors in the original plan. The Policy Unit must also do spot studies of specific policy issues as they arise.

It is notable that policy units in Ministries of Agriculture are normally deficient in size and access to financial and personnel resources for fulfilling these functions. That requires priority given to training. Foreign aid should play a major role in increasing human and financial resources for this essential function, but it rarely does so. In practice, these functions tend to be filled in an ad hoc manner by the collectivity of individuals in the various departments. It is far better to systemize filling these needs.

Ministerial Coordinating Body: Several Ministries

The agriculture plan requires major coordination of inputs from several ministries, most obviously roads, electrification, education, finance, and the central bank. That requires a coordinating body reporting to the Chief of State, to ensure delineation and budgeting of major inputs, and ensuring that the final plan is fully implemented by each of the component ministries.

Setting Priorities

Everyone knows that everything cannot be done at once. That knowledge seems rarely to show itself when setting narrow priorities for the short run and sequencing over time for the long run. As an example, our discussion of finance has made the case for its importance, but suggested that its priority and hence timing should be later than for the research extension complex. Similarly, major improvements in marketing may lag behind farm production increasing actions. It is difficult to set priorities because of vested interests, but they need to show in implementation.

DISTINGUISHING FEATURES OF THIS BOOK

This chapter draws policy-oriented conclusions that generally differ from the conventional views expressed in much of the literature and more so by decision makers in foreign assistance bodies and in governments of low- and middle-income countries. It is consistent with the observations of those many who have worked intensively in diverse, high- and low-potential agricultural areas in traditional agriculture and early stages of modernization.

Part 1: The Economic Transformation

Small commercial farmers are the focus of this book. They have sufficient farm income to be above the poverty line and produce the bulk of agricultural output and comprise in the order of half of rural households. They are commercial farmers selling a substantial proportion of their agricultural production and are not poor by the standards of their community. Large-scale, urban-oriented farmers are not included. That leaves a large rural population whose income is largely from rural non-farm sources. The bulk of the rural poor fall into that class.

The bulk of the rural-oriented literature makes a much simpler assumption that agricultural production takes place on what is, in effect, a simple average of our two classes of households. That simple average depicts a poor subsistence or even below-subsistence farmer. The difference between our assumption and the central tendency of the literature drives the departure of a whole host of findings in this book from conventional views. As an important aside, all research in rural areas must separate small commercial farmers from the rural non-farm sector and its large number of subsistence farmers. Now that distinction is rarely made.

There is now substantial recognition that the rural non-farm sector is large. However, the common focus in the literature has been on how the urban sector can provide a growing market for the labor of the rural non-farm sector. Indeed, it is seemingly implicit in much of the literature that rural non-farm production is marketed largely in urban areas. That is completely wrong. The common view fits logically with the view that farming is largely subsistence farming and hence cannot provide that market.

This book draws on substantial literature that small commercial farmers are the market for the rural non-farm sector and that they spend in the order of half of their income, and specifically of their incremental income from modernization, on the rural non-farm sector. That sector produces labor-intensive, largely non-tradable, income-elastic goods and services, largely consumption goods, for the small commercial farmer. They remain competitive with other goods and services because of low wage rates and the labor intensity of the goods and services they provide.

This book then measures the impact of increased income from modernization of the small commercial farmer on the rural non-farm sector. It does so with a simplified approach that focuses on a small number of policy variables and uses an Excel spreadsheet for the analysis that facilitates testing the impact of alternative assumptions on the employment impact. That facility for testing sensitivity is important because some of the key assumptions, although backed with strong logic, have only modest amounts of empirical evidence to draw upon. These measurements explain the finding of a large literature showing agricultural growth as the primary correlate of poverty reduction.

The calculations show that rapid agricultural growth dominates employment reduction in both low- and middle-income countries and while it is important to gross domestic product (GDP) growth in middle-income countries it is not dominant as for low-income countries. The difference between a six percent and three percent rate of agricultural growth is the difference between essentially no decline and rapid decline in rural poverty. In Pakistan, where large-scale farms are considered to be important, such a difference in growth rates of those farms is inconsequential to rural employment and poverty reduction.

The exposition explains the dynamism in the market towns of prospering agricultural areas and why a substantial proportion of the economic transformation (the rapid growth of the non-agricultural sector) occurs in market towns with a consequent geographic dispersion of urbanization. Conversely, it explains why a few large cities dominate urbanization when agriculture is stagnant. It follows that the principal poverty trap is in the geographic areas physically constrained from responding to opportunities for yield-increasing agricultural technology.

Most countries, although dominated by high-productive potential areas, also have significant geographic areas that are unresponsive to modernizing biological science technology. The response is migration to other areas, with a consequent skewing of the age distribution in that area towards older ages. The migration is facilitated because the rapidly modernizing areas will leave the job openings in major urban areas largely for those from the stagnating areas. The market towns of the progressive areas will also be able to absorb net in-migration. That transition is facilitated by orienting education to facilitating the shift to non-agricultural occupations and by good central infrastructure.

Most modern analysis of rapid growth in low- and middle-income countries makes trade, based on labor-intensive manufacturing comparative advantage, a major factor in achieving high growth rates. Trade is also important to a high agricultural growth rate strategy. However, growth with rapid agricultural growth fosters rapid growth in the large non-tradable sector and hence has a much lower trade component than more traditional models of growth. That reinforces the case for rapid agricultural growth as high-income countries play a less active role in trade expansion.

Finally, it is shown how a dynamic agriculture can make significant capital as well as labor contributions to accelerating growth of the urban sector, drawing on a detailed historical analysis of Taiwan to substantiate the case. That is in contrast to exploitation of a relatively stagnant agriculture, as in post-revolution Russia and in one stage of China's rapid economic growth. The bulk of the literature, especially the terms of trade literature, sees these transfers as negative for agricultural growth. However, that literature does not emphasize the large reductions in cost of production rising from the technological change in agriculture.

There is broad acceptance of the point by Professor Amartya Sen that poverty and hence lack of food security is due to lack of income not lack of food supply. This book fully documents how the income of the rural poor is to be increased. It differs radically from influential views of many of Sen's followers in showing that increased agricultural production is the means by which incomes of the rural poor are to be increased. Agricultural growth is central to both sides of poverty reduction: the supply of food and the incomes of the poor creating the effective demand for that food.

This book discusses the potential for safety nets and price stabilization for the short-term alleviation of poverty while the long-term solution in agricultural growth provides the dominant solution. Non-fungible foreign aid plays an important role in that context.

Part 2: Traditional Agriculture: The Base for Modernization

The unusually wide dispersion of yields in traditional agriculture arises from choices about work effort (labor input) that are substantially influenced by limited consumption choices. The context of modernization greatly expands those choices and results in greater homogeneity of decision making and production outcomes. This analysis further strengthens the case for the rapid spread of all-weather physical infrastructure and formal education. The result is greater homogeneity of farming practices at high levels of output and income. These forces also explain why, in high-productivity agricultural areas that appear to have extreme population pressures on land resources, as modernization occurs a substantial proportion of the output increase is attributable to an increased area under cultivation. In brief, with modernization the consumption incentives change as well as the production incentives. That brings greater homogeneity in production decisions.

Professor T. W. Shultz made the important point that farmers in traditional agriculture are poor, have a low productivity, but are efficient. This book notes that the slow pace of change in traditional agriculture provides ample time for even the most backward farms to adjust, but that the faster pace under modernization results in a dispersion that can usefully be reduced by effective public extension services.

Traditional agricultures in Asia and Latin America often had a predominance of land in large-scale feudal holdings. Part 2 on traditional agriculture explains why and where such systems arose, with important implications to post-land-reform decisions. Most of the Asian feudal systems were converted, by expropriation of land to the tiller, to systems dominated by small commercial farmers.

The impact of rapid agricultural growth on rural employment and poverty reduction is measured in the feudal context and compared to the situation when those feudal holdings are converted through expropriation into small commercial farms. The contrast in poverty reduction is immensely in favor of expropriation, driven substantially by the multipliers from now small commercial farms on income in the poor rural non-farm sector.

It is shown that in traditional agricultures population puts pressure on the environment that can be relieved by modernization. Likewise, in traditional agricultures women have access to information that is important to family decision making and know how to bring that information into decision making, setting the stage for loss of influence as information moves outside the village and institutional structures limit wives' access to that information. That loss of access to information is the product of decisions in the new institutions of modernization, particularly extension programs. That point is dwelled upon in Part 3 on modernization from the point of view of how to redress that unfortunate situation.

Part 3: Modernization of Agriculture

The major departure of this book from current conventional wisdom on the development of agriculture is in placing the centrality of government intervention at the core of that process. Failure in the modernization of agriculture occurs because governments fail to provide vital national leadership and essential institutional structures. That is reinforced by failure to make large public investment in rural infrastructure and education.

Of course, the very scarcity of government resources, both human and financial, require carefully set priorities. Part 3 details, chapter by chapter, what those priorities are. It accepts as essential to success the carefully developed African Union target of ten percent of government expenditure on agriculture and points out that this target is rarely met, or even discussed, and provides an important explanation for the failures in agriculture.

The dominant public expenditure for agricultural modernization is on rural physical infrastructure—roads and electrification—and education. Modernization cannot occur without constantly improving rural infrastructure and education. Agricultural modernization requires a high and constantly increasing level of expenditure on these two requirements.

It is emphasized that rural populations will continue to increase in low- and middle-income countries and more so with rapid modernization of agriculture and its accelerated growth of the rural non-farm sector. Thus, rural infrastructure and education are to ensure a healthy educated population in rural areas, many of whom will migrate to urban areas. Because they are essential for reasons other than modernizing agriculture, those expenditures are not counted in the ten percent figure stated above.

It is common for low- and middle-income countries to contemplate and even implement expensive input and output subsidy programs. Learned articles discuss the pros and cons of these policies. They miss the overriding point that these programs are bad for modernization because of the huge opportunity cost in the fundamentals of agricultural modernization. Public resources are scarce due to the innately poor economic environment for raising government revenues and the requirements for agricultural modernization are large. Those resources must be allocated to the highest rate of return activities. Agricultural subsidies for other than institutional development never make that priority list. All that is in the context that research/extension continually offer profitable productivity-increasing technologies. The literature to the contrary is built on an analysis of those with smaller holdings than our defined small commercial farmer.

The book does argue for food safety nets to protect the poor from periods of intense privation. It does so in the context that for low-income countries foreign aid tends to pick up a substantial share of the cost with resources that are not readily available for other uses.

Our quantitative analysis shows that in a low-income country (and by extension to some extent a middle-income country) change in cereal production, both weather and growth induced, tends to have only a small effect on agricultural prices. That is because of the significant transmission of income change from agricultural production to demand for food, through the poor rural non-farm population. That is in sharp contrast to the strong price depressing effects of increased agricultural production in high-income countries. In the relatively stable domestic cereal price environment of low- and middle-income countries major price fluctuations driven by forces external to a specific low- or middle-income country bear heavily on the poor and can be reduced by trade restrictions.

Asian countries' food consumption is usually dominated by a single cereal. National level data in Africa shows close correlation between different cereal prices so stabilization of one tends to stabilize the whole set.

The core of modernization as is emphasized throughout this book is modern science-driven technology. The rate of return to research literature corroborates that low- and middle-income countries underspend on research and also, but to a somewhat lesser extent, on extension. Concurrently, the international system (Consultative Group on International Agricultural Research—CGIAR) also shows substantial underinvestment. The marginal returns are well above the cost of capital and therefore more capital should be allocated to these institutions. Of course, problems of misallocation of resources and the changing research needs over time call for improvements in decision making, but the basic point stands.

One of the effects of improved technology is an increase in the productivity of the more responsive land with a consequent incentive to ensure that all such land is brought into cultivation. Thus increased land in production accounts for a substantial portion of the output growth in a modernizing agriculture.

Middle-income countries have a huge opportunity for growth in domestic demand for high-value agricultural commodities that is not at all reflected in research and extension expenditure on these commodities. That is the primary reason for failure of rural employment growth and poverty reduction in rural areas of those countries. Expansion of research and extension will be, in significant part, from a largely cereal emphasis to coverage of a wide range of livestock and horticultural commodities. Similarly, tropical export commodities tend to be neglected in research. As the scope for such commodities increases, the research extension systems for them must be built.

The literature on agricultural development generally emphasizes that it is a long-term process with delayed results. However, many low-income countries have not made a start on modernization. They can get quick results, i.e. a large impact in a year or two, by exploiting existing improved varieties with a massive push on chemical fertilizer use and improved seed and a priority given to the most responsive crops and areas. That requires a focus on the seed fertilizer complex including on adaptive research and demonstrations, a large but inevitably modestly trained extension service, and a strong fertilizer supply push from the government. The same is required for improved seed.

It is unlikely that the required growth can occur without the private sector dominating both fertilizer supply and improved seed production. Urgency in getting on with both may call for an initially activist government policy on fertilizer inputs and supply channels and in initiating improved seed production, particularly in the case of hybrids. The danger is that government input will be more than necessary and extend for too long with a consequent constraint on competiveness, efficiency, and most important, on the total size of the sector.

The case is made that long-term agricultural growth requires a specialized quasi-government rural finance system, much as essentially exists in all high-income countries. The small commercial farmer can self-finance a significant increase in fertilizer use and purchase of improved seed, but will be able to invest more with greater impact on production if external finance is available.

In the early stages of modernization of agriculture in Asian countries, most of them developed specialized agricultural finance institutions such as those in all high-income modernized agriculture countries. Because of poor discipline those institutions had large, in the order of 40 percent, overdues on repayment. In response, foreign aid agencies stopped investing in such institutions and they and the academic literature emphasized other sources of finance—none of which worked on the scale required. The result is that the laggard countries in Asia (e.g., Nepal) and essentially all African countries lack effective supplies of finance to small commercial farmers.

This book debates the timing of the provision of finance. It need not be early in the modernization process as better to delay and get it right on repayment. However, indefinite delay, as per the foreign aid programs, has proved costly. It is clear that what works in contemporary high-income countries from when they were middle-or even low-income ones is the correct institutional approach. That will be supplemented by other types of institutions, including commercial banks and micro-credit, providing not only specialized services but efficiency-increasing competition. However, the core is a specialized quasi-governmental institution.

The rapid growth in the proportion of agricultural production marketed, the rapid growth of large cities, and equally important the radical changes in marketing systems, including the rise of supermarkets, provide a challenge to the small commercial farmer.

It is clear that a strong cost of production advantage continues for the small commercial farmer but that the new requirements for uniformly high quality, substantial scale of purchases, traceability, and rapid response to changing consumer tastes represent major challenges for the small commercial farmer. They can be met but require organization and technical assistance. Failure to provide essential government institutional support will result in a shift to imports from high-income countries, as has already happened in a few Asian countries. The consequent unnecessary and uneconomic loss of national income and poverty reduction is unfortunate and can be avoided. What would be very helpful is expansion of foreign technical assistance into building the required large-scale expansion in university teaching and in research/extension into a broad range of sophisticated marketing and business management areas.

In the order of six percent rate of agricultural growth in low- and middle-income countries is possible because of the opportunity to catch up to advanced countries. Obviously, foreign technical assistance can be immensely valuable in the catch-up process. That potential is particularly large in agriculture given the advanced state and relevant history of institutional growth in high-income countries.

There was period in the 1960s and 1970s, continuing somewhat into the 1980s, when foreign aid played an important leadership role in accelerating agricultural growth. That was, sensibly, primarily in the areas of agricultural university development and agricultural research and extension, but included other areas as well. It was oriented to building technical capacity and drew heavily on technical assistance personnel from successful home, and in some cases, colonial systems. Since then quantity of aid to agriculture and even more the quality and relevance to agricultural growth have declined precipitously. That resulted in low rates of poverty decline and low popular support for national government.

The book closes on the need for a clear vision and strategy for the agricultural sector in order to rally not only farmers to the cause but the larger public as well. That motivation is important to the incentive structures for agricultural growth. Further, the expenditure on vital rural infrastructure and education, and building large critical institutions for research and extension, require broad support that comes from vision, strategy, and detailed planning.

NOTE

1. His story was "Baby shoes for sale. Never used."

ANNEX: ANALYTICAL HISTORY OF AGRICULTURE AND THE ECONOMIC TRANSFORMATION

The modern concept of agriculture's role in the economic transformation starts with Nobel Laureate W. Arthur Lewis and evolves over several decades to the complex position stated in this book. The data component lies with corroborating that agricultural growth is the prime source of poverty reduction, that continuous profitable technological change in agriculture is possible, that prospering farmers spend a high proportion of their income increments on the rural non-farm sector that harbors the bulk of the poor, and that the employment elasticities for that sector are high.

EVOLUTION OF A CONCEPT

W. Arthur Lewis's (1954) concept was that agriculture supplied the labor force for the economic transformation by increasing labor productivity so that the wage goods, food, were available for labor transferred from agriculture to the non-agricultural sector. That labor would produce capital goods for increasing the capital stock as the basis for growth.

To Lewis the agricultural labor force was just able to support itself with adequate food. Only by increasing agricultural productivity could the economic transformation get underway. There was no underemployed labor as everyone was busy producing the food required for subsistence. If they left agriculture, the increased labor productivity of the remaining households would have to produce the food to support them. Although, as we will see, Lewis did not have it all correct he started his enquiry down the correct path. Increased agricultural productivity was essential.

There were several well-publicized models derived from the Lewis position notably by Ranis and Fei (1961), Jorgenson (1961), and much later Lele and Mellor (1981). Fei and Ranis assumed marginal labor productivity had been driven to zero with a large stock of underemployed labor. Agricultural productivity did not have to increase to compensate for a transfer of labor to the urban

© The Author(s) 2017
J.W. Mellor, *Agricultural Development and Economic Transformation*,
Palgrave Studies in Agricultural Economics and Food Policy,
https://doi.org/10.1007/978-3-319-65259-7

non-agricultural sector. Jorgenson assumed that the marginal productivity of labor was positive and that there was no stock of underemployed labor. Agricultural productivity, as for Lewis, would have to be increased in order to provide the food for labor transferred to the urban sector. Without increased agricultural productivity labor transfer would cause an increase in the relative price of food, which through various mechanisms would remove the capital formation benefit of the labor transfer.

These papers gloss over the mechanism by which food would be transferred to the urban sector. Lele and Mellor (1981) provide a more complex classical model that started with the agricultural production increase and deals with how that would facilitate the labor transfer. A deficiency of all these models was a focus on only one of several means by which agriculture could contribute to capital formation in the urban sector. In this context, Mellor (1963) analysed the effect of price changes associated with different rates of agricultural growth on the distribution of income with a focus on the lowest-income groups. Mellor (1973), substantially based on meticulous conceptual and empirical work by T. H. Lee (1971), stated the inter-sectoral transfer of resources from agriculture.

Johnston and Mellor in a widely quoted *American Economic Review* article (1961) and further in (1984) presented a far more complex picture. They delineated a set of contributions of agricultural growth to the economic transformation. One in that set, that would later rise to a dominant position, was expenditure by farmers on consumer goods produced by the non-agricultural sector. In effect, as for Lewis, increased agricultural productivity was required but one of its impacts was to increase demand for the output from the non-agricultural sector. The concept also implied a large underemployed agricultural labor force. Their work drew, from Johnston's time with the postwar land reform in Japan, on related work by Japanese economists Ohkawa and Ishikawa, on Japan and China.

Mellor expanded all these elements as well as describing traditional agriculture and the means of its modernization, in a prize-winning book, *The Economics of Agricultural Development* (1966). Mellor, in a paper (1967) that won the American Agricultural Economics Association award for best published research in that year, developed the ideas into a clear conceptual framework. Much of the foregoing assumes a large underemployed labor force. Mellor and Ranade (2006) model the fundamental relationships of agriculture and poverty reduction for Pakistan in the context of an open economy with full employment. They draw attention to the critical role of the large, rural, non-tradable sector in poverty reduction and show that the poverty-reducing effects of agricultural growth, while still large, are substantially less if the supply of labor is less than perfectly elastic.

Mellor and Stevens (1956) showed from comparative analysis of production functions how the marginal productivity of labor and the size of the underemployed labor force would differ among agro-ecological regions and that in some regions a large underemployed labor force was consistent with a positive marginal product of labor. That set the stage for a major role in the economic transformation of a large, underemployed, rural labor force. It also confirmed that the problem was not one requiring increased labor productivity in agriculture as being essential to release labor for the non-agricultural sector. The increased productivity was required to provide purchasing power for rural non-agricultural goods and services. A later work by Mellor (1963) pursued further the scope for differences in marginal productivity and the extent of employment of the family labor force.

There is an immense literature showing high returns to agricultural research and the impact of a wide range of technological innovations on agricultural productivity. However, the paper by Herdt and Mellor (1964) written shortly before the green revolution contrasts US and Indian research in response to chemical fertilizer input. They in effect showed what was required of a green revolution. The Indian research was driven by the view that Indian farmers were too poor to afford purchased fertilizer and so bred for varieties that improved yields at low levels of fertilizer input and of course low output (see Fig. 12.1). The US graph shows output rising sharply and continuing to a far higher level than that of the Indian research. That is of course exactly what the work of IRRI and CYMMT were about to do and thereby unleash the green revolution. The conceptual case is succinctly made for research-based, high-input, high-output agriculture. IRRI and CYMMT revolutionized the approach to agricultural research in low- and middle-income countries and thus opened the way for agriculture to make a continuous large contribution to the economic transformation.

Mellor and Lele (1973) showed that the size of the consumption expenditure on the labor-intensive, non-tradable non-agricultural sector was substantial. That was a counter to the position by Hirschman (1958) that "Agriculture certainly stands convicted on the count of its lack of direct stimulus to the setting up of new activities through linkage effects—the superiority of manufacturing in this respect is crushing." The Mellor and Lele position was that yes, the production linkages were weak, but the consumption linkages were very strong. Johnston and Kilby (1978) followed that by showing much stronger production linkages than stated by Hirschman but still much less than the powerful consumption linkages.

Mellor in *The New Economics of Growth* (1976) provided a book-length, India-based statement of the means of agriculture's stimulation of the non-agricultural sector with considerable emphasis on the consumption linkages and the means by which agriculture could grow to provide those stimuli.

That was followed by a book edited by Mellor of country case studies, *Agriculture on the Road to Industrialization* (1995), that documented how various countries had seen strong agriculture-based consumption linkages to growth of the rural non-agricultural sector. The title was a misnomer since it was not large-scale urban industry but rural non-farm. This book was read by Prime Minister Meles, a true intellectual, when he was leading the forces that later took over the government of Ethiopia and he set forth his strategy of agricultural development led industrialization.

Mellor and his colleagues did country studies consistent with the foregoing. The country studies showed farmers' expenditures in the rural sector were high even in relatively developed Egypt (Mellor and Gavian 1999), Rwanda (Mellor 2002b), Guatemala (Barrios and Mellor 2006), and Pakistan (Mellor and Ranade 2006). Farmers did not travel to urban centers to make their purchases and vice versa. Thus, the stimulus was shown in case after case to be to the rural non-farm sector, including retail establishments in market towns.

Mellor and Malik (2017) clarified that rural households in low- and middle-income countries fell into two roughly equal classes in numbers of households— a rural non-farm sector that was generally poor and derived a very modest share of income from direct agricultural production and small commercial farms that produced the bulk of agricultural output that were not poor, were commercial and therefore were able to drive growth of the rural non-farm sector by substantial expenditures on that sector. Much of the contemporary literature incorrectly described an agriculture that was, in effect, a subsistence-oriented average of all rural households that could therefore not drive the rural non-farm sector by its expenditures.

Mellor and Kumro (2017) showed how those process resulted in the rural non-farm sector purchasing the bulk of incremental cereal production and thereby keeping the price from falling with increased output. That left the income in the hands of the small commercial farmer to be spent, in substantial part, on the rural non-farm sector.

Evolving Data Support

The seminal data-based research on agricultural growth–poverty relationships was carried out by Ahluwalia (1978) in a time series analysis of agricultural growth and poverty reduction in India. He showed that the relationships were very strong. Although not explained in this or the following references, they show that somehow income from agricultural growth was getting into the hands of the rural poor who used it to increase food consumption and lift themselves out of poverty.

A series of studies based on cross-section studies of international data corroborated the Ahluwalia findings (Ravallion and Datt 2002; Thirtle 2001; Timmer 1997). They also showed a lag in the impact, consistent with the complex relationship discussed by Mellor and his colleagues, and in this book. Timmer also showed that the effect did not hold for large-scale agriculture, again consistent with our exposition.

A quite different literature, based on micro-data from farm level studies, corroborates that small commercial farmers spent a substantial portion of incremental income on the rural non-farm sector. Peter Hazel, fully aware that the role of agriculture depicted by Mellor and colleagues required that the small farmers producing that output must spend a high proportion of their incremental income on the rural non-farm sector, and set out, first at the World Bank and then at IFPRI, to measure that impact. The study that most directly attacked that task was on Malaysia (Bell et al. 1982) and documented that about half of incremental income from agricultural growth was spent on the rural non-farm sector. Hazell followed that effort by comparing African countries with Malaysia (Hazell and Röell 1983) and then with a monumental study of the green revolution in South India (Hazell and Ramasamy 1991) that also corroborated farmers' expenditure in the rural non-farm sector. Delgado and colleagues at IFPRI then summarized the massive evidence on this point (Delgado et al. 1998).

Over a period of years Mellor and his colleagues authored a series of country studies that quantified the impact of a high agricultural growth rate on expenditure on the rural non-farm sector, stimulating rapid increase in employment, for example Rwanda (Mellor 2002a), Egypt (Mellor and Gavian 1999), Pakistan (Mellor and Ranade 2006), Ethiopia (Dorosh and Mellor 2013), Guatemala (Mellor and Barrios 2006), and Afghanistan (Akbarzad and Mellor 2005). Most of these studies used a simplified growth accounting framework shown by Haggblade et al. (1991) as more practical compared to more sophisticated models.

Mellor and Malik (2016) refined the definitions and quantified the distinction between the small commercial farmer and the rural non-farm households. The latter were either landless or subsistence farmers who depended on the rural non-farm sector for much of their income. The former produced the bulk of agricultural output, 80–90 percent, and the income; and prior to accelerated agricultural growth the rural non-farm population encompassed substantial underemployment.

Mellor and Kumro (2017) extended the Mellor and Malik analysis to show that the increased income of the rural non-farm population was largely spent on food, providing the bulk of the market for increased cereal production and thereby not only lifting themselves out of poverty but also ensuring food security. In that process, it was shown that even with high growth rates in cereals and overall agricultural production the relative prices of those commodities were unlikely to decline. That maintained incentives to increase production with continuous technological change.

REFERENCES

Abate, G. T., Rashid, S., Borzaga, C., & Getnet, K. (2016). *Rural finance and agricultural technology adoption in Ethiopia: Does the institutional design of lending organizations matter?* (IFPRI discussion paper no. 1422). Washington, DC: International Food Policy Research Institute.

Adams, D. W. (1988). The conundrum of successful credit projects in floundering rural financial markets. *Economic Development and Cultural Change, 36*(2), 355–367.

African Union. (2010). *Comprehensive African Agricultural Development Plan (CAADP)*. Addis Ababa: The New Partnership for Africa's Development.

Ahluwalia, M. S. (1978). Rural poverty and agricultural performance in India. *Journal of Development Studies, 14*, 298–323.

Ahmed, R., & Hossain, M. (1990). *Developmental impact of rural infrastructure in Bangladesh* (Vol. 83). Washington, DC: International Food Policy Research Institute.

Akbarzad, & Mellor, J. W. (2005). *All the Afghan policy analyst needs to know about agricultural growth and poverty reduction* (occasional paper). Kabul: Ministry of Agriculture, Government of Afghanistan.

Aker, J. C. (2011). Dial "A" for agriculture: A review of information and communication technologies for agricultural extension in developing countries. *Agricultural Economics, 42*(6), 631–647.

Alabi, R. A. (2014). *Impact of agricultural foreign aid on agricultural growth in sub-Saharan Africa: A dynamic specification* (AGRODEP Working Paper No. 6). Washington, DC: International Food Policy Research Institute.

Ali, D. A., Deininger, K., & Duponchel, M. (2014). *Credit constraints and agricultural productivity and rural nonfarm participation: Evidence from rural Rwanda* (Policy Research Working Paper No. 6769). Washington, DC: World Bank Group.

Alston, J. M., & Pardey, P. G. (2001). Attribution and other problems in assessing the returns to agricultural R&D. *Agricultural Economics, 25*(2–3), 141–152.

Alston, J. M., Marra, M. C., Pardey, P. G., & Wyatt, T. J. (2000). Research returns redux: A meta-analysis of the returns to agricultural R&D. *Australian Journal of Agricultural and Resource Economics, 44*(2), 185–215.

© The Author(s) 2017

J.W. Mellor, *Agricultural Development and Economic Transformation*,
Palgrave Studies in Agricultural Economics and Food Policy,
https://doi.org/10.1007/978-3-319-65259-7

Alston, J. M., Andersen, M. A., James, J. S., & Pardey, P. G. (2011). The economic returns to US public agricultural research. *American Journal of Agricultural Economics, 93*(5), 1257–1277.

Anderson, K. (2010). *Krueger, Schiff, and Valdes revisited: Agricultural price and trade policy reform in developing countries since 1960* (Policy Research Working Paper No. 5165). Washington, DC: World Bank Group.

Anderson, K., Ivanic, M., & Martin, W. J. (2014). Food price spikes, price insulation, and poverty. In J. P. Chavas, D. Hummels, & B. D. Wright (Eds.), *The economics of food price volatility* (pp. 311–339). Chicago: University of Chicago Press.

Anik, A. R., Manjunatha, A. V., & Bauer, S. (2013). Impact of farm level corruption on the food security of households in Bangladesh. *Food Security, 5*(4), 565–574.

Antle, J. M., & Pingali, P. L. (1994). Pesticides, productivity, and farmer health: A Philippine case study. *American Journal of Agricultural Economics, 76*(3), 418–430.

Bachman, D. (2006). *Bureaucracy, economy, and leadership in China: The institutional origins of the great leap forward.* Cambridge: Cambridge University Press.

Banerjee, A., & Duflo, E. (2012). *Poor economics: A radical rethinking of the way to fight global poverty.* New York: Public Affairs.

Barker, R., & Levine, G. (2012). *Water productivity in context: The experiences of Taiwan and the Philippines over the past half-century.* Colombo: International Water Management Institute.

Barnes, D. F. (2007). *The challenge of rural electrification: Strategies for developing countries.* Washington, DC: Resources for the Future Press.

Barrett, C. B. (1996). On price risk and the inverse farm size-productivity relationship. *Journal of Development Economics, 51*(2), 193–215.

Barrett, C. B. (2007). Displaced distortions: Financial market failures and seemingly inefficient resource allocation in low-income rural communities. In E. Bulte & R. Ruben (Eds.), *Development economics between markets and institutions: Incentives for growth, food security and sustainable use of the environment* (pp. 73–86). Wageningen: Wageningen Academic Publishers.

Barrett, C. B. (2010). Measuring food insecurity. *Science, 327*(5967), 825–828.

Barrett, C. B., & Maxwell, D. (2007). *Food aid after fifty years: Recasting its role.* Abingdon: Routledge.

Barrett, C. B., Sherlund, S. M., & Adesina, A. A. (2008). Shadow wages, allocative inefficiency, and labor supply in smallholder agriculture. *Agricultural Economics, 38*(1), 21–34.

Barrett, C. B., Bellemare, M. F., & Hou, J. Y. (2010). Reconsidering conventional explanations of the inverse productivity-size relationship. *World Development, 38*(1), 88–97.

Barrett, C. B., Garg, T., & McBride, L. (2016). Well-being dynamics and poverty traps. *Annual Review of Resource Economics, 8*, 303–327.

Barrios, J. M., & Mellor, J. W. (2006). *Agriculture and employment growth in Guatemala* (Occasional Paper No. 26). Guatemala City: IARNA.

Bates, R. H. (2014). *Markets and states in tropical Africa: The political basis of agricultural policies.* Berkley/London: University of California Press.

Bates, R. H., & Block, S. A. (2013). Revisiting African agriculture: Institutional change and productivity growth. *The Journal of Politics, 75*(2), 372–384.

Bell, C., Hazell, P., & Slade, R. (1982). *Project evaluation in regional perspective: A study of an irrigation project in Northwest Malaysia.* Baltimore: Johns Hopkins University Press.

Besley, T. (1995). Savings, credit and insurance. In J. Behrman & T. N. Srinivasan (Eds.), *Handbook of development economics* (Vol. 3A, pp. 2123–2207). Amsterdam: Elsevier.

Binswanger-Mkhize, H. P., Bourguignon, C., & Van Den Brink, R. J. (2009). *Agricultural land redistribution: Toward greater consensus*. Washington, DC: World Bank Publications.

Birkhaeuser, D., Evenson, R. E., & Feder, G. (1991). The economic impact of agricultural extension: A review. *Economic Development and Cultural Change, 39*(3), 607–650.

Blimpo, M. P., Harding, R., & Wantchekon, L. (2013). Public investment in rural infrastructure: Some political economy considerations. *Journal of African Economies, 22*(2), ii57–ii83.

Bocquet-Appel, J. P. (2011). The agricultural demographic transition during and after the agriculture inventions. *Current Anthropology, 52*(S4), S497–S510.

Boserup, E. (1965). *The conditions of agricultural growth: The economics of agrarian change under population pressure*. Abingdon: Routledge.

Brooks, J. (2010). *Agricultural policy choices in developing countries: A synthesis*. Paris: Organisation for Economic Co-operation and Development.

Buck, J. L. (1937). *Land utilization in China: A study of 16,786 farms in 168 localities, and 38,256 farm families in twenty-two province in China, 1929–1933*. Shanghai: University of Nanking.

Burnside, C., & Dollar, D. (2000). Aid, policies and growth. *The American Economic Review, 90*(4), 847–868.

Carletto, C., Corral, P., & Guelfi, A. (2017). Agricultural commercialization and nutrition revisited: Empirical evidence from three African countries. *Food Policy, 67*, 106–118.

Case, T., Farms, B., Johnson, M., & Owusu, V. (2013). *Revisiting agricultural input and farm support subsidies in Africa: The case of Ghana's mechanization, fertilizer, block farms and marketing programs* (IFPRI Discussion Paper No. 1300). Washington, DC: International Food Policy Research Institute.

Charron, N. (2011). Exploring the impact of foreign aid on corruption: Has the "anti-corruption movement" been effective? *The Developing Economies, 49*(1), 66–88.

Chaudhury, N., Hammer, J., Kremer, M., Muralidharan, K., & Rogers, F. H. (2006). Missing in action: Teacher and health worker absence in developing countries. *The Journal of Economic Perspectives, 20*(1), 91–116.

Chenery, H., & Strout, A. (1966). Foreign assistance and economic development. *The American Economic Review, 56*(4), 679–733.

Christiaensen, L., Demery, L., & Kuhl, J. (2011). The (evolving) role of agriculture in poverty reduction: An empirical perspective. *Journal of Development Economics, 96*(2), 239–254.

Christiaensen, L., Weerdt, J., & Todo, Y. (2013). Urbanization and poverty reduction: The role of rural diversification and secondary towns. *Agricultural Economics, 44* (4–5), 435–447.

Cohen, B. (2006). Urbanization in developing countries: Current trends, future projections and key challenges for sustainability. *Technology in Society, 28*(1), 63–80.

Collier, P., & Dercon, S. (2014). African agriculture in 50 years: Smallholders in a rapidly changing world. *World Development, 63*, 92–101.

Crist, E., Mora, C., & Engelman, R. (2017). The interaction of human population, food production, and biodiversity practice. *Science, 356*(6335), 260–264.

De Janvry, A. (1981). The role of land reforms in economic development: Policies and politics. *American Journal of Agricultural Economics, 63*, 384–392.

De Janvry, A., Fafchamps, M., & Sadoulet, E. (1991). Peasant household behaviour with missing markets: Some paradoxes explained. *The Economic Journal, 101*(409), 1400–1417.

Deininger, K., & Byerlee, D. (2012). The rise of large farms in land abundant countries: Do they have a future? *World Development, 40*(4), 701–714.

Delgado, C. L., Hopkines, J., Kelly, V. A., Hazell, P., Mckenna, A. A., Gruhn, P., et al. (1998). *Agricultural growth linkages in sub-Saharan Africa*. Washington, DC: International Finance Corporation.

Deng, T. (2013). Impacts of transport infrastructure on productivity and economic growth: Recent advances and research challenges. *Transport Reviews, 33*(6), 686–699.

Dercon, S., & Christiaensen, L. (2011). Consumption risk, technology adoption and poverty traps: Evidence from Ethiopia. *Journal of Development Economics, 96*(2), 159–173.

Dercon, S., Gilligan, D. O., Hoddinott, J., & Woldehanna, T. (2009). The impact of agricultural extension and roads on poverty and consumption growth in fifteen Ethiopian villages. *American Journal of Agricultural Economics, 91*(4), 1007–1021.

Desai, G. M. (1982). *Sustaining rapid growth in india's fertilizer consumption: A perspective based on composition of use* (International food policy research institute (IFPRI) research report 031). Washington, DC.

Desai, G. M., & Hazell, P. B. (1982). *Sustaining rapid growth in India's fertilizer consumption: A perspective based on composition of use*. Washington, DC: International Food Policy Research Institute.

Desai, B. M., & Mellor, J. W. (1993). *Institutional finance for agricultural development. An analytical survey of critical issues and food policy review* (1st ed.). Washington, DC: International Food Policy Research Institute.

Dickovick, J. T. (2014). Foreign aid and decentralization: Limitations on impact in autonomy and responsiveness. *Public Administration and Development, 34*(3), 194–206.

Donnges, C., Edmonds, G., & Johannessen, B. (2007). *Rural road maintenance – Sustaining the benefits of improved access*. Bangkok: International Labour Organization (ILO).

Dorosh, P. A., & Mellor, J. W. (2013). Why agriculture remains a viable means of poverty reduction in sub-Saharan Africa: The case of Ethiopia. *Development Policy Review, 31*(4), 419–441.

Dorosh, P., Wang, H. G., You, L., & Schmidt, E. (2012). Road connectivity, population and crop production in sub-Saharan Africa. *Agricultural Economics, 43*(1), 89–103.

Doucouliagos, H., & Paldam, M. (2014). *Finally a breakthrough? The recent rise in the size of the estimates of aid effectiveness* (Economics Working Papers No. 7). Washington, DC: World Bank Group.

Duflo, E., Kremer, M., & Robinson, J. (2011). Nudging farmers to use fertilizer: Theory and experimental evidence from Kenya. *The American Economic Review, 101*(6), 2350–2390.

Duranton, G. (2015). Growing through cities in developing countries. *The World Bank Research Observer, 30*(1), 39–73.

Eicher, C. K., & Staatz, J. M. (1998). *International agricultural development* (3rd ed.). Baltimore: Johns Hopkins University Press.

Ethiopia. (2010). *Ethiopia's agriculture sector policy and investment framework: Ten year road map (2010–2020)*. Addis Ababa: Fedral Democratic Republic of Ethiopia.

Fan, S., & Chan-Kang, C. (2005). *Road development, economic growth, and poverty reduction in China* (Vol. 12). Washington, DC: International Food Policy Research Institute.

Fan, S., & Hazell, P. (2001). Returns to public investments in the less-favored areas of India and China. *American Journal of Agricultural Economics, 83*(5), 1217–1222.

Farag, M., Nandakumar, A. K., Wallack, S. S., Gaumer, G., & Hodgkin, D. (2009). Does funding from donors displace government spending for health in developing countries? *Health Affairs, 28*(4), 1045–1055.

Feder, G., & Nishio, A. (1998). The benefits of land registration and titling: Economic and social perspectives. *Land Use Policy, 15*(1), 25–43.

Financial Times. (2016, April).

Fink, R. (2002). *Corruption and the agricultural sector*. Washington, DC: Management Systems International.

Food and Agriculture Organization. (2011). *The state of food and agriculture: Women in agriculture, closing the gender gap for development*. Rome: Food and Agriculture Organization.

Gage, T. B., & DeWitte, S. (2009). What do we know about the agricultural demographic transition? *Current Anthropology, 50*(5), 649–655.

Galor, O., & Weil, D. (2000). Population, technology, and growth: From Malthusian stagnation to the demographic transition and beyond. *The American Economic Review, 90*(4), 806–828.

Garenne, M., & Joseph, V. (2002). The timing of the fertility transition in sub-Saharan Africa. *World Development, 30*(10), 1835–1843.

Gavian, S., El-Meehy, T., Bulbul, L., & Ender, G. (2002). The importance of agricultural growth to SME development and rural employment in Egypt. In G. Ender & J. S. Holtzman (Eds.), *Does agricultural policy reform work? The impact on Egypt's agriculture, 1996–2002* (pp. 395–435). Bethesda: Abt Associates Inc.

Giller, K. E., Witter, E., Corbeels, M., & Tittonell, P. (2009). Conservation agriculture and small holder farming in Africa: The heretics' view. *Field Crops Research, 114*(1), 23–34.

Gollin, D., & Rogerson, R. (2014). Productivity, transport costs and subsistence agriculture. *Journal of Development Economics, 107*, 38–48.

Gómez, M. I., & Ricketts, K. D. (2013). Food value chain transformations in developing countries: Selected hypotheses on nutritional implications. *Food Policy, 42*, 139–150.

Gómez, M., Mueller, B., & Wheeler, M. K. (2016). *Private sector extension activities targeting small farmers in developing countries*. Washington, DC: United States Agency for Development.

Goyal, A. (2010). Information, direct access to farmers and rural market performance in central India. *American Economic Journal: Applied Economics, 2*(3), 22–45.

Griffin, K. B. (1974). *The political economy of agrarian change: An essay on the green revolution*. Cambridge, MA: Harvard University Press.

Grosh, M., Del Ninno, C., Tesliuc, E., & Ouerghi, A. (2008). *For protection and promotion: The design and implementation of effective safety nets*. Washington, DC: World Bank Publications.

Haggblade, S., Hammer, J., & Hazell, P. (1991). Modeling agricultural growth multipliers. *American Journal of Agricultural Economics, 73*(2), 361–374.

Haggblade, S., Hazell, P. B., & Dorosh, P. A. (2007). Sectoral growth linkages between agriculture and the rural nonfarm economy. In S. Haggblade, P. B. Hazell, & T. Reardon (Eds.), *Transforming the rural nonfarm economy: Opportunities and threats in the developing world* (pp. 141–182). Baltimore: Published for the International Food Policy Research Institute by Johns Hopkins University Press.

Hanjra, M. A., Ferede, T., & Gutta, D. G. (2009). Reducing poverty in sub-Saharan Africa through investments in water and other priorities. *Agricultural Water Management, 96*(7), 1062–1070.

Hayami, Y., & Ruttan, V. W. (1985). *Agricultural development: An international perspective* (2nd ed.). Baltimore: Johns Hopkins University Press.

Hazell, P. B., & Ramasamy, C. (1991). *The green revolution reconsidered: The impact of high yielding varieties in South India*. Baltimore: John Hopkins University Press.

Hazell, P. B., & Röell, A. (1983). *Rural growth linkages: Household expenditure patterns in Malaysia and Nigeria* (Vol. 41). Washington, DC: International Food Policy Research Institute.

Headey, D. (2011). Rethinking the global food crisis: The role of trade shocks. *Food Policy, 36*(2), 136–146.

Herdt, R. W., & Mellor, J. W. (1964). The contrasting response of rice to nitrogen: India and the United States. *Journal of Farm Economics, 46*(1), 150–160.

Herz, B. K., & Sperling, G. B. (2004). *What works in girls' education: Evidence and policies from the developing world*. New York: Council on Foreign Relations.

Hesketh, T., Lu, L., & Xing, Z. W. (2005). The effect of China's one-child family policy after 25 years. *New England Journal of Medicine, 353*(11), 1171–1176.

Hirashima, S. (1977). Zamindars and kammees in the Punjab: An economic analysis of non-farm households in the Pakistan Punjab. In S. Hirashima (Ed.), *Hired labor in rural Asia*. Tokyo: Institute of Developing Economies.

Hirashima, S. (2008). The land market in development: A case study of Punjab in Pakistan and India. *Economic and Political Weekly, 43*(42), 41–47.

Hirschman, A. O. (1958). *The strategy of economic development*. New Haven: Yale University Press.

Hossain, M. (1988). *Credit for alleviation of rural poverty: The Grameen Bank in Bangladesh*. Washington, DC: International Food Policy Research Institute.

Huisman, J., & Smits, J. (2009). Effects of household-and district-level factors on primary school enrollment in 30 developing countries. *World Development, 37*(1), 179–193.

Hurley, T. M., Rao, X., & Pardey, G. (2014). Re-examining the reported rates of return to food and agricultural research and development. *American Journal of Agricultural Economics, 96*(5), 1492–1504.

Inocencio, A., Kikuchi, M., Merrey, D., Tonosaki, M., Maruyama, A., Jong, I. D., & Sally, H. (2005). *Lessons from irrigation investment experiences: Cost-reducing and performance-enhancing options for sub-Saharan Africa*. Colombo: International Water Management Institute.

International Energy Agency. (2016). World energy outlook 2016 – Electricity access database. Retrieved from http://www.worldenergyoutlook.org/media/weowebsite/2015/WEO2016Electricity.xlsx

International Finance Corporation. (2011). *Scaling up access to finance for agricultural SMEs policy review and recommendations*. Washington, DC: International Finance Corporation.

International Food Policy Research Institute. (2016). *2016 Global Food Policy Report survey*. Washington, DC: International Food Policy Research Institute.

International Technological University. (2016). Statistics: ICT facts & figures, mobile phone subscriptions. Retrieved from www.itu.int/ict

Islam, N. (2011). *Foreign aid to agriculture review of facts and analysis* (IFPRI Discussion Paper No. 1053). Washington, DC: International Food Policy Research Institute.

Jack, W., & Suri, T. (2011). *Mobile money: The economics of M-Pesa* (NBER Working Paper Series No. 16721). Cambridge, MA: National Bureau of Economic Research.

Jayne, T. S., Mather, D., & Mghenyi, E. (2006). *Smallholder farming under increasingly difficult circumstances: Policy and public investment priorities for Africa* (MSU International development working paper no. 86). East Lansing: Michigan State University.

Jayne, T. S., Mather, D., Mason, N., & Ricker-Gilbert, J. (2013). How do fertilizer subsidy programs affect total fertilizer use in sub-Saharan Africa? Crowding out, diversion and benefit/cost assessments. *Agricultural Economics, 44*(6), 687–703.

Johnson, D. L., & Lewis, L. A. (2007). *Land degradation: Creation and destruction.* Lanham: Rowman & Littlefield.

Johnston, B. F., & Kilby, P. (1978). *Agriculture and structural transformation: Economic strategies in late developing countries.* New York: Oxford University Press.

Johnston, B. F., & Mellor, J. W. (1961). The role of agriculture in economic development. *The American Economic Review, 51*(4), 566–593.

Johnston, B. F., & Mellor, J. W. (1984). The world food equation: Interrelations among development, employment, and food consumption. *Journal of Economic Literature, 22,* 531–574.

Jorgenson, D. W. (1961). The development of a dual economy. *The Economic Journal, 71* (282), 309–334.

Juselius, K., Møller, N. F., & Tarp, F. (2014). The long-run impact of foreign aid in 36 African countries: Insights from multivariate time series analysis. *Oxford Bulletin of Economics and Statistics, 76*(2), 153–184.

Kaminski, J., & Christiaensen, L. (2014). Post-harvest loss in sub-Saharan Africa: What do farmers say? *Global Food Security, 3*(3), 149–158.

Kaminski, J., Christiaensen, L., & Gilbert, C. L. (2016). Seasonality in local food markets and consumption: Evidence from Tanzania. *Oxford Economic Papers, 68*(3), 736–757.

Karlan, D., Osei-Akoto, R., & Udry, C. (2012). *Agricultural decision after relaxing credit and risk constraints* (NBER working paper series no. 18463). Cambridge, MA: National Bureau of Economic Research.

Kazeem, A., Jensen, L., & Stokes, C. S. (2010). School attendance in Nigeria: Understanding the impact and intersection of gender, urban-rural residence and socioeconomic status. *Comparative Education Review, 54*(2), 295–319.

Kennedy, E., Bouis, H., & Von Braun, J. (1992). Health and nutrition effects of cash crop production in developing countries: A comparative analysis. *Social Science & Medicine, 35*(5), 689–697.

Khandker, S. R., & Koolwal, G. B. (2014). *Does institutional finance matter for agriculture? Evidence using panel data from Uganda* (Policy Research Working Paper No. 6942). Washington, DC: World Bank Group.

Khandker, S. R., Bakht, Z., & Koolwal, G. B. (2009). The poverty impact of rural roads: Evidence from Bangladesh. *Economic Development and Cultural Change, 57*(4), 685–722.

Kihara, J., Nziguheba, G., Zingore, S., Coulibaly, A., Esilaba, A., Kabambe, V., et al. (2016). Understanding variability in crop response to fertilizer and amendments in sub-Saharan Africa. *Agriculture, Ecosystems & Environment, 229*, 1–12.

Krishnan, P., & Patnam, M. (2014). Neighbors and extension agents in Ethiopia: Who matters more for technology adoption? *American Journal of Agricultural Economics, 96*(1), 308–327.

Krueger, A. O., Schiff, M., & Valdés, A. (1988). Agricultural incentives in developing countries: Measuring the effect of sectoral and economywide policies. *World Bank Economic Review, 2*(3), 255–272.

Kumar, S. K. (1987). Women's role and agricultural technology. In J. W. Mellor, C. L. Delgado, & M. J. Blackie (Eds.), *Accelerating food production in sub-Saharan Africa* (pp. 135–147). Baltimore: Johns Hopkins University Press.

Kumar, S. K. (1988). Effect of seasonal food shortage on agricultural production in Zambia. *World Development, 16*(9), 1051–1063.

Kumar, S. K. (1994). Meeting the food security needs of the poor: Perspective from Asia. In E. Linusson, M. Beaudry, & M. Latham (Eds.), *Cornell International Nutrition Monograph No. 26. Right to food and good nutrition*. Ithaca: Cornell University Press.

Kumwenda, J. D. T., Waddington, S. R., Snapp, S. S., Jones, R. B., & Blackie, M. J. (1996). *Soil fertility management research for the maize cropping systems of smallholders in southern Africa: A review* (NRG paper 96–02). Mexico: CIMMYT.

Lam, W. F. (1996). Institutional design of public agencies and coproduction: A study of irrigation associations in Taiwan. *World Development, 24*(6), 1039–1054.

Lancaster, C. (2008). *Foreign aid: Diplomacy, development, domestic politics*. Chicago: University of Chicago Press.

Lee, T. H. (1971). *Inter-sectoral capital flows in the economic development of Taiwan, 1895–1960*. Ithaca: Cornell University Press.

Lee, R. (2003). The demographic transition: Three centuries of fundamental change. *The Journal of Economic Perspectives, 17*(4), 167–190.

Lele, U. (1971). *Food grain marketing in India. Private performance and public policy*. Ithaca/London: Cornell University Press.

Lele, U. (1975). *The design of rural development. Lessons from Africa*. Baltimore: Johns Hopkins University Press.

Lele, U. J. (1991). *Aid to African agriculture. Lessons from two decades of donors' experience*. Baltimore: Johns Hopkins University Press. pp. xix + 627pp.

Lele, U., & Mellor, J. W. (1981). Technological change, distributive bias and labor transfer in a two sector economy. *Oxford Economic Papers, 33*(3), 426–441.

Lele, U., & Nabi, I. (1991). Concessionary and commercial flows in development. In I. Nabi (Ed.), *Transitions in development: The role of aid and commercial flows*. San Francisco: ICS Press.

Lentz, E. C., Barrett, C. B., Gómez, M. I., & Maxwell, D. G. (2013). On the choice and impacts of innovative international food assistance instruments. *World Development, 49*, 1–8.

Levine, G., Sheng, K. H., & Barker, R. (2000). The evolution of Taiwanese irrigation: Implications for the future. *International Journal of Water Resources Development, 16*(4), 497–510.

Lewis, W. A. (1954). Economic development with unlimited supplies of labour. *The Manchester School, 22*(2), 139–191.

Linusson, E., Beaudry, M., & Latham, M. (1994). *Cornell International Nutrition Monograph No. 26. Right to food and good nutrition*. Ithaca: Cornell University Press.

Lu, C., Schneider, M. T., Gubbins, P., Leach-Kemon, K., Jamison, D., & Murray, C. J. (2010). Public financing of health in developing countries: A cross-national systematic analysis. *The Lancet, 375*(9723), 1375–1387.

Lutz, W., & Samir, K. C. (2011). Global human capital: Integrating education and population. *Science, 333*(6042), 587–592.

Malapit, H. J., Sproule, K., Kovarik, C., Meinzen-Dick, R., Quisumbing, A., Ramzan, F., et al. (2014). *Measuring progress toward empowerment: Women's empowerment in agriculture index: Baseline report.* Washington, DC: International Food Policy Research Institute.

Malik, S. J. (2008). Rethinking development strategy: The importance of the rural non-farm economy in growth and poverty reduction in Pakistan. *Lahore Journal of Economics, 13*(Special Edition), 189–204.

Marenya, P. P., & Barrett, C. B. (2009). State-conditional fertilizer yield response on western Kenyan farms. *American Journal of Agricultural Economics, 91*(4), 991–1006.

Martin, T. C. (1995). Women's education and fertility: Results from 26 demographic and health surveys. *Studies in Family Planning, 26*(4), 187–202.

Maumbe, B. M., & Swinton, S. M. (2003). Hidden health costs of pesticide use in Zimbabwe's smallholder cotton growers. *Social Science & Medicine, 57*(9), 1559–1571.

Maxwell, D., & Fitzpatrick, M. (2012). The 2011 Somalia famine: Context, causes and complications. *Global Food Security, 1*(1), 5–12.

McCullough, E. B. (2016). Labor productivity and employment gaps in sub-Saharan Africa. *Food Policy, 67*, 133–152.

Mead, D. C., & Liedholm, C. (1998). The dynamics of micro and small enterprises in developing countries. *World Development, 26*(1), 61–74.

Mellor, J. W. (1963). The use and productivity of farm family labor in early stages of agricultural development. *Journal of Farm Economics, 45*(3), 517–534.

Mellor, J. W. (1966). *The economics of agricultural development.* Ithaca: Cornell University Press.

Mellor, J. W. (1967). Toward a theory of agricultural development. In H. M. Southworth & B. F. Johnston (Eds.), *Agricultural development and economic growth* (pp. 21–60). Ithaca: Cornell University Press.

Mellor, J. W. (1969). Agricultural price policy in the context of economic development. *American Journal of Agricultural Economics, 51*(5), 1413–1420.

Mellor, J. W. (1973). Accelerated growth in agricultural production and the intersectoral transfer of resources. *Economic Development and Cultural Change, 22*(1), 1–16.

Mellor, J. W. (1976). *The new economics of growth: A strategy for India and the developing world.* Ithaca: Cornell University Press.

Mellor, J. W. (1978). Food price policy and income distribution in low-income countries. *Economic Development and Cultural Change, 27*(1), 1–26.

Mellor, J. W. (1989). Agricultural development in the third world: The food, poverty, aid, trade nexus. *Choices, 4*(1), 4–8.

Mellor, J. W. (Ed.). (1995). *Agriculture on the road to industrialization.* Baltimore: Published for the International Food Policy Research Institute (IFPRI) by Johns Hopkins University Press.

Mellor, J. W. (2002a). *How much employment can rapid agricultural growth generate? Sectoral policies for maximum impact in Rwanda* (Occasional Paper No. 19).

Bethesda: Prepared for United States Agency for International Development by Abt Associates Inc.

Mellor, J. W. (2002b). *Poverty reduction and biodiversity conservation: The complex role for intensifying agriculture. A viewpoint series on poverty and environment.* Washington, DC: WWF Macroeconomics Program Office.

Mellor, J. W. (2017). *Ethiopia: An African land productivity success story.* Under review by John Mellor Associates.

Mellor, J. W., & Ahmed, R. (Eds.). (1988). *Agricultural price policy for developing countries.* Baltimore: Johns Hopkins University Press.

Mellor, J. W., & Dorosh, P. (2010). *Agriculture and the economic transformation of Ethiopia* (ESSP II Working Paper No. 10). Washington, DC: International Food Policy Research Institute.

Mellor, J. W., & Gavian, S. (1987). Famine: Causes, prevention and relief. *Science, 235*, 539–546.

Mellor, J. W., & Gavian, S. (1999). *The determinants of employment growth in Egypt—The dominant role of agriculture and the rural small scale sector* (Impact Assessment Report No. 7). Cairo: Abt Associates Inc.

Mellor, J. W., & Johnston, B. F. (1984). The world food equation: Interrelations among development, employment and food consumption. *Journal of Economic Literature, 22*(2), 531–574.

Mellor, J. W., & Kumro, T. (2017). *Rapid growth in cereals production generates much of its own demand in low income countries.* Under review by John Mellor Associates.

Mellor, J. W. (1973b). Accelerated growth in agricultural production and the intersectoral transfer of resources. *Economic Development and Cultural Change, 22* (1), 1–16.

Mellor, J. W., & Lele, U. J. (1973). Growth linkages of the new food grain technologies. *Indian Journal of Agricultural Economics, 28*(1), 35.

Mellor, J. W., & Malik, S. J. (2017). The impact of growth in small commercial farm productivity on rural poverty reduction. *World Development, 91*, 1–10.

Mellor, J. W., & Masters, W. A. (1991). The changing roles of multilateral and bilateral foreign assistance. In U. Lele & I. Nabi (Eds.), *Transitions in development: The role of aid and commercial flows* (pp. 331–372). San Francisco: ICS Press.

Mellor, J. W., & Pandya-Lorch, R. (1992). Food aid and the development in the MADIA countries. In U. Lele (Ed.), *Aid to African agriculture: Lessons from two decades of donor experience.* Baltimore: The Johns Hopkins University Press.

Mellor, J. W., & Ranade, C. (2006). Why does agricultural growth dominate poverty reduction in low and middle income countries? *The Pakistan Development Review, 45* (2), 221–240.

Mellor, J. W., & Stevens, R. D. (1956). The average and marginal product of farm labor in underdeveloped economies. *Journal of Farm Economics, 38*(3), 780–791.

Mellor, J. W., Weaver, T. F., & Lele, U. (1968). *Developing rural India: Plan and practice.* Ithaca: Cornell University Press.

Mellor, J. W., Delgado, C. L., & Blackie, M. J. (1987). *Accelerating food production in sub-Saharan Africa.* Baltimore: The Johns Hopkins University Press.

Mellor, J. W., Nabi, I., & Tusneem, M. E. (2008). Agricultural development and food security [with comments]. *The Pakistan Development Review, 47*(4), 357–380.

Mgbenka, R., Bah, E., & Ezeano, C. (2015). The role of local government council in agricultural transformation in Nigeria: Need for review of policy. *Agricultural Engineering Research Journal, 5*(2), 27–32.

Minten, B., Reardon, T., Singh, K., & Sutradhar, R. (2014). The new and changing roles of cold storages in the potato supply chain in Bihar. *Economic and Political Weekly, 49* (52), 98–108.

Montenegro, C. E., & Patrinos, H. A. (2014). *Comparable estimates of returns to schooling around the world* (Policy Research Working Paper No. 7020). Washington, DC: World Bank Group.

Morris, M. L. (2007). *Fertilizer use in African agriculture: Lessons learned and good practice guidelines.* Washington, DC: World Bank Publications.

Moser, C., Barrett, C., & Minten, B. (2009). Spatial integration at multiple scales: Rice markets in Madagascar. *Agricultural Economics, 40*(3), 281–294.

Nagarajan, G., & Meyer, R. L. (2005). *Rural finance: Recent advances and emerging lessons, debates and opportunities* (Reformatted version of Working Paper No. AEDE-WP-0041-05). Columbus: Department of Agricultural, Environmental, and Development Economics, The Ohio State University.

Narain, D., Mellor, J. W., & Desai, G. M. (1985). *Agricultural change and rural poverty: Variations on a theme by Dharm Narain.* Baltimore: Johns Hopkins University Press.

Nelson, G. C., Rosegrant, M. W., Koo, J., Robertson, R., Sulser, T., Zhu, T., et al. (2009). *Climate change: Impact on agriculture and costs of adaptation* (Vol. 21). Washington, DC: International Food Policy Research Institute.

Nin Pratt, A., & Fan, S. (2009). *R&D Investment in national and international agricultural research: An ex ante analysis of productivity and poverty impact* (IFPRI Discussion Paper No. 00986). Washington, DC: International Food Policy Research Institute.

North, D. (1987). Institutions, transaction cost and economic growth. *Economic Enquiry, 25*(3), 419–428.

Ortmann, G. F., & King, R. P. (2007). Agricultural cooperatives I: History, theory and problems. *Agrekon, 46*(1), 18–46.

Palacios-Lopez, A., Christiaensen, L., & Kilic, T. (2017). How much of the labor in African agriculture is provided by women? *Food Policy, 67*, 52–63.

Pardey, P. G., Andrade, R. S., Hurley, T. M., Rao, X., & Liebenberg, F. G. (2016). Returns to food and agricultural R&D investments in sub-Saharan Africa, 1975–2014. *Food Policy, 65*, 1–8.

Pingali, P. L., Marquez, C. B., & Palis, F. G. (1994). Pesticides and Philippine rice farmer health: A medical and economic analysis. *American Journal of Agricultural Economics, 76*(3), 587–592.

Pinstrup-Andersen, P. (1988). *Food subsidies in developing countries: Costs, benefits, and policy options.* Baltimore: Published for the International Food Policy Research Institute by Johns Hopkins University Press.

Pinstrup-Andersen, P., & Watson, D. D., II. (2011). *Food policy for developing countries: The role of government in global, national, and local food systems.* Ithaca: Cornell University Press.

Pratt, A. N., & Fan, S. (2010). *R & D investment in national and international agricultural research: An ex-ante analysis of productivity and poverty impact.* Washington, DC: International Food Policy Research Institute (IFPRI).

Qaim, M. (2001). Transgenic crops and developing countries. *Economic and Political Weekly, 36*(32), 3064–3070.

Ranis, G., & Fei, J. C. (1961). A theory of economic development. *The American Economic Review, 51*(4), 533–565.

Rao, C. H. (1975). *Technological change and the distribution of gains in Indian agriculture* (Vol. 17). Delhi: Macmillan Company of India.

Rashid, S., Tefera, N., Minot, N., & Ayele, G. (2013). Can modern input use be promoted without subsidies? An analysis of fertilizer in Ethiopia. *Agricultural Economics, 44*(6), 595–611.

Ravallion, M., & Datt, G. (2002). Why has economic growth been more pro-poor in some states of India than others? *Journal of Development Economics, 68*(2), 381–400.

Reardon, T. (2015). The hidden middle: The quiet revolution in the midstream of agrifood value chains in developing countries. *Oxford Review of Economic Policy, 31*(1), 45–63.

Reardon, T., Timmer, C. P., Barrett, C. B., & Berdegue, J. (2003). The rise of supermarkets in Africa, Asia and Latin America. *American Journal of Agricultural Economics, 85*(5), 1140–1146.

Riddell, R. C. (2008). *Does foreign aid really work?* Oxford: Oxford University Press.

Riddell, R. C., & Robinson, R. (1995). *Non-governmental organizations and rural poverty alleviation*. Oxford: Oxford University Press.

Rosegrant, M. W., & Binswanger, H. P. (1994). Markets in tradable water rights: Potential for efficiency gains in developing country water resource allocation. *World Development, 22*(11), 1613–1625.

Rosegrant, M. W., Ewing, M., Yohe, G., Burton, I., Huq, S., & Valmonte-Santos, R. (2008). *Climate change and agriculture: Threats and opportunities*. Eschborn: GTZ.

Sachs, J. D. (2005). *Investing in development: A practical plan to achieve the millennium development goals*. London: Earthscan.

Saito, K. A., & Weidemann, C. J. (1990). *Agricultural extension for women farmers in Africa* (World Bank Discussion Paper No. 103). Washington, DC: World Bank Group.

Schäfer, H. B., & Lipton, M. (1979). *Why poor people stay poor: Urban bias in world development*. London: Harvard University Press.

Schiff, M. W., Valdés, A., & Krueger, A. O. (1992). *The political economy of agricultural pricing policy: A synthesis of the political economy in developing countries*. Washington, DC: World Bank Publications.

Schultz, T. W. (1964). *Transforming traditional agriculture*. New Haven: Yale University Press.

Schultz, T. W. (1975). The value of the ability to deal with disequilibria. *Journal of Economic Literature, 13*(3), 827–846.

Sen, A. (1981). *Poverty and famines: An essay on entitlement and deprivation*. Oxford: Oxford University Press.

Sharpley, A. N., Smith, S. J., & Naney, J. W. (1987). Environmental impact of agricultural nitrogen and phosphorus use. *Journal of Agricultural and Food Chemistry, 35*(5), 812–817.

Stifel, D., Minten, B., & Koru, B. (2016). Economic benefits of rural feeder roads: Evidence from Ethiopia. *The Journal of Development Studies, 52*(9), 1335–1356.

Tadesse, G., & Bahiigwa, G. (2015). Mobile phones and farmers' marketing decisions in Ethiopia. *World Development, 68*, 296–307.

Tamboli, P. M., & Nene, Y. L. (2011). *Revitalizing higher agricultural education in India: Journey towards excellence*. Secunderabad: Asian Agri-History Foundation.

Thirtle, C. (2001). *Relationship between changes in agricultural productivity and the incidence of poverty in developing countries* (DIVD report no. 7946). London.

Thirtle, C., Irz, X., Lin, L., Mckenzie-hill, V., & Wiggins, S. (2001). *Relationship between changes in agricultural productivity and the incidence of poverty in developing countries* (Report No. 7946). London: Department for International Development.

Thirtle, C., Lin, L., & Piesse, J. (2003). The impact of research-led agricultural productivity growth on poverty reduction in Africa, Asia and Latin America. *World Development, 31*(12), 1959–1975.

Tiffen, M., Mortimore, M., & Gichuki, F. (1994). *More people less erosion: Environmental recovery in Kenya.* London: Overseas Development Institute.

Timmer, C. P. (1986). *Getting prices right: The scope and limits of agricultural price policy.* Ithaca: Cornell University Press.

Timmer, C. P. (1997). *How well do the poor connect to the growth process?* (CAER Discussion Paper No. 17). Cambridge, MA: Harvard Institute for International Development.

Timmer, C. P. (2015). *Food security and scarcity: Why ending hunger is so hard.* Philadelphia: University of Pennsylvania Press.

Todaro, M. P., & Smith, S. C. (2011). *Economic development* (10th ed.). New York: Prentice Hall/Addison-Wesley.

Trostle, R., & Seeley, R. (2013). Developing countries dominate world demand for agricultural products. *Amber Waves, Economic Research Service.* Washington, DC: United States Department of Agriculture.

Urmee, T., Harries, D., & Schlapfer, A. (2009). Issues related to rural electrification using renewable energy in developing countries of Asia and Pacific. *Renewable Energy, 34*(2), 354–357.

Van de Walle, D. (2002). Choosing rural road investments to help reduce poverty. *World Development, 30*(4), 575–589.

Vandercasteelen, J., Tamru, S., Minten, B., & Swinnen, J. (2016). *Cities and agricultural transformation in Africa: Evidence from Ethiopia* (ESSP Working Paper No. 91). Washington, DC: International Food Policy Research Institute.

Vanlauwe, B., Wendt, J., Giller, K. E., Corbeels, M., Gerard, B., & Nolte, C. (2014). A fourth principle is required to define conservation agriculture in sub-Saharan Africa: The appropriate use of fertilizer to enhance crop productivity. *Field Crops Research, 155*, 10–13.

Verhofstadt, E., & Maertens, M. (2014). *Can agricultural cooperatives reduce poverty? Heterogeneous impact of cooperative membership on farmers' welfare in Rwanda* (Bioeconomics Working Paper Series No. 2). Leuven: Department of Earth and Environmental Sciences, University of Leuven.

von Braun, J., & Webb, P. J. R. (1989). The impact of new crop technology on the agricultural division of labor in a West African setting. *Economic Development and Cultural Change, 50*, 313–338.

Webb, P., & Block, S. (2012). Support for agriculture during economic transformation: Impacts on poverty and undernutrition. *Proceedings of the National Academy of Sciences, 109*(31), 12309–12314.

Wiebe, K., Lotze-Campen, H., Sands, R., Tabeau, A., van der Mensbrugghe, D., Biewald, A., et al. (2015). Climate change impacts on agriculture in 2050 under a range of plausible socioeconomic and emissions scenarios. *Environmental Research Letters, 10*(8), 085010.

William, G. K., Foster, V., Archondo-Callao, R., Briceño-Garmendia, C., Nogales, A., & Sethi, K. (2008). *The burden of maintenance: Roads in sub-Saharan Africa* (AICD Background Paper No. 14). Washington, DC: World Bank Group.

Williamson, J. G. (2013). Demographic dividends revisited. *Asian Development Review, 30*(2), 1–25.

World Bank Group. (2007). *Poverty and the environment: Understanding linkages at the household level.* Washington, DC: World Bank Group.

World Bank Group. (2008). *World development report 2008: Agriculture for development.* Washington, DC: World Bank Group.

World Bank Group. (2009). *World development report 2009: Reshaping economic geography.* Washington, DC: World Bank Group.

World Bank Group. (2012). *World development report 2012: Gender equality in development.* Washington, DC: World Bank Group.

World Bank Group. (2014). *Ethiopia poverty assessment* (Report no. AUS6744). Washington, DC: World Bank Group.

Yang, J., Huang, Z., Zhang, X., & Reardon, T. (2013). The rapid rise of cross-regional agricultural mechanization services in China. *American Journal of Agricultural Economics, 95*(5), 1245–1251.

You, L., Ringler, C., Wood-Sichra, U., Robertson, R., Wood, S., Zhu, T., et al. (2011). What is the irrigation potential for Africa? A combined biophysical and socioeconomic approach. *Food Policy, 36*(6), 770–782.

INDEX

Note: Page numbers followed by "n" refer to notes.

© The Author(s) 2017
J.W. Mellor, *Agricultural Development and Economic Transformation*,
Palgrave Studies in Agricultural Economics and Food Policy,
https://doi.org/10.1007/978-3-319-65259-7